TRACE

Rachael Brown is a broadcast journalist. In 2002, after graduating from RMIT, she began her career with the ABC, where she has held several postings, including Europe correspondent from 2010 to 2013. In 2008, she won her first Walkley Award for Best Radio Current Affairs Report, for her investigation into the Victorian Medical Practitioners Board whose negligence contributed to the sexual assaults of a dozen women.

Rachael is the creator, investigator, and host of the ABC's first true-crime podcast, *Trace*, which won the 2017 Walkley Award for Innovation. The podcast also won two 2017 Quill Awards: for Innovation, and for Best Podcast. Rachael lives in Melbourne, Victoria.

Rachael Brown

TRACE

Who killed
Maria James?

SCRIBE
Melbourne • London

Scribe Publications
18–20 Edward St, Brunswick, Victoria 3056, Australia
2 John St, Clerkenwell, London, WC1N 2ES, United Kingdom
3754 Pleasant Ave, Suite 100, Minneapolis, Minnesota 55409 USA

First published by Scribe 2018

The publishers gratefully acknowledge receiving permission from ABC
Commercial for the use of selected transcripts from *Trace* and the
photograph of Mark James (taken by Jeremy Story Carter) that appears
on the inside front cover.

This book addresses some distressing stories and themes. If it raises
concerns for readers, they can contact Lifeline on 13 11 14, or
Beyond Blue on 1300 22 46 36.

Typeset in 11.75 on 16.5pt Sabon by the publishers
Printed and bound in Australia by Griffin Press.

The paper this book is printed on is certified against the
Forest Stewardship Council® Standards. Griffin Press holds
FSC chain of custody certification SGS-COC-005088. FSC
promotes environmentally responsible, socially beneficial
and economically viable management of the world's forests.

9781925713091 (Australian edition)
9781911617853 (UK edition)
9781925693218 (e-book)

CiP records for this title are available from the National Library of
Australia and the British Library.

scribepublications.com.au
scribepublications.co.uk
scribepublications.com

To the fighters. To Maria.
To her sons, who couldn't forget.
To a detective who wouldn't let go.
And to all the silent heroes.

Contents

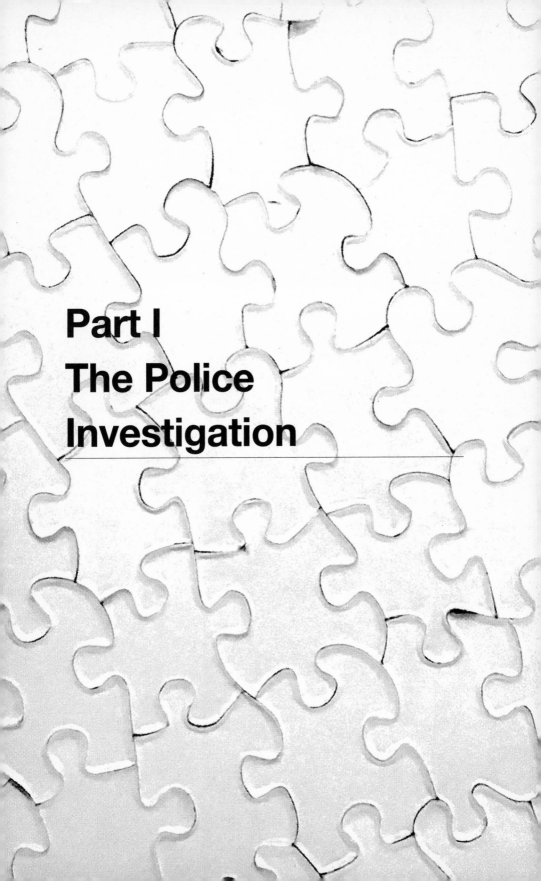

Part I
The Police
Investigation

June 1980

He doesn't know it yet, but this one will bury its hooks into him.

He arrives at 736 High Street, Thornbury, with a lot more to prove than the other detectives. This is his first homicide case. Ron Iddles takes mental photographs of the crime scene. *Click*. The front window: every square inch plastered with book jackets. *Click*. Bookshop interior: shelves upon shelves of second-hand books. *Click*. Lounge: two empty coffee cups on a table. Another small table with a broken leg. *Click*. Kitchen: chopping board on a counter. Beside it, a dirty footprint. Nearby, an open cutlery-drawer. *Click*. Bedroom one: a red rotary-dial telephone, the receiver out of its cradle. A turntable with a pile of LPs, the majority of them Elvis. *Click*. Bedroom two, across the passage: the victim, female, at the base of a bed, head closest to the door, legs pointing towards a wardrobe. Right leg bent at the knee, right calf and foot pointing outwards. The victim's shoes have been kicked or taken off. Multiple stab wounds, to the chest, neck, and back. Hands tied with twine. No apparent bruising on the wrists. One pillow at the victim's head, and another at her feet. Heavy blood stains on the carpet and on a corner of a bed quilt. Some smearing further along the carpet, and on the wardrobe. A lock on the back of the bedroom door.

Ron Iddles is 100 per cent certain of two things. The killer is someone the victim knew and was originally comfortable with. Frenzied attacks usually point to a relationship—possibly an intimate one, but definitely some kind of connection. The coffee cups, too, back up this theory.

This end to Maria James's life is the start of Ron Iddles' dream job. He's waited for this break since he was a boy rushing through his milking and hay-carting chores on his parents' dairy farm in Victoria's north-west so he'd be in time for *Homicide*. He used to sit glued to the 1960s TV series, in awe of actors John Fegan and Leonard Teale, who would march down the steps of Victoria's Russell Street police headquarters in their pork-pie hats and proceed to solve cases every week in under an hour. If it wasn't *Homicide*, it was *Columbo*, the seemingly forgetful but cunning American TV detective. From him, adult Ron has borrowed his trademark crumpled jacket. He's bought himself a London Fog overcoat, so through all the dark nights to come, Ron will be the one in off-white amid a sea of black and blue.

He cut his teeth on the mean beat of Collingwood, where the only people who moved after 1.00am were crooks, police, and prostitutes. Here, as a green 19-year-old, he took on the feared members of the Painters and Dockers Union. And he drew a line that would come to define the rest of his decorated career, shooing away a bribe from a local justice of the peace to 'fix something up'. Compassion would later bud in various shades of grey, but in terms of duty, his world has been black and white from the get-go.

Now a plucky 25-year-old, Ron has a lot riding on this homicide job. The core crew members are his boss, Senior Sergeant Brian McCarthy, then Sergeant Jack Jacobs, Senior Constable Roland Legg, and himself, Detective Senior Constable Ron Iddles. R. Iddles. Riddles—a befitting name for a mystery-solver. For now, his job is to find out who killed Maria James.

April 2016

1.00pm Coroners Court w Ron

— Diary note, 21 April 2016

I lean over the crime scene photo-booklet in a stark white meeting room at the Coroners Court of Victoria. Its thin cardboard cover is in Victoria Police blue, and the 25 photographs slide along a plastic binding-comb. The early photos are interiors of the second-hand bookshop at 736 High Street, Thornbury. Next to a sign, 'Tales of war and adventure', novels jostle on the shelves—piles and piles of them, stacked not with their spines out, but flat, so more can be crammed into the heaving bookcases. These and the book covers plastering the front window choke the room.

The store's counter has a sign in front, 'No smoking'. A little note, '30 cent exchange', hangs beside a door with a white curtain separating Maria James's bookshop from the home she lived in with her two young sons. Behind this door, and down a passage, is the kitchen, where everything is in meticulous order, except for a cutlery drawer that gapes like an open mouth. On the kitchen bench, an onion sits on a chopping board, beside a newspaper cutting about an upcoming dinner dance. Hanging from the wall is a wilted fern and a banner with the proclamation, 'Mothers are the most wonderful people in the world.'

Off the passageway, on the left, is the bedroom of 11-year-old Adam, Maria's youngest son. Boats sail across the wallpaper. On a dresser is a Bata Scout shoebox—school shoes perhaps?—a stack of Elvis records, and a mirror with a magazine cut-out of the crooner's face taped to it. Underneath is a red telephone, the handset resting idly beside it. In the bedroom opposite there's a sea of 1970s floral, on the bedspread, curtains, and wallpaper. All mismatched. Darker blotches add new blooms to the carpet and quilt. Elvis Presley looks on from a framed photo on a bedside table. Above the bedroom door is a reprint of Gustav Klimt's painting *The Kiss*. And below Klimt's testament to lovers lies Maria James, at the base of her bed.

I wince at Maria's bruised face in the autopsy photos. Her left eye is slightly opened; the right, swollen and closed. Her skin looks puffy and translucent. Her scalp is missing some clumps of her dark hair. I wonder whether this was the killer's doing, or the pathologist's. I've seen post-mortem photos before, during my days as a court reporter. Some days, during those grim prosecution sessions aimed at swaying a jury, I'd look; other days, I'd drift. Common journo distractions were newspapers, Sudoku, doodling, or scratching one's initials into the Supreme Court media desks. I have no doubt this would have looked disrespectful to those crammed into the rigid wooden pews of the public gallery. But once you see, you can't unsee. And these pictures can creep into your dreams, so sometimes it's best not to look.

Today I have to, because a seeming contradiction in this cold case has inspired my promise to Maria's sons that I'll look into it. A promise, for two boys, now middle-aged men, who've lived in a holding pattern for as long as I've been alive. It's promises that can be our undoing, I'll later learn from Ron Iddles. For now, as I look at all the white crumbs on Maria's black jumper, which turn out to be her white shirt peeking through the slashes in the wool, I make her a silent pledge that I'll do my best.

When Ron arrives to walk me through this final photo album of Maria James's life, he says he can't look at these photos through the same sentimental prism I'm using. My sad crumbs are his priceless clues. 'I see that as part of a jigsaw puzzle,' he tells me. 'If I looked at that in some other way, I don't think I would've lasted 25 years.' He's been a constant figure at police doorstops throughout my career as a journalist with the ABC, but I've never worked with him personally. He's 61, burly, and he wears that appraising stare, synonymous with any cop. But there's a gruff warmth about him, a reassuring presence. He's known for his no-bullshit approach and his compassion towards victims, families, and even crooks.

'Most aren't bad people,' he tells me. 'They just make bad choices in life.' He has a certain knack. I've watched a killer go to water in an interview room when Ron put a hand on his shoulder and said, 'It's a big burden to carry, don't let it eat you up.' The killer dragged his chair forward, put his hands around Ron's, and confessed. I remember a fellow journalist commenting, 'If I had anything to confess, I'd confess to Ron'.

The lines on Ron's forehead and around his piercing blue eyes read like a diary of those 60-hour shifts he's spent at horror scenes. And there's something of myself I recognise in him—sheer stubbornness. But this has made him a divisive figure within the Victorian police force. Ron is part of the old guard, a copper who'll buck the system by releasing information if he feels it'll help a case. Some of the new guard, however, would prefer that the force's information, and secrets, remain internal. Many of my colleagues lament that over the past decade the force's media-liaison unit has morphed into more of a shield than a channel. Which is why I need Ron. He's approaching retirement from his position as secretary of the Police Association, the police union. It'll mean handing in his badge—number 18150—for good. He should be daydreaming about fishing trips with his son off the coast of Cairns, or bike rides, or, finally, getting some decent sleep. Instead, he's graciously fielding questions from me, about his very first case, which still grates like hell.

June 1980

Ron Iddles' crew moves into the ill-fated bookshop on High Street, hoping the walls might talk. Or that the locals will. The thinking is that the detectives' presence might encourage people to drop in with information about the stabbing. Sixty-eight wounds. Christ. This tells Ron that the killer's emotions have outrun their intelligence. It was unplanned, he suspects, but furious all the same. He's seen death before, but this is something else. And the force doesn't employ cleaners, so each time he walks past the bedroom he sees the victim's blood soaked into the carpet.

For this Homicide rookie, it feels very strange for his crew to be treating this house like their own. A woman has been viciously killed in here, and they're going about their lives as if it's all normal. They're using her cutlery, crockery, kettle, even the outside barbecue for dinners, as they usually don't knock off till 22:00 or 23:00 most nights. Then they go home, shower, maybe chat to their wives, pass out, and return by 07:00 to do it all again. His crew has turned the dining table—a billiard table with a board perched on top—into their communal desk. It's now a nest of paperwork being peered over by detectives sporting brown suits and moustaches.

Ron spots Mark James, the victim's 13-year-old son. Mark and his little brother, Adam, have been shipped off to live with their dad, but Mark's occasionally allowed back in for clothes. Ron quietly wonders about Mark, what he's making of all this, of his house being commandeered, his home forever lost.

March 2016

I am grateful for what you are doing. Thanks.

— Text from Mark James to Rachael Brown, 14 March 2016

The 49-year-old version of Mark James sits beside me in his lounge-room, south-east of Melbourne. Each time he moves, the leather of the sofa creaks. The room's bare, save for a photo beside the TV of his younger brother, Adam, and his late mother, and his voice bounces off the floorboards. Mark has painful memories of his childhood home. He tells me that during one of his visits back, in those early days, he saw something no kid should ever have to see.

'There were a couple of times that I was let back into the house, and I was strictly told not to go into Mum's bedroom. Well, telling a 13-year-old that is almost like an invitation, and I opened the bedroom door, and all of the furniture was gone but there were blood stains all over the carpet. That was very distressing.'

This bloodied image has never dulled. 'Just about every day, Mum is on my mind. It's painful that there's no resolution. Our mum was taken away from us, and I think with a little extra effort we could get an answer as to who the murderer was.'

Mark has a round face with soft features and his mum's brown eyes. He has a heavy-set stature and an ambling way about him—the way he moves, the way he speaks—but it's loaded with graciousness. He adored his mother. She was the daughter of immigrants whose Italian roots were infused in her cooking and sometimes her temper. Mark smiles, remembering an incident when he was nearly knocked off his bike during his morning paper-round. The driver did the courtesy of ferrying Mark home, only to be ripped into so ferociously by Maria that he probably regretted his courtesy more than his poor driving. Mark says she'd have done anything for her boys. Her other love was Elvis. 'I think "Kentucky Rain" was her favourite,' Mark says. The mournful song tells of an anxious man's search for his missing love. *Kentucky rain keeps pouring down, and up ahead another town that I'll go walking through.*

As for their little town, Mark has warm memories of growing up in Thornbury, in Melbourne's north. Before its wine bars and eateries appeared during the gentrification of the nineties, it was an unromantic working-class suburb—one full of battlers. But Maria had the safety net of the bookshop, which originally belonged to her parents-in-law. Mark says when his parents separated in 1978, his dad, John James, left the shop to Maria so it would provide an income for her and the boys. And Mark says he loved curling up with a book in there.

'I used to read the Biggles books, which were about a flying ace, a pilot, that my dad had read as well and encouraged me to read. As well as those books, I loved the science-fiction books, particularly the very colourful pictures of spaceships on the front covers. Sometimes I would wander in at night times, and when Mum and Dad went out. And when my cousin would come over, we'd actually use the bookshop as a little play area.'

Mark looks sheepish for a second. 'At the time, a lot of newsagents and bookstores started to have light, even heavy, pornographic magazines, and in order to compete, Mum put a box of these in the corner and covered every one in plastic so that they couldn't be opened. So she had this porno box.' Mark laughs at his 13-year-old self. 'I used to, at two in the morning, sneak into the shop, and I couldn't open the books up and have a look because they were all in plastic, but I could see the covers, and I was shocked enough.' In a small way, this little bookshop showed Mark the world. 'There would be customers coming in: sometimes they would talk to me, and I would see my mum interacting with them. That's an opportunity I had because Mum had a bookshop. Without that, I would be a less interesting person.'

After that day in 1980, this home, his anchor, became a foreign world of fingerprint dust and police tape. Mark doesn't think the detectives knew he'd snuck into his mum's bedroom, but saying goodbye was important to him.

'That was my home for 13 years. I needed to reconnect with the place before I could let it go. And I really wanted to take more of my possessions, more of my toys, the things that were in my bedroom.'

This is only the second time we've met. Earlier in the year I'd called Mark, asking for his blessing to do a journalistic deep-dive into the cold case of his mum. Because in 2014 a best mate and colleague, Kerri Ritchie, told me that a witness had made an explosive police statement. 'You should keep in touch with Ron Iddles,' she told me, as she headed off on maternity leave. 'It could be big'. So I did. And nothing came of it. Ron Iddles was at the Police Association by then, so he was off the case that had frustrated him for all those years, and he was stumped as to why this witness's statement had never seen the light of day. This also niggled at me—enough for the Iddles baton change that's now landed me in Mark's sparse lounge-room. I don't know it yet, but it will become all-consuming. There's the murder, and then things get dark.

I want to review his mum's case through a podcast. I feel this intimate medium will allow for sensitive treatment. But some true-crime podcasts treat crime like a spectator sport. Maria James's story should be both forensic and respectful, so my early caveat was getting Mark's blessing. Had he said no, I wouldn't have pursued the case. That was the line I drew. I'd imagined that, after all the news stories over all the years, Mark might be lugging around fatigued surrender. He'd most likely be wondering whether he'd be let down all over again. But he's on board. So here we are.

'Even though it's been so many years—I mean, we're talking about 36 years—given modern forensic techniques, including DNA, I'm certain that if enough resources are thrown behind it [the cold case], they could definitely find the killer,' Mark says.

He's confident that an ABC podcast could revive interest in dusty files about his mum, which sit in boxes in a police storage room alongside the unfinished stories about another 280 Victorians. Mark has a desperate hope about him, the sort of hope that either fuels people or breaks them. But, like Ron Iddles, he has an unwavering conviction that there's someone in the community who holds the missing puzzle-piece. It's just a matter of finding them, and tugging on their conscience.

Mark James speaks so fondly of Ron, whom he met as a 13-year-old when he was getting under the heels of those detectives at his dining table, throwing questions at them.

'I wasn't upset that they were there. I was encouraged that something's happening, they're doing their job, and gee, wow, there's a lot of police here, they're taking it very seriously. I was probably a bit annoying to them sometimes, coming up and talking, [while] they were trying to do their job.'

Ron's been a constant in Mark's lifetime of upheaval.

'Ron stayed in touch, and how he kept in touch with me, I don't know. I mean, I moved address and always would forget to tell Ron, but Ron would find me and stay in touch, and he would say, "We are still looking at certain suspects." And he was the source of encouragement for me—I guess probably the only source of encouragement, that maybe one day there could be a solution.'

What a thing to carry from your teenage years. When I was a kid, I remember dressing up with my best mate, Sarah, for a school-costume day. Detectives Brown and Puttick we were, with trench coats and crudely made cardboard name-badges. We used to patrol the local neighbourhood for mysteries to solve. But when we saw a knife lying in someone's garden one day, we decided the job might be over our heads. I think that's about the time all the girls changed their career ambition to dolphin trainer. But here's Mark, his trajectory severed so cleanly from mine with 68 flashes of a blade.

He revisits that day all the time. He's just back from his daily paper-round for the local newsagent, Terry Gannon. His mum's at the stove, cooking the boys scrambled eggs, their favourite breakfast. She turns from the stove and asks something strange.

'She said to me in a very kind of solemn and unusual way, "If anything happens to me, make sure Adam is looked after." She actually made me promise. And she was looking anxious and worried. And that was the second time. She'd said it to me on the weekend as well. It was something out of character. Mum cared about us very much, and she would never put that kind of burden on us.'

Now, in hindsight, her plea chimes ominously. 'She would do anything for her children, and she was quite perceptive. If something was wrong with Adam or me, she would know about it before we even said anything.' But at the time, Mark just thought she was being a bit weird. So he promised, scoffed his breakfast, and headed off for his weekly school excursion to the local bowling alley. His mum, as she did every day, walked his 11-year-old brother, Adam, to the bus stop. Because he had cerebral palsy and Tourette's, he went to a special school. Maria put Adam on the bus and waved him goodbye.

17 June 1980

John James returns to Fitzroy Town Hall, where he's the town clerk. He'd forgotten his glasses, so had to quickly duck home to get them. Back in the office, his secretary, Isabella Fabris, tells him his ex-wife just called. John and Maria James have been separated for about 18 months now, but they're still on good terms—they were childhood sweethearts, after all. He's remarried, and lives with his second wife, Patricia, in North Fitzroy. But he still sees Mark and Adam every weekend for fishing and skiing trips, cinema excursions, and city lunches at Italian cafés. He's left Maria his parents' bookshop to run, and she seems happy, dividing her time between the shop and her boys.

John dials his old house. Maria answers and says, 'Hang on, please,' so he waits on the line. He hears a muffled discussion in the background. He thinks it might be an argument, but he can only really make out Maria's voice. Then he hears her give a yelp—more of a startled noise, he thinks, rather than a fearful one. There's more one-sided conversation; she almost sounds like she's giving directions. It must be someone she knows, someone she's confident enough to argue with. Then there's silence—several minutes of it. John starts to get a bit edgy, so he whistles into the phone to get Maria's attention. Nothing. Then her voice gets a little louder. After about four minutes, she yelps a second time. John's now sure that something is wrong. He tells Isabella he's worried, that he needs to check on Maria, that he'll be back soon.

He jumps in his car for the 15-to-20-minute journey

through Northcote, and arrives at the bookshop around 12.10 to 12.20pm.

He finds the shop locked up. He knocks, and buzzes the doorbell, but there's no reply. So he heads round the back, down a little lane off Mansfield Street that leads to the backyard. The back door's locked, too. Weird. He knocks and calls out. Nothing. He feels around for a spare key that Maria sometimes keeps in the laundry. It's not there. He heads back around the front. Again, no response. Then back again. Futile. He drags a ladder around the front, and peers over a wall that seals the gap between the bookshop and the neighbouring 'Celia's', a clothes shop, to see if he can get in that way. No good. Something is very wrong, but John can't work out what. When he drags the ladder back, he notices Maria's car. This usually means she's home.

On his fourth lap, he notices a curtain move, on the door behind the shop counter that separates the store from the residence. John races around to the back. Meanwhile, at the front door, Michael Mel, an architecture student who's hoping the bookshop has a magazine he needs for his studies, peers through the window. He, too, notices the curtain move, and then remain still, but he can't make out a figure or face. Mr Mel gives up and walks off. On the next of John James's panicked laps, he hears the front buzzer going. There's a man with a dark complexion and short black hair at the door, carrying a green folder. It seems that no one is having any luck in raising the bookseller's attention. John James runs into Mrs Rennie's place, which butts up against the lane, to call his ex-wife. But the line's engaged—the phone is still off the hook.

John is now desperate to get in any way he can. He remembers the side window, where he'd installed an air-conditioner, and he climbs in, crawling over the kitchen bench. The house is in darkness. The whole place seems cold, and he feels a terrible sense of dread. He calls out, but gets no reply, so he takes a knife from the cutlery drawer, and unlocks the back door as an escape route. First he checks the lounge room. Nothing there. Then he creeps down the hallway. He glances to his right, into Adam's bedroom. Then he turns to his left and switches on the light to Maria's bedroom. He sees her on the floor. Her eyes and mouth are open, and there is blood everywhere. He's too late.

As John James's heart pounds in his ears, the killer is most likely a breath away, hiding behind the door. Had John walked into the bedroom, he might've been the second victim. But he backs away, horrified, and rushes out the back door to the neighbour's place to call Triple 0. As he waits for police, he paces up and down the back lane, thinking, *What the hell happened? How am I going to tell the boys? I should've got here sooner. How am I going to tell the boys?* Up and down, up and down. On one weary lap, he comes to the front of the bookshop, and notices someone in there. It's a woman, casually perusing the shelves like it's any other Tuesday. As he anxiously shoos her out, she tells John she'd found the bookshop door unlocked. She'd also noticed that the door from the shop to the residence was ajar. Had it been a few minutes earlier, they'd both have seen him—a man running from the direction of the bookshop who was nearly hit by a passing car as he sprinted across High Street and down Hutton Street towards the railway line. He has a small head start. Or, possibly, a huge one.

April 2016

'It was a fairly horrific scene. In 25 years of investigating homicides, I haven't come across one where someone's been stabbed that many times.' In the meeting room of the Coroners Court, Ron Iddles points out various wounds from Maria's autopsy photos, 'I look at that, especially around the chest and that they're grouped together ... this is not isolated, this is someone who knows her.' He relays his theory. 'I'm guessing what happened [is], she's having a coffee with someone when John James rings and she expresses some concern. Whoever the person is there realises whatever he's done or said is going to be uncovered because the ex-husband's coming out. And from that point on, it clearly escalates. I think she's tried to make her way to the bedroom where she knew there was a lock on the door. She's been followed in and attacked.'

Ron thinks the weapon was the Staysharp knife that was missing from Maria's kitchen. 'So, again, that shows you that the person who's responsible didn't go there with an intention initially to kill her. This is something that's got out of control—emotions have run out of control.' Given the furious nature of the attack, Ron bets that the killer injured himself. 'So, as he's stabbing her, his hand slips down on the knife blade and he cuts his fingers.' Ron says detectives were pretty confident the killer's blood would have been mixed amongst Maria's, on her pillow, but DNA technology only existed in the realm of science-fiction in 1980. 'DNA first came to the fore in about 1994, when we started to use it, very minimally—it's reasonably sophisticated now.'

There were no wounds on Maria's arms and hands from

self-defence injuries, suggesting to Ron that she was first attacked from behind. 'Stabbed in the back, then turned over, multiple stabs to the chest, throat cut, and then, for whatever reason, the hands are tied up. I've had a case where someone was hog-tied after death—it doesn't make sense. Sometimes we try to look for a logical answer, but it's not there.' He says there were no marks on Maria's wrists, so they were most likely bound after she died; otherwise, there'd be bruising.

It's a perspective I hadn't expected, but Ron sees his work as a privilege. 'I've often said there's no greater honour than to investigate the death of a fellow human being, and you do it regardless of race, creed, criminal history, colour of their skin.' He remembers each and every one of the 320 homicides he's investigated. And after 25 years with the Homicide Squad, he has a stellar strike rate of 99 per cent of cases solved. But Maria's is the case that got away.

'Mark James still rings me: "Ron, what's happening?"' Neither of them can let go. 'People talk about closure. It's never closure; there's no such thing. It's about providing an answer for them so they might understand what happened. It does get to you a bit, say when Mark would ring constantly, "Ron, where you at? I want to know what's happened to my mother."'

17 June 1980

Nearly lunchtime, Allan Hircoe thinks, as he finishes working on the electricity box on the wraparound porch of St Mary's presbytery. Now he can get out of the hair of the grumpy housekeeper. He'd knocked to ask if he could turn the power off for a bit, and she'd slammed the door in his face. *Lovely Catholic hospitality.* As he's tinkering, something to the left, across the churchyard, catches his eye. It's a chap who looks to have blood on his hands and face. *Gawd, what's he gone and done to himself? Maybe he fell over, poor sod.* Allan tells the man to wait right there, that he has a first-aid kit in his van, he'll just run and get it. The van's not far, but when he grabs the kit and turns around, the injured man has disappeared. *Weird.* He wraps things up, turns the power back on, and heads back to the office. A colleague advises him to avoid High Street for the afternoon, that something's happened. *Hmmm, cops must've blocked it off*, Allan thinks fleetingly before he attends to the next call-out.

In the space of an afternoon, 13-year-old Mark James has to grow up. There's the promise he made about being Adam's protector. And he might have to be his mum's defender as well. He marches two doors south down High Street, from the bookshop to the real estate office on the corner of Mansfield Street, detectives in tow. They have asked if he has any ideas about who might have attacked his mum, and his mind immediately jumps to the last man she had a relationship with, Peter ___. Mark had sometimes seen the real estate agent after school, having coffee with his mum in the rumpus room. But all that was before he found her crying at the kitchen table, a few months back. She told Mark she'd discovered Peter was married. She felt anguished, but it went against everything she stood for, so Maria called it off.

The only other person Mark has seen around his mum

lately is a man who sometimes chats to her around 5.00am, when Mark gets up for his paper-round. He must be a garbage man or council worker, or something. Mark can't think who else would be up so early. This man has tried to be friendly with his mum, but given her morals, and her tendency to take relationships slowly, Mark thinks the furthest this friendship has got is chats through the doorway. So Mark is only suspicious of one person. He strides into the real estate office, sees Peter ___, and says, 'That's him.' He wants to help the detectives, and pointing at this man is the best he can do for now.

January 2017

I have known the deceased for LIFE years.

Pain suffocated within a blank space. On the final page of Maria James's autopsy report is a victim-identification form. It was Maria's older brother, Tony Aleandro, who had this gutting task. On the form, in the blank space asking how long the identifier had known the victim, Tony wrote, 'life', in capital letters. *I have known the deceased for LIFE years.* The shoemaker's calculation is somehow more stark than the pathologist's 14 paragraphs detailing the length, depth, and angle of each of the 68 stab wounds.

I head out to visit Tony Aleandro with Kerri Ritchie, who's helping with my investigation. We only have an address for him unfortunately, no phone number, and we catch him in the middle of dinner. He opens the door warily in boxer shorts and a stained T-shirt. As soon as I see his eyes, I know it's him. He has the eyes of a ghost—the same ones I've been staring at for a year, in studying photos of Maria. There's one in particular that's transfixing: she's staring straight at the camera, sad, wary, *Mona Lisa*-esque. Out of courtesy, we have to let Tony know we're doing this investigation. True-crime stories aren't stories to the loved ones left behind, who have to shrug off a blanket of grief each morning just to fumble through the day. Our being on his doorstep, however well intentioned, has clearly propelled Tony back more than 36 years to that horrific day.

We explain that we're reviewing his sister's cold case, looking for witnesses or details that might've been overlooked. Kerri gently adds, 'Maria was the same age as us, and I've got two little kids, too. There's nothing I wouldn't do for them, and she sounds like a similar woman'. But he doesn't want to talk about his sister. 'It happened a long time ago, and every now and then it pops up, you know.' Amid his polite apology, he sighs, 'You have a lot of let-downs, you think something's going to happen, and they were so sure at one stage they had someone, but anyway … I don't really feel like talking about it, if that's OK.' He slowly closes the door. We've shaken him, and I feel guilty. I don't blame him for not wanting any part of this. I'm not sure I'd be able to get back on that sickening rollercoaster either.

June 1980

The murder is all over Melbourne's newspapers: 'Sex killing'; 'Police seek help in two murder inquiries'; 'Shop murder; man sought'; 'The horror deaths without a motive'.

Malcolm Fraser is prime minister, and the country is on the cusp of its first test-tube baby. Soon, the Lindy Chamberlain case about a dingo stealing her baby will overshadow Maria James's death. But, for now, it's a media frenzy. Ron Iddles' team has a precious 72-hour window to get this right. That's when the trail's hot—when peoples' memories are fresh, and the killer is more likely to slip up. If the police don't achieve a breakthrough now, it's going to be an uphill battle. Their top priority is finding eyewitnesses.

The best lead so far comes from Jeanette Hodson. She was driving past the bookshop around the time of the murder when a man ran across the road in front of her car. She had to brake violently to avoid hitting him. She says he even reached out a defensive hand on her car bonnet, then kept running. Ron's crew believes this man might be Maria's killer, and, with Jeanette Hodson's help, they compile a photofit to pass around the community. Her description is of a man in his late thirties to early forties, about 166 centimetres tall, with a dark complexion, short, black brushed-back hair, with a balding patch at the rear, and somewhat stockily built, with a thick neck and rather thick arms.

Hoping to get some new tips from the public, Ron's boss, the head of the Homicide Squad, Paul Delianis, fronts the press about the murder that he describes as 'most disturbing'. 'It's a bizarre killing where a woman was tied by her hands, and it seems as though afterwards the killer has tortured the woman or played with her during the killing process. Thereafter he has moved the body into a number of positions. We believe he's possibly a sexual maniac.'

August 2016

Path i/v 11am

— Diary note, 12 August 2016

Forensic pathologist David Ranson is well versed in reconstructing victims' final moments. He has glasses, greying hair with a neatly clipped beard and moustache, and an eloquent, professorial delivery. His grim job doesn't seem to have dented his big, warm personality. He has an eagerness about him to humanise the unfathomable. David tells me he often consults on TV crime series, to ensure they get the details right. And I remember during a Melbourne festival, The 24 Hour Experience, when patrons got the chance to peek behind some of the city's closed doors, David and his colleagues from the Victorian Institute of Forensic Medicine (VIFM) performed a play in the usually off-limits state mortuary. It's here that post-mortems from about 2,500 unexpected deaths take place each year.

I'm keen to get David's fresh eyes over Maria James's autopsy report from 1980. He looks at the pathologist's name, and raises a knowing eyebrow. 'He was an interesting character. I used to hear old stories of him rolling up to court with the wrong case file and giving the wrong evidence to the court.' These were the bad old days of drinking on the job, of tales of cops working in a haze of cigarette smoke, and of pigs being let loose in newsrooms. 'The old coroner's mortuary and court, the Flinders Street extension, where Melbourne's World Trade Centre is now, were considered a disgrace. During court hearings you'd hear the roar of the mortuary saw, and smells would waft into the corridors and courtroom.' David says this culture wasn't conducive to the important work needing to be done, hence the establishment of VIFM.

He picks up the same crime-scene photo book that I flinched at, and leafs through it like it's a Sunday newspaper.

'Hmmm. No skull fractures. Sixty-eight stab wounds. Blood-alcohol analysis: minimal level of alcohol. It depends how soon after death the autopsy was done and the sample was taken, because you can produce a little alcohol after death with decompositional changes. The external jugular vein's incised in the neck. We've got head injuries, we've got neck injuries, we've got front of chest, we've got back of chest, we've got abdomen, we've got loins, we've got lower back. So a wide variety of areas have been stabbed in this individual. Much easier having 68 stab wounds in court than it is having one, although it's a very long and complicated autopsy.'

'The next picture in the book, photograph 24, is very interesting'. David zeroes in on a distinctive stab pattern above Maria's breasts. 'Particularly discrete clusters above both breasts in the upper pectoral region under the collarbones, and you've basically got six one side, and I think is it eight the other side? Seven? So we've got a very, very similar pattern here.' David's seen this before. 'Sadly, this kind of offending is generic. It is not an uncommon predilection to that site—if you like a particular ritualistic type of injury. If someone's going to inflict something of a sort of psychosexual nature, then they'll go for structures like the breasts. They'll also go for the face.' A line from a newspaper article wriggles uncomfortably in my thoughts—the suggestion that a potato masher was pressed down on Maria's face.

'Tied around the wrists: that's interesting.' David studies the twine wound around Maria's wrists, binding her left one over her right. 'There could be a number of reasons for this, depending on whether her wrists were bound while she was alive, as a means of controlling the individual, or after death, sometimes as part of stabilising a body so it can be moved around, or it may just be part of some ritualistic behaviour.' I tell him Ron Iddles thinks they were bound after Maria died. He agrees. 'The thing you are looking for particularly is any vital reaction to a struggle against a ligature. There may be pin-prick haemorrhages in the skin, and you may see them distal, that is, more away from the heart.' Because there were no such haemorrhages in the hands and fingers from a blood blockage or an alteration in oxygenation, it seems the binding was tied after death.

Finally, David notes that there's been blunt force applied to Maria's head. So perhaps, and this would be one small mercy in this whole horrific nightmare, she wasn't awake to the worst of it. 'Significant blunt force to the head may, of course, affect the brain and result in a lowered conscious state—enabling them to be, if you like, more ritualistically assaulted.' David's now said the word 'ritualistic' three times.

June 1980

An information caravan is set up in front of the Thornbury bookshop, displaying special phone-numbers: anyone with information can call 480 3311 or 480 1750. A photofit of a man who has sometimes been seen leaving Maria James's place in the early hours of the morning is being circulated amongst taxi drivers. Inside the house, detectives work furiously at Maria James's dining table—an improvisation that's never been resorted to before and mightn't be repeated. But for now, it's handy that the detectives are close to each other, because in the flood of tips a lot of the intel isn't recorded, and just ends up inside their colleagues' heads. They don't have a computer, so everything is done manually. Information reports are either written in longhand, typed on the sole typewriter, or indexed. The poor sucker with this last tedious job is Sergeant Jack Jacobs. Everything goes into a little red book, like an A–Z address book. A tip-off about a red car, say, will go under R for red, C for car, and perhaps H for Holden. It's monotonous work.

Decades later, Ron Iddles will quietly question whether they eliminated everybody properly, whether leads that seemed urgent overcrowded more important ones. Perhaps in abandoning a file on, say, Bob Smith, to chase someone else, detectives never eliminated old Bob properly. Or if they *did* so, didn't record their reasons, but just stored it in their heads, making it impossible for current cold-case detectives to know their predecessors' thinking should they ever need to revisit Mr Smith.

But for now, Ron and his colleagues are inundated, and

he's a little nervous. He's only ever worked on small criminal cases. This is something else. Information reports will soon top 1,400. He's the new boy on the block, watched on by his more-weathered crew members to see if he'll perform. So he relies on many coppers' greatest tool: his gut instinct. And on an A.B.C mantra: Assume nothing. Believe nothing. Check everything.

As he was taught at detective school, 'You'll never solve a job sitting at your desk.' In these early days, a lot of shoe leather is worn out finding and interviewing tens of persons of interest. And Ron's unit borrows a strategy from the US, scoping Maria's funeral. Detectives think that, given 98 per cent of murders are committed by someone known to the victim, it's not unrealistic to assume their killer will attend the funeral. Because not doing so might arouse suspicion.

March 2016

I would've got as many photographs as I could of Mum.
She was a Christian woman, and I would've liked to have taken her cross, and I would've taken my toys, I had a remote-control car.

— Mark James's interview with Rachael Brown, 14 March 2016

It was Father Anthony Bongiorno who presided over Maria's funeral at her parish, St Mary's Thornbury. But that's all a blur for Mark James. He tells me all he remembers is white noise. The church was crawling with cops, and it made him anxious.

'That day, I was really uncomfortable to be out in public. It was a big funeral, and police were there filming. Rather than it being a private, quiet family event, it was an exposed thing. My dad had bought me a brand-new computer game [console] back then, called an Atari, and I actually had the box for this. I didn't really want to be involved with other people or interacting in that funeral, so I carried that Atari box around, to kind of shield me from other people. Totally inappropriate, but I just didn't want to be around anyone.'

When I was around this age, I remember playing 'Double Dragon' on an Atari with my crush from down the road, hoping to impress him. And here's Mark James, lugging around its box because he just can't cope. His Atari memory takes me back to those crime-scene photos. There's one of a trampoline — the old-school kind with exposed exterior springs that would deliver electric shocks or scrapes on misjudged landings. It leans on its side, against the house under the shade of a lemon tree, never to be played on again. So much of Mark and Adam's childhood was abandoned that day.

Mark says he wasn't allowed to take keepsakes from the house.

'I really wanted to keep a few things of Mum's, and to get as many of my things as possible, but Dad said they would bring too many painful memories. And at that time the police were still taking fingerprints, and I couldn't take anything. Later on, I was allowed to take out a few toys of mine, but it was more or less *Get in, rush, get out*, and my dad didn't want me taking too much. He said, "Don't worry about your old stuff — I'll buy you all new stuff."'

The Atari was a nice idea, but Mark wanted his favourite sci-fi books, some toys, and things that reminded him of his mum. Anything. I look around his sparse lounge room, and wonder whether he's carried this minimalism with him into adulthood. Yet another subconscious fracture. One of the only things Mark managed to hold on to was the family's Bible.

'It was important to me because Mum's handwriting was in it, and so was my dad's. It was a huge leather-bound Catholic Bible. It had been a source of pride for Mum and Dad to have bought this Bible, which they paid a lot of money for. And it had a section at the front for birthdays.'

The local church had loomed large in the family's life. Mark was an altar boy, Maria James would regularly make the short trip three doors down for masses, and sometimes she'd leave Adam with Father Bongiorno. The 11-year-old demanded a lot of attention, with his cerebral palsy and Tourette's, so his time with the priest also allowed Maria to run errands or have some quiet time.

But Mark says the brash Italian priest had upset his devout Catholic mother in a very public roasting, the year she died. It was about those magazines she kept under the counter.

'They were inside sealed plastic, so it's not as though people could come in and open up and look at them, but he made a big deal about this in church and actually referred specifically to my mum, which was a little odd because at the time there were a few other shops in the area that had similar or worse material, and he made no mention of them, just of my mum. She was embarrassed and humiliated. It upset her a lot.'

It was actually Father Bongiorno who broke the tragic news to Mark, with the delicacy of a sledgehammer. Usually after his weekly bowling excursion, the bus would drop Mark off at the bookshop, as it was on the way. This time, the bus went straight back to his high school, Immaculate Heart College, Preston, where his local parish priest was waiting for him.

'I remember Father Bongiorno was there. I think there was a police car there as well. We were heading towards the school office and he broke the news to me, and I could barely stand up ... I was in shock, I kind of collapsed and had difficulty walking. I would've expected Father Bongiorno to pick me up and to help carry me, but he wasn't really doing much. He was having to half-drag me into the principal's office. I've reflected on the way he said it. It didn't appear to come out in a compassionate or sympathetic way—it was more like something he just wanted get over, you know, finish off and get it over with. I think Father Bongiorno and I drove back either in a police car or in a taxi to the bookshop. Police were everywhere.'

'It was almost like my life stopped. Everything just stopped dead. I can see the flurry of activity, the police are there, later on the media arrived, there are passers-by standing around watching, and there are also some shopkeepers, and these people were all agitated obviously, interested to know what transpired. Everyone was upset.'

'My dad was there. He'd been crying, and he was giving me hugs and he was in shock. He just told me that Mum had been murdered, he didn't give me any other details.'

Then the two bereft sons were shipped off to their dad's with nothing more than the school uniforms on their backs.

July 1980

This isn't where she thought her life would be. She's 25 years old, been married for just 18 months, and she's now a stepmother to two traumatised children, one with an intellectual impairment. Patricia James pads through the children's house that's caked in grey fingerprint dust. Thank God for her girlfriend Margaret, who's come to help clean the place and put things back in order. The police have finished the initial forensics, leaving chalky traces and a decision to make. Can they live here? Talk about living in a woman's shadow. But the boys are upset enough—she doesn't want to drag them out of their comfort zone.

Thankfully, her husband, John James, decides the kids will come and live with them in North Fitzroy. Life becomes all about the boys, pulling them through, just putting one foot in front of the other. John's been quite amazing, really, with his sometimes annoying propensity for distraction. Never one to throw his arms in the air and say, 'I can't cope', he's decided they can't put their lives on hold until the cops catch the guy. They have to make life as normal as possible for his two sons. It's Mark's birthday at the end of the month, so they should probably plan a dinner.

She's trying to teach Adam things, like using cutlery. He's been used to ruling the roost at home, sitting on the floor and eating with his hands. Maria let him get away with a lot because, Patricia thinks, she felt guilty. Adam was deprived of oxygen at birth, so Maria blamed herself for his disability. Irrationally, obviously. *Well, let's talk about the obstetrician*, Patricia thinks. *That's a conversation that should've happened*. She's worried people will see her as that cliché, the cold stepmother, making Adam sit at the dinner table with a knife and fork, but she's only trying to help.

So they go through the motions until it feels real. John doesn't bring up that day much. It rattles her, of course, that her new husband was by all accounts standing right beside the killer, shielded only by a door. It could've been John's funeral, too. But he rarely talks about it, and only occasionally muses about who Maria might've been speaking to. He tells Patricia that he just can't make a connection. Everything is as hazy as the voice was.

January 2017

I was the Mayor of Fitzroy at the time of Maria James's murder. I attended Maria's funeral, which was conducted by Father Bongiorno. I was shocked and appalled to hear Father Bongiorno denounce John James from the pulpit, saying that if John had not left her, she would still be alive. John James was distraught and had to be almost carried out of the Church.

— Email from Tim Harding to the *Trace* team, 23 July 2017

'Like, jaw-dropping. I mean, really? A priest with any integrity, with any compassion, with any love of Christ and being Christ-like, would not have uttered even one of those syllables.' None of the fury has diluted for Patricia James, who Kerri Ritchie and I meet at the home of her childhood friends Santo and Pat Barbante. Patricia couldn't believe this blow from the pulpit — Father Bongiorno using Maria's funeral to chastise her for selling soft porn. 'Attacking someone who could not defend themselves, it was so un-Christian, you would have to say there was an underlying motive there. So what was that motive? He was very condemning, and was hurting, not only us adults, but those two children. It's just ...' She can't even finish her sentence. During the funeral address, while Mark James was hiding behind his Atari box, Patricia James was seething.

She's 62 now, a widow — she lost her husband, John, to non-Hodgkin lymphoma in 1996. She smiles over the photo album that Kerri and I are poring over as Kerri finds a young one of John James.

'He's like a movie star, Pat!'

'The thing with John is that he had a baby face — he never looked his age.'

As Patricia, Santo, and Pat dive back into the past, their gentle ribbing of each other hints at a friendship that's weathered a great many things since their youth. They used to while away afternoons at the local milkbar, with their slicked-back hair and angora sweaters. Then everything got more confusing with age, and next thing they knew they were sitting in St Mary's at their friend's funeral, listening to the priest imply she had loose morals.

'What healing did he bring? What light did he bring? None.' Patricia says the pornographic magazines were very tame in today's terms. 'Even what you can get at a newsagent's or service station these days is more risqué than those magazines. She was a very faithful Catholic. But selling these magazines was just a case of, "We've got to pay the rent. We've got to make ends meet." At that particular point, John was still working his way up, still doing night school, so there wasn't a lot of money to spare, so it would have been a case of, "Okay, it's a necessary part of the business". Not one that she would advertise or speak out about. It would be a case of, "okay, there'd be certain people who'd know that certain things were available" and that's it.'

Santo chimes in, equally defensive of Maria. 'You get the Italian priests that come over from Italy, and they're tyrants. They were tyrants in their little villages because they were the most educated people, they could do what they liked. He had the same attitude when he came to Thornbury, like everyone was ignorant except him.'

'In the week leading up to Maria's murder, how was she doing?' I ask. 'You've said you don't think she had a boyfriend, or anything like that. Was she stressed out? Did she have anything going on?'

'My only comment would be, again through John, not through personal observation, she was in a really good place. Maybe if she did have a love interest, that may have contributed to that?'

'But you'd think John would have spoken about it, if there'd been one,' Kerri says.

'Yeah,' Patricia says, 'because this is the thing, John and Maria were friends. They were friends before they became an item, before they got married. Yes, over the years as they grew apart, there were obviously marital tensions. But the foundational element of all of that was that they were friends. And Maria said to John, "As long as I get the kids, you can do what you want." For her, her life was those two boys. It was really a case of being a superbly dedicated mum, and the reason that I know that is because of the way that Maria and John organised things. It was a case of visitation, you know. John wanted to see the kids? Not a problem, he could pop in any time he liked. And, literally, John was on the doorstep and available 24/7, and that was never in question.'

'Well, we know that, from that terrible day, too, she called him and he was there,' I say. 'In all those years you were with him afterwards, he obviously would've wanted it solved. When you talked about it, who did he think did it?'

'He always maintained that he felt like Maria knew that person.'

'I would have thought, if John had known that person, she would've said, "Jack's here" or "The priest is here". She said, "Someone's here," so I find that quite interesting.'

'John operated on two levels,' says Patricia. 'I know he would've had the phone there [waiting for her], and he would've been also been doing something else.'

And after her yelps?

'I don't think he would have thought the worst. It would have been a case of maybe she slipped over, or something like that. Something more mundane. He would've jumped in the car and driven there with curiosity.'

'Not dread?'

'Yeah, exactly.'

But he didn't go to his deathbed dogged by questions. He'd ploughed on. I confess to Patricia that the idea of the boys starting with a blank slate at their dad's sits uneasily with me. But she doesn't remember banning keepsakes. She doesn't remember Maria owning that much stuff. She was a basic woman—maybe she owned some jewellery, but she didn't have little knick-knacks everywhere. What Maria did have, Patricia suspects, would've gone to her brother Tony or sister Rose.

As Patricia and Santo share their memories of Maria, two things seem irrefutable. She was pretty tough, street-wise, so you wouldn't try putting anything over her or you'd risk the wrath of her Italian temper. And Santo says she'd do anything for her boys. 'Maria would give in to Adam a lot, but she loved him that much she would just give him anything, you know'.

'Saintly,' Patricia adds.

Santo stirs her: 'Then Patricia came along, and back then I'd say, "She's a bit cruel," but now that I've thought about it, it's probably what he [Adam] needed, because he was going to have to stand on his own eventually.'

'You were the bad cop, Patricia?' asks Kerri.

'Yeah.'

Patricia says she was just fumbling through, like everyone else. And for the first time in this conversation, her voice breaks.

'There's no manual, but the thing that to this day grieves me, and really, just even speaking about it, my heart is hurting ... In answer to your question before, how was Maria? She was in a really good place. She had the shop, she had her independence, she had her kids, and the relationship with me and John was all coasting along really nicely. In all honesty, I think had we had the opportunity, we would've gotten to be good mates.'

'You used to go to picnics and everything with her,' Pat Barbante says.

'We were in a good place. That, to me, is the future that we were robbed of.'

When we leave the three friends, and they farewell us from the front yard, Pat puts her arm around Patricia, who seems a little shaken. 'Glass of bubbly?', I hear Pat whisper as she gently steers her friend back into the house. Kerri's solution would've been exactly the same—the universal prescription of caring girlfriends.

Left, right, left, right. The Japanese writer Haruki Murakami sees running as a metaphor for life, and for writing. I run to get out of my own crowded head, or to wade through it, for an answer. The jaunty calls of kookaburras filter down through the gum trees along the Yarra River. Merri Creek lies past the end of Hutton Street. Could the killer have thrown the knife in there? But the driver, Jeanette Hodson, who nearly crashed into the man sprinting across High Street, didn't notice a knife in his hand when he slapped it down on her car bonnet. Maybe he tossed it away beforehand? But, then, wouldn't the cops have found it? Maybe he threw it down a drain? Surely he'd have left behind a crumb of information, a trace? Maybe we should call the podcast that. *Trace*. Left, right, left, right. Oooh, pretty butterflies—they always remind me of my late grandma, Nanny Anne. Wonder if she's met Maria up there. Maria, if you can throw me down some signs, that would be great. Who were you talking to? Did you tell a girlfriend who you were meeting that day? Your sister? Man, where do I even start? Left, right, left, mind the dog leash, right.

And what margin do I set for human error? I'm relying on cops' memories and assumptions. What if the guy sprinting across High Street wasn't the killer? That then negates the photofit. What if the killer didn't leave any blood behind in Maria's room? What if her coffee guest wasn't her murderer? So these events that have been crucial coordinates of the investigation may have simply plotted a lifetime of wild-goose chases? Left, right, left, right.

Cops always start with the husband or the lover. But John James's story checked out, and he had his secretary to vouch for him. Was Maria seeing someone? That might explain the lock on the back of her bedroom door. Or maybe any single mother would occasionally want her privacy? We'd tried asking Tony Aleandro, and Patricia James, and the dredging rattled them and made us feel guilty. If nothing comes of this investigation, all we will have succeeded in doing is to have upset a lot of haunted people. Left, right, left, right. 'Pain is inevitable. Suffering is optional' says the Japanese writer. You must have more kilometres in your legs than me, buddy. And we're not machines, are we, Mr Murakami?

April 2016

They shoot at him on the rooftop every few months. It's always the same. It's around 2.00am, Ron Iddles is driving a divisional van through Abbotsford, the scanner beeps with a potential break-in at a nearby factory, so he stops to check. As he's searching the roof of the factory, the shots ring out. Then he wakes. He never knows what triggers these nightmares. Just the job, he guesses. The factory is near where Ron once intercepted a car with a boot-full of stolen cigarettes. The thieves took off, and there was a small pursuit. The factory is also near an armed robbery he was once called to. But that's as real as it got. Yet his subconscious has added bullets to his dreams. Annoying, because there are enough nightmares during waking hours.

As he sits beside me in this sterile Coroners Court meeting room, he shares one of Homicide's unwritten rules: 'Don't let yourself become emotionally involved, because if you do, your judgement becomes clouded.' He's slipped up a couple of times. He'd promised Elvira Buckingham he'd solve her daughter's murder. The stabbed body of 16-year-old Michelle Buckingham was found dumped beside a rural road in 1983. Twenty-nine years later, a Shepparton newspaper journalist,

Tammy Mills, nagged Ron to reopen the case. He did, and Tammy's subsequent articles in the *Shepparton News* inspired a local, Norm, to invite Ron to a clandestine meeting in the middle of a country footy oval. It was here that Norm dobbed in his brother-in-law, Stephen Bradley. 'Him and a couple of other blokes put the hard word on her. She wouldn't put out, so they continued. They stabbed her', Norm later told the Shepparton Magistrates Court.

A couple of hours after those dark family secrets were spilled on the footy oval, Ron remembers visiting Elvira.

'I hadn't met her before, and I remember it's 8.30 at night, the light's on in the house. I walk down the drive, my heart is pounding. I knocked on the door and she came out, and she's a big German woman. She said, "Who are you?" and I said, "I'm Ron Iddles, Senior Sergeant from Homicide." "Come in," she said. I told her, "I think I can solve your daughter's murder."'

'"The last detective told me that," she said. "And you know what, Ron, for 28 years I haven't had a daughter, 28 years, and after 20 years my doctor told me to get over it, and get on with my life. Now you're knocking on my door, you're going to tell me you can solve it. You've just brought back the emotion that is so raw, as if it's day one. You're going to take me on a rollercoaster ride. But if you don't solve it, you'll destroy me."

'I said, "You're going to have to trust me", and she got up and she gave me a big hug, and said, "I trust you." Before the trial, she rang me up and said, "I'm worried about the trial, Ron, I'm worried they'll trash my daughter's name in the media, and trash her reputation in court." I said, "Don't worry about that, your daughter was 16."'

Four days before the trial started, Elvira Buckingham had

a massive heart attack and died. 'In the end, I think that's
what killed her, just the stress of having to go through the
process.' A tear rolls down Ron's cheek, and he doesn't even
bother brushing it away. He's a million miles away. 'You're
resurrecting something from the past. You might go to
a family, sometimes there's been no contact for 10, 15, 20
years, but all of a sudden you go to their house and you say
to them, "You know what, we're going to relook at this, and
we've got some information, I think I can solve it". Well, it's
like it's yesterday, that emotion for them is raw, and you take
them on a rollercoaster ride. It's like Elisabeth Membrey.'

The 22-year-old arts graduate disappeared in 1994. Blood
was discovered in her flat and car, but her body's never been
found. Her parents, Joy and Roger Membrey, desperately
want to find Elisabeth's remains so they can finally have a
funeral. 'I say to Roger and Joy, "I think we're going to do all
right, we're working on something." We arrested a suspect,
but in the end I eliminated him.' The suspect, Shane Bond,
a patron at the hotel Elisabeth worked at, was acquitted in
2012 in the circumstantial case against him. 'So it was like
taking them to the top, and then there is no result: "I'm sorry,
Rog, he hasn't done it." Bang, they're at the bottom, and
they're low, low, low.

'Then for the investigator, it's about, *Is there anything
else in the file? What else can I do?* Because you look at the
parents and you think, *I've caused it, basically*, so you find
something else, and away you go again. I took them to the
top twice without a result, took 'em there three times, but the
person in the end was acquitted. It's a journey you take them
on, and there's always a risk you mightn't get there.'

July 1980

Detectives learn that risqué comics might've sparked an argument on the morning of Maria James's murder. A salesman tells Ron Iddles' team that when he was making a delivery that morning, at the service station across the road, he saw someone knocking on the bookshop door. Another witness says they saw Maria in a heated argument with a man around the same time. Detectives believe this man is Mario Falcucci, a bit of a local loner with a short fuse who lives with his mother in Hutton Street, which runs from the bookshop down past the railway line.

Mario will long sit high on Ron Iddles' 'persons of interest' list. When police interview Mario, numerous times, either his temper flares up, or at critical junctures he complains that his memory's foggy because he had the Asian flu. Detectives have to remind him, 'Mario, we just need to go through this.' He finally admits to being in the bookshop that morning, and to arguing with Maria as he tried to sell her some Parade comics. Ron Iddles sees the comics in his briefcase. Some relate to sexual killings. But Mario is adamant that when Maria refused to buy his comics, he left peacefully.

Ron's gut says something's not right about Mario, though. And when they execute a warrant on his house, they make two interesting discoveries. In the backyard, they find green twine tying tomato plants to stakes. It's very similar to what was used to bind Maria's wrists. However, there's only one major company in Footscray that makes this stuff. The same twine would often be tied around the stacks of magazines that customers brought into Maria's shop, which suggests that the killer didn't necessarily bring the twine with him. But something else is off. Detectives find a dry cleaner's receipt for a pair of grey trousers. The shop's city address catches Ron's attention: Fletcher Jones, in Flinders Street. And the date: 18 June. It's the day after Maria's murder. Why would Mario make a 20-kilometre round trip when surely there's a dry-cleaner in Thornbury? When officers visit Fletcher Jones, the receipt documentation notes there was a stain on the grey trousers that appeared to be blood. But the detectives are too late—the stain has been washed away forever.

As well as Mario Falcucci, there are strong contenders for other possible suspects. And the motive might be passion. Ron's team has ruled out John James, but there are three other men whom Ron wants to investigate. He wonders whether any of them were behind the bunch of flowers that was delivered to Maria, along with an affectionate card, around a week before her murder. Detectives visit the local florist but the best the staff can remember is that a man came in, paid for the flowers in cash, and relayed the comment he wanted written on Maria's card.

A very important clue comes from Mark James. The 13-year-old tells police that his mum had been seeing someone, but she discovered he was married, so she called it off. A revenge killing perhaps? This man, a real estate agent, comes into the shop while detectives are working, confesses to having had a sexual relationship with Maria, but asks the officers not to jeopardise his marriage. They say if he can supply an alibi, there'll be no need to question his wife. So he tells officers that at the time of the murder, he and his colleague were showing a client through a house for sale. Ron contacts this colleague, and, yep, the real estate agent's alibi checks out.

Next person of interest: Mr Telecom. One of the thousands of slivers of information that flood in, in these early months, is from someone who says that Maria James was in, or intending to be in, a relationship with a man who worked for Telecom. Ron's team's inquiries eventually lead to a man living in South Yarra. This Telecom worker admits to visiting the bookshop, and buying books from Maria, but he says he wasn't in a sexual relationship with her. And he denies any knowledge of the murder. This whole avenue of inquiry is striking Ron as pretty innocuous ... until Mr Telecom commits suicide. Not long after Maria's murder, once detectives have moved out of her house and back to their Russell Street office, the Telecom worker kills himself. On a small typewriter in his South Yarra flat, he's left a typed note. It makes reference to his interview by Homicide detectives, but that's it—no confession, no explanation. Ron wonders, *Was this man crippled by guilt? Or was he already suffering from a mental illness?*

The loose threads start to pile up, and time's getting away from them. They're getting so desperate for information that they resort to hypnotism. It's the first time that Victoria Police has employed the technique in a murder investigation. A local council garbage man has come forward who remembers seeing someone at Maria's around five o'clock on the morning of her murder. Detectives dub this person of interest 'The Five-A-M man'. A police doctor, Peter Bush, at Royal Melbourne Hospital, performs hypnosis on the garbage man to see if he can remember any distinguishing features of the man he saw, so police can compile a better sketch or face-fit. Dr Bush swings a fob watch in front of the garbage man, asks if his eyes are getting heavy, then questions him for half an hour. To no avail. The garbo says he never really felt out to it.

Ron wonders whether this is true, or whether he just wanted to insert himself into the investigation. You get those types. Those who are lonely, who just want to be part of something. His colleagues soon charge someone for just that. Michelle O__'s story about Maria having a relationship with a Mordialloc butcher who was into kinky sex cost detectives a week's work, and Ms O__ a conviction and fine for perverting the course of justice.

Needing someone who won't lie to them, Ron's team leans on the local priest, Father Anthony Bongiorno, for information. They're hoping the devout Maria, or her killer for that matter, might have dropped a clue in the confessional box that the priest might be willing to share. Turns out he won't, not even if his life depended on it. Father Bongiorno tells detectives that to do so would fly in the face of canon law — what's said in the confessional stays there. This doesn't go down well with Ron's boss, Inspector Brian Ritchie, who throws the priest's own book, the Bible, at him, opened at a psalm about how one should obey state laws as well as God's ones. 'Just tell us if she was having an affair,' Inspector Ritchie asks the priest. But he won't be budged.

ABC reporter Norm Beaman also presses Father Bongiorno on this point, in a TV interview aired shortly after the murder.

If you were free to make comment about information you gained in confessional, would you do so?

'I can't even make a comment on your presumption or your hypothesis that I might be free to give valuable information.'

Were you aware at any time that you were speaking to Mrs James in the confessional?

'I can't make any comment on whether she went to

confession, or whether or not I spoke to her inside the confessional or outside the confessional, or what was the nature of our discussions, of a personal nature referring to her personal background or associations, or anything she said of a confidential nature to me.'

You knew Mrs James rather well?

'Of course, I'd have to admit that. I'd have to also admit I spoke to her—only a fool would deny that.'

Then you'd know her voice?

'I can't comment on that, whether or not she was in the confessional box, whether I knew she was there or not.'

Norm Beaman presses on, but gets nowhere ...

But if you know Mrs James well, you'd know her voice, wouldn't you?

'I can't comment on that.'

Don't you think you have a moral obligation to the public to divulge every piece of information that you have?

'I think it's been well proven I've been of valuable assistance to them [the police], but in this case, of course, respecting my status as a priest, my professional status and her rights, and my confidences, I can make no further comment than that.'

How will you feel personally if some other woman falls victim to this murderer?

'Well, I can't see how I'm involved. My status as a priest does not really convey any responsibility for me to solve every murder that might or might not happen in the city of Melbourne.'

'We say as priests, I know less about confession than something I know nothing about.'

August 2016

Brian Ritchie is on for 3pm. He says his memory is not great but he remembered all about Father Bongiorno.

— Text from Andy Burns, *Trace* producer, 11 August 2016

Brian Ritchie is now 78, with kind eyes and ruddy cheeks. He's a perfect fit for his summer job at the local shopping centre. Ron Iddles has let slip that Brian's been moonlighting as Santa Claus. Brian chuckles, 'They were short of Santas, so I went in. Actually, Ron Iddles turned up. He's a talker, isn't he?'

I tell him I love it. It's about as far away as you can get from a grouchy Homicide detective. As he thinks back to his three years as Inspector of Victoria's Homicide Squad, his wife, Helen, potters in the kitchen, occasionally yelling out anecdotes and filling in the gaps in her husband's memory. It's interesting, as I chase the past, when older versions of those I've read about in coroner reports or newspaper clippings jump off those pages and sit right in front of me. Now it's Brian, at a doilied dining table in Melbourne's eastern suburbs, under a German cuckoo clock.

Brian is still angry about his confrontation with Father Bongiorno. 'I still believe, once she is dead that the privacy of the confessional no longer should apply. Common sense to me was, *It's not going to affect her now, but it could clear up the murder and put somebody behind bars, where they belong*. He rejected it in a big way, and I think he actually went to the media about it, and so I had to go to the media about it with my side.'

I ask Brian about the lengths they went to back then,

to try to solve this thing, and about the hypnotism. As we speak about the then new-agey technique, his clock chimes with comedic timing. *Cuckoo*. 'Hypnotism was a handy tool, actually. It was interesting: the first time I saw him [the hypnotist] operate, they called all the officers in the crime department, all the inspectors, chief superintendent, everybody, into the big muster room area, and this guy was explaining hypnotism to us, and they called out a fella named Bill Little. Bill was Senior Sergeant at Footscray, and Bill volunteered to be hypnotised. The guy took him back to his childhood days when he went to school, and Bill broke down when he said, "Oh, we are so poor I've got no shoes", so they had to stop it. That was the extent that this thing could go.' Brian laughs that he once volunteered as a guinea pig. 'We had a guy when I was doing an officer's course, he hypnotised me, and during a class he'd just do a whistle or something, and I'd jump up and run round the desk. Well, the instructors weren't very impressed!'

Brian Ritchie remembers Maria James's house well. In fact, so does Helen. It was quite the family affair. 'We basically lived there, you know. The wives came out with meals for us.' Helen chips in, 'You wouldn't see them otherwise. Brian was off to work before the kids woke in the morning, and home after they were in bed. I said to our youngest, "When did you last see Daddy?" and he said, "Live or on TV?"' The couple laugh, then Brian's face clouds a little. 'I was devoted; my time was just gone. And, actually, we had a kidnapping attempt on my eldest son at primary school by two crooks, who were charged with murders—that's all history, of course.'

I ask whether unsolved cases like Maria James's keep him up at nights wondering. 'No, that was a long time ago, no. I used to. I'd be thinking 24 hours a day, *What haven't I done?*

And actually, I was lucky. When I took charge of the squad, we had 80 murders that year, and we solved 79 of them, but I changed the system. If a crew got a murder, they stayed on that case and didn't go on call again until they'd gone as far as they could—that way, they could devote themselves to it. That'd make a big difference. They weren't happy about it, though, because until then the rosters were permanent, and they'd say, "I've got next Christmas off." ... Uh-uh, bad luck.' Bad Santa. 'I loved the challenge, but I was always a worrier, you know, that we missed something. I suppose you naturally get affected by it one way or the other. Even poor old Ron, he was breaking down in the end, wasn't he? Crying and stuff. It certainly does impact on you.'

September 1989

Ron Iddles is burnt out. The 18-hour days are taking a toll. He's been in the force for 17 years now, the last nine in Homicide, days consumed by death and misery. No rest *from* the wicked. And he's missing precious times he'll never get back—Christmases, his children's birthdays, sports days, school concerts, far too many milestones to count. Thank God for his wife, Colleen, he thinks—the kids wouldn't be what they are without her. His body and his mind need a break. But there are no such things as mental-health initiatives and understanding bosses. He fears that any admission he's struggling will mean ostracism and an instruction to 'Harden the hell up.' He's right. When he finally unravels, a police psychologist tells him, 'Well, that's just part of policing.' Ron will later learn that this shrink—the one advising officers on how to best cope with their jobs—was part of a paedophile ring.

So Ron quits, and finds solace on the road. He's no longer Victoria Police member 18150, but a Debco contract truck driver, delivering potting mix to nurseries around Melbourne. He's dealing with a different kind of muck, but he likes it. He follows that up with new-furniture deliveries, and is successful enough to afford a second truck and driver. He's no Lindsay Fox, but it's an interesting lesson in entrepreneurialism. There's no sick leave if the wheels of the truck don't turn, so he's regimented, in a very different manner to his last job. He teaches himself how to fix problems. The mechanics of a truck are easier to navigate than those of the human psyche.

2016

Sad I won't get to meet Brian. Please pass on my best wishes. I just wanted to ask him about 'Joe'. Ron Iddles mentioned that Brian 'liked him as a person of interest' in the Maria James case … A shopkeeper sometimes saw him with a gun (because he was a night watchman) and thought 'Joe' might've been visiting Maria James that day.

— Email from Rachael Brown to John Delphin

Ron Iddles has brought me up to speed on those who were considered the major 'persons of interest' in 1980, and I'm keen to revisit them. Easier said than done. The generation I need, it's not like they're on Facebook, Twitter, or LinkedIn. So a big chunk of my life begins being chewed up poring over federal rolls and the Australian Electoral Commission database. My initial Holy Grail is Jeanette Hodson, the driver who nearly crashed into the man sprinting from the bookshop. I find a woman in Newborough—not her. Another Jeanette in Neerim South—also not her, although she endearingly tells me she wishes she were. The closest my producer, Kerri Ritchie, and I come to the elusive Jeanette is finding out she might have worked for a cat-protection society in Greensborough. *Might* have.

I bomb out on Mario Falcucci, too. I learn he's now in a nursing home with dementia, so even if I visit, it's not going to help. Also now in a nursing home is Brian McCarthy, Ron's former colleague who worked out of the bookshop with him. Brian's family would prefer I didn't interview him. Fair enough. So his buddy and former colleague John Delphin graciously asks Brian some questions on my behalf.

I'm most interested in a guy we'll call 'Joe'. This security guard—or night watchman, as they called them back then—has come up in local scuttlebutt as potentially being linked to the murders of two other local women in the early 1980s. And since then, if I have the right Joe, he has served jail time for being an accessory after the fact in the murders of two drug couriers. So ex-Senior Sergeant McCarthy liked him as a suspect in the Maria James case. But that was then, and when Mr Delphin presses him on it now, he comes up blank. And, unfortunately, nothing else Brian can remember provides the lead I need. The name of the Telecom worker who committed suicide, for example. Or the name of the 5.00am man. These are still gaping holes for me. Ron's memory is usually impeccable, but these names escape him.

Mr Telecom could very well be the killer. He was never eliminated. I consult the man I've come to regard as the unofficial mayor of High Street, a goldmine of all the local gossip. Terry Gannon used to run a newsagency down the road from Maria's bookshop, and our regular phone chats have taught me a lot about the colourful characters who gravitated around that little pocket of Thornbury. Mark James worked for him, and he had a soft spot for Adam James, who'd often wander in asking to be a paperboy, 'just like Mark'. Terry used to chat with Maria most mornings, and two things stood out for him: 'Her kindness, and her fierce loyalty to those boys'.

Terry vaguely remembers a Telecom worker—a Greek man, he thinks, who Maria had described as 'a bit of a spunk'. He wonders if this was who Maria was referring to on the morning of her death.

'She was off to buy a cake,' Terry tells me. "Going to meet a friend of ours," she'd said. It was a foreign name.'

I'm desperate to learn more about Mr Telecom. Ron Iddles tells me his former colleague Dave ___ conducted the police interview, so he'd be worth a call. Dave's now retired, and when I call, he says some notes might be in his garage—but he's not prepared to look, to check for the name of this mystery man.

'That's all in the past now,' he says.

'Not for Maria's sons,' I gently point out.

But it makes no difference. I get the feeling Dave shut that door some time ago. As for Mr Telecom's family, Ron doesn't remember him having any. Yet another suspect is parked for now.

Then there are those who dropped onto the police's radar later in the piece. Like Frank Todd. It was around 2006, Ron thinks, when a detective asked if his crew had ever checked out this man, who was a regular at the James house and was later convicted for paedophilia. No, Ron has to admit to me a decade on, they never looked at Frank Todd. He used to work with John James at the Fitzroy Town Hall, and the two had been firm mates since childhood—John even asked Frank to be Mark's godfather. But as for motive, there doesn't seem to be one. Nonetheless, I make a mental note to check with Mark about his godfather.

Kerri and I wear down our own shoe leather, canvassing local shopkeepers. Celia and her clothes boutique might have gone, but Calvin and his records are still here, tubs and shelves of them, in tight stacks that would have rivalled Maria's Tetris book-packing. 'Being on this strip, you never really forget it,' Calvin Hills says of Maria's murder. 'Thornbury was an innocent place comparatively, so it left a huge impression on a lot of people. A lot of us were teachers in the area, and bookshops were special places. So for something that violent, in a place regarded highly, a bookshop ...' He drifts off, then tells us it's terrific that Maria's story isn't lost.

He can't help us, though, with the real estate agent who was having an affair with Maria before she was murdered. Ron Iddles thinks his name is Peter ___. His old real estate office is now a community legal practice, but a land title search tells us the building is still owned by the same person, Denis Gabriel, so perhaps he can shed some light on all this. After too many failed attempts trying to call him, we land on his doorstep, and he welcomes us in and regales us with stories about the colourful locals. No intel on our Peter, though. 'Try Peter P. Peters,' he says, 'the man who owned the real estate practice. I think he lives up north now.' We track down the alliterative former agent in Queensland, and our call drags him away from his gardening. He's gracious, but doesn't remember the Peter we're after. A lot of employees went through his office, Peter P. Peters tells us. Some moved on quickly.

Kerri and I canvass about half-a-dozen real estate agents who used to work that beat. Again, no luck on the Casanova. One phone call usually necessitates another three, which can lead to another nine. Now I understand the sentiment behind something a cold-case detective once said to me, which infuriated me at the time. I'd explained that the podcast would call for leads from listeners.

'Yeah,' the detective said, 'but that might result in 100 emails about a white car.'

'Isn't that a great thing?' I replied naively.

'But now we have to follow up 100 emails about a white car.'

I get it. It's exhausting, and very often comes to nothing.

Then there's my favourite lead that's also careering nowhere. The enduring niggle I've had about this case has to do with an electrician. Ron Iddles says this electrician saw a man with blood on him in the St Mary's churchyard around the time of Maria's murder. The electrician apparently made a police statement, yet Ron's never heard what came of it, and I don't recall ever seeing it in the press. So this electrician is my new Holy Grail. Ron can't remember his name, but he thinks the police interview was facilitated by the electrician's detective mate, Howard Beer.

So I text Howard. And email. And call. And email again. Poor Howard has probably had a gutful. He tells me he's emailed the electrician, but has heard nothing back. 'Well, are you sure that's his email? Have you called him? Can you? Can you at least tell me his name?' Yes, I'm annoying. But I feel this electrician could be the missing puzzle-piece that the James boys are so desperately counting on. But every reply from Howard, *if* one comes, is the same. *No word yet.*

This has to go on the backburner. Along with people like Will McGenniskin—the garbo who was hypnotised in the hope he might offer a better description of the 5.00am man. Along with Jeanette Hodson. Along with peripheral suggestions like, 'Try to find the Italian receptionist from Peter P. Peters. I don't think she knew Maria, but she knew everything that went on in that office'.

So, so many people to track down. So many dead ends. I crave to look inside Maria's ten cold-case boxes, which are usually piled in a Victoria Police warehouse, out in the south-western suburbs. The time it would save me, and the help it would bring! But Victoria Police maintains it's an open investigation, so this information is off limits, especially to pesky journalists. Every spare second around my actual job—radio current affairs shift work—is being poured into finding answers for a woman I've never met. Yet there's still been no indication from the ABC that it'll even commission this podcast. I'll end up waiting eight months, and for most of this time the investigation 'team' is just me. This is too big for one person.

One Sunday in July, sleep deprived and pissed off, I wonder whether I should just have a break from this. Permanently, or at least for a while, to do normal human things like dinners and dating and exercise, instead of spending hours lost down rabbit holes of ancestry.com. I return from a teary debrief with Kerri, and open my letterbox to a waiting little face-slap from the universe. It's a junk-mail flier for a real estate agent—the one-and-only Peter ___, with his mobile-phone number and all. Okay, Maria. You win. I'm not going anywhere.

March 1994–2001

Come the early 1990s, Australia's recession hits, and many companies fall into a heap. Ron's potting-mix business with Debco is strong enough to weather the economic battering, but the scare is enough to make a certain phone call seem like a blessing.

It's Superintendent Geoff O'Loughlin. The boys in blue want him back. It's the second time that Geoff's called. Colleen didn't tell Ron about the first time. For her, it's going to mean basically being a single parent again. But she knows policing is in his blood. Ron's 39 now, and the time he's spent running his own business has made him appreciate the security, conditions, and holidays of Victoria Police, so his decision is an easy one. But the obligatory refresher at the Police Academy is slightly demoralising. He's now a 're-tread', the slur for cops who leave and want to return. And he can't have his old number back: he's now 30065. Initially, he thinks it's going to be a drag, back driving a divisional van in Collingwood, or on a beat that'll be equally taxing. Instead, he's streamlined back into Homicide, and after four years he's slogged it back to the rank of senior sergeant. Around a year later, he's awarded his old badge number. He's back.

He's careful, this time, of his mind. He knows people will think it's crazy, but in 1999 he starts driving overnight Firefly passenger coaches to Adelaide or Sydney ... to relax. After, say, a three-week homicide job, when his colleagues might be picking up their golf clubs, Ron's heading over the Westgate Bridge to leave that world behind for a while. Well, most of it. One guy boards in Adelaide, a gold chain around his neck, and says to Ron, 'I know you—we're on opposite sides of the fence'. Ron replies, 'Well, if you know me, you know you're in safe hands.' The drug dealer boards and sleeps soundly all night. Another night, a passenger tells Ron, 'I know your voice. You've either got a cooking show or you're on 3AW (a Melbourne radio station).' Most nights, these trips for Ron are a nice reminder of the better side of human nature. Instead of his regular sceptical officer prism, he has a rear-view mirror full of adventurers.

In 2001, when Ron Iddles is in charge of the Missing Persons Unit, a colleague gets a lead on the Maria James murder: a punter has suggested they re-look at a bloke by the name of Keogh. Ron is keen to revisit the James file. Usually, the trifecta of murder-solving hinges on knowledge of the victim's identity; his or her cause of death; and the motive. But 18 years on, this last cog still eludes him. And it's a case frustratingly lacking in forensic evidence. The murder weapon was never found. No fingerprints were able to be dusted off the coffee mugs. There was a lot of blood splatter, and Ron thinks the killer's blood might be mixed up in it somewhere, but police have only been able to test for blood groupings—nothing more specific. Until now. Come the turn of the century, as Ron dives back into the James file, technology is now on his side. DNA testing is coming to the fore, and Ron has a win ... a genetic profile of the killer.

August 2016–January 2017

> Peter ___ has agreed to meet me in 20 minutes. If I can get
> him to agree are you happy for me to interview? Will iPhone be
> quality enough — and any partic qs?

— Text from *Trace* producer Andy Burns to Rachael Brown, 8 August 2016

The needed nudge from the universe sitting in my letterbox begins a very odd pursuit of Peter ___. I dial the mobile number on the junk-mail flier, and explain that I'm looking into the cold case of Maria James, and that I understand they used to be friends. Can I come and have a chat? Peter says he remembers the murder, but didn't know Maria. I've expected this, so I explain that I understand the certain sensitivities involved, and that I'll be discreet, because I'm desperate to talk to people who knew Maria, who might help shed light on her killer. Again, he's adamant he's not *that* Peter. Confused, I call Kerri Ritchie, and can hear her smirking through the phone when she says I've been played. 'Of course he's going to deny it. Also, he's a smooth-talking real estate agent'.

So I send in Andy Burns. She's helping me produce a pilot episode that will hopefully, finally, get *Trace* commissioned. Andy arrives—trenchcoat and all—at a pub opposite the real estate office and calls the mysterious Peter. He tries to send his PA instead, but Andy explains that's not a good idea, given the personal nature of the inquiry. He brings the PA anyway. Andy calls me for a debrief.

'She (the PA) definitely was very helpful in remembering stories about random other stuff. It felt like they were running a tag team on me of obfuscation.' Andy continues that she'd told Peter she was working on *Trace* to help Maria's sons, Mark and Adam. Not long after, Peter asked if Maria has kids. 'I repeated, "Yeah, she has two sons", and he said, "Were they there? Did they see anything when it happened?" And it just struck me as an odd question.'

'Do you think he was fishing for information on possible witnesses?'

'It crossed my mind.'

This makes me a little uneasy, because if we're right about Peter, he would've known the boys, known when they were at school. Was this an anxious question from someone who thinks the boys might've remembered something incriminating? Andy adds that she tried to offer Peter an out.

'I said it's completely understandable that someone who's had an extra-marital affair wouldn't want their wife to know, and they could just contribute anonymously to *Trace*. But he just kept coming back to this point, "I'm not your guy, you need to go back to your sources." He was fairly good-humoured through the whole thing.'

As it turns out, Peter kept saying it wasn't him because … it *wasn't*. During a chat with Rowland Legg, one of the original detectives on the Maria James case, Rowland tells me he recalls a different surname for the real estate agent. It's not the guy from the flier. We've just spent the past six months chasing the wrong Peter. Sorry, Peter.

So now it's back to square one. With the name from Rowland Legg, we chase the right Peter, but we never catch him. And I can't leave a message with his wife, because I'm not here to wreck a marriage. So this is one lead I've frustratingly had to leave alone. Kerri does, however, track down his former colleague, who we'll call Carlo, who provided Peter's alibi. Ron Iddles once told me that in unsolved cases he'll always revisit the alibi, because they've been known to crumble. 'Ten to 15 years later the relationship might've broken down, the person says, "You know what, I'm going to tell you who actually killed her."'

When we talk to Carlo, his first reaction is, 'Wow, they still haven't caught the bloke?' He tells Kerri he didn't know about the affair—he thought Peter was a happily married man. 'It's not as if we went for drinks every weekend and talked about social things. I was new to the industry, just trying to do the job. I really don't know what happened with Peter and Maria.' But he tells Kerri he had no reason to lie for Peter, then or now, and that if he told police in 1980 that he was doing a house inspection with Peter in Greensborough at the time of the murder, then that's exactly where they were.

So, in short, I'm ten months in, and have made no great inroads into the initial persons of interest. Then my phone beeps with a text from Ash Gannon, the son of Terry the newsagent. Hopefully, it's news of an interview time. I've been holding off meeting Terry, as he's been unwell, and, as he always chuckles conspiratorially, his wife's a little wary of him talking to me.

'Ask Ron if a *Herald Sun* or *Age* was found in the bookshop,' he has suggested to me recently, hinting he might know something I don't. Terry was questioned himself once, as many of the local shopkeepers were, but cops interrupted one of his beloved games with the Northcote Cricket Club to do it. The avid batsman's reply of 'Piss off until after' only encouraged detectives to stop the match.

The first time I see Terry's face, it's smiling back from the front of his memorial-service brochure. Ash Gannon's text had conveyed the sad news of his death. Terry had only recently found out he was sick, but the ravages of liver cancer despatch its victims pretty quickly. My cheeks are soon wet for a man I'd only known through a phone line. A man who'd told his nurse the weekend before, 'She better hurry up and solve it—I won't be around for much longer'. A man who said to his son Ash, 'Tell that little warrior to be careful'.

And such are the creeping bonds in journalism that I find myself at a funeral for someone I've never met, during an investigation into the murder of someone I never knew. Terry's brother has the mourners chuckling at memories of Terry's trademark hat. 'Just because you're poor doesn't mean you should look poor,' the Thornbury battler used to say. I internally debate the pros and cons of introducing myself to his wife, Jeanette, worried she mightn't want me here. But when I do, she engulfs me in a hug and then pulls back, puts her hands on my shoulders, and whispers, 'It dominated his life, you know. He just wanted to know who did it'.

'He'll now know before any of us,' I say.

This is the toll of cold cases: they're never that temperature for those affected. And this is just one. There are another 1,300 cold cases sitting in boxes around the country. You can regard such a statistic with a feeling of futility. Or you can remember that starfish parable: of a beach littered with stranded starfish after a storm, and of a little boy trying to throw them back into the sea. An old man chuckles, 'There's too many—you can't make a difference.' The boy picks up another, throws it to safety, smiles, and says, 'I made a difference to *that* one.'

2002

Maria James's exhibits are back from the forensics lab, and, two decades on, police have their strongest lead yet. Ron was always pretty confident that some of the blood found on Maria's pillow would have belonged to her killer. That pillow has now yielded a male DNA profile, which detectives can use to compare against that of suspects—Mario Falcucci, for example, whose twine and bloodied trousers have long bugged Ron. He finds Mario in a nursing home, but Mario, now elderly, no longer has all his faculties, so Ron seeks permission from Mario's sister for a buccal swab. The old man licks the cotton bud like an ice-cream, and the sample is sent away for comparison to Maria's pillow. It turns out to be no match.

As for the other initial persons of interest, DNA testing will be tricky. Ron has an idea that Mr Telecom—who committed suicide—was cremated, so detectives would have to find relatives for familial DNA samples. The same goes for Frank Todd: cremated, no children, so they'd need to test siblings. Ron's crew never worked out who the 5.00am man was, so DNA is no help there, and there's no need to test the real estate agent, because his alibi holds up. The only real progress for now is having Mario ruled out.

But sometimes the strike-outs are just as important. It's a different kind of closure. Take Phil Cleary, for example. The former independent federal MP and star half-forward flanker for the Victorian Football League has been at Ron for ages to look into Peter Keogh, who killed his sister, Vicki, in 1987. She'd initially taken pity on the violent and drunken criminal; then, when it got too hard, she ended it, and he stabbed her outside a Coburg kindergarten. Yet Keogh was acquitted of murder, went down for manslaughter instead under the old provocation defence, and Phil Cleary has been an advocate for victims' rights ever since.

Police spoke to Keogh about the Maria James murder in 1980, but eliminated him as a person of interest when his partner provided him with an alibi. Falsely, as it turns out. Phil has information that she'd been leaned on. So, yep, Ron would have to agree, Keogh is a strong person of interest. Also, as a teenager, Keogh was shot in both knees during a knife attack on a policeman, which could fit with reports that the man seen running from the bookshop had a limp.

But as police look into Keogh, he commits suicide. Detectives make a last-minute appeal to the coroner to take Keogh's DNA before he's cremated. His DNA profile is tested against Maria's bloody pillow, and ... no match. But at least that's another one off the list, and Phil Cleary can rest easier that Keogh's CV of assault, child rape, arson, and manslaughter didn't also extend to the killing of another loved woman who happened to be in the wrong place at the wrong time.

A decade sails by, frosting over the trail of Maria's killer. This equates to around 120 homicide investigations for Ron, including the 2001 disappearance of arts graduate Elisabeth Membrey, the 2005 murder of Fairfield solicitor David Robinson, and the 2006 shooting of security guard Erwin Kastenberger. Time, and evil, march on.

Then, in 2013, Adam James drops a bombshell that Ron never saw coming. Adam's revelation alerts Ron to the possibility that at Maria's funeral, when detectives were scrutinising the congregation for her killer, maybe they were all looking in the wrong direction. Maybe they should've been looking up at the altar.

Part II
The Church

March 2016

Adam lives in Wantirna. It would be better to interview him at my place. I will speak with him over the weekend and text you then.

— Text from Mark James to Rachael Brown, 17 March 2016

Adam James takes very deep breaths. He's only ever told this story privately before: to his brother, and to police. He's just met me, so I'm already impressed by his nerve. Adam's now 47 years old, with an infectious humour and a childlike booming voice. His cerebral palsy and Tourette's means he has the intellectual and emotional capacity of an 18 year old. His older brother, Mark, sits beside him on the couch. He's kept his promise to his mum: he's looked after his little brother all this time. Adam lived with Mark for a bit, and now he's in a residential care facility. Mark fills me in, 'Adam's confident, in the sense he can walk, eat, and do all the things the rest of us do, but he can't really cook or file a tax return.'

'You're not alone there,' I joke to Adam.

He still clings to one of his favourite memories of his mother. Literally. He's wearing a brown-and-white Disneyland bomber jacket, and he tells me about a happy family trip to the US theme park. He thinks it's hilarious that my parents went to Disneyland and enjoyed rides like Splash Mountain … *without* me. Adam lost his life raft as an 11-year-old.

'My dad rang my school and he spoke to the headmaster, he told me to come home right away, and I arrived home at the bookshop …' Adam's booming voice starts to crack. 'I said to him, "Dad, where's Mum?" and he said, "She's gone, son."' Adam collapses into sobs and slaps his leg a couple of times, shaking his head. 'I'm sorry, Rach, I don't want to be like this.'

No, Adam. I'm sorry. So very sorry. The lump in my throat will feel like a boulder by the time I've finished putting him through this harrowing interview. But it's crucial; Adam may just prove the key to cracking his mum's cold case.

For 33 years he kept a secret, because someone told him to, someone he trusted. And now it comes out in a flood.

The morning before Maria was murdered, she'd left Adam at St Mary's with Father Anthony Bongiorno. 'He said to me, "Adam, I want you to trust me. I don't want you to tell your mum or Mark what I'm going to do."' Adam says the priest led him into a little room behind the altar. As he claws his way through this memory, his eyes remain fixed on the floor, he rocks back and forth, and his splayed right hand rubs metronomically between the webbing on his left. His right leg jiggles. Sometimes his head cocks to the right and nestles into his right shoulder. He rubs under his nose, his eyes, and then through his hair. Over and over and over. 'He told me to pull my pants down halfway, and he, then he put his hand …'

Adam's breathing is getting heavier; his rocking, faster. I lean in to stop the tape, to give him some air. He says he wants to push through.

'... then he put his hand down there, and he was touching me. I asked him to stop, and he wouldn't stop. I asked him what he was doing. He didn't say.'

Adam remembers the abuse being halted by footsteps. It was his mum coming to collect him.

'As we went, he said to me, "Adam, remember what I told you. You can trust me. Don't tell your mum or Mark about this." As me and my mum left the parish, Father Bongiorno said to her ... in a whisper ... "Goodbye, Maria ... I will be seeing you."' Adam's voice cracks again on repeating these words from the priest.

These few sentences have taken Adam close to seven minutes to utter. He stutters and repeats words. 'Um yeah, um yeah, well, Rach, um yeah, well, Rach ...' This is the state where he's working up to something. Sometimes it comes; sometimes it doesn't. Often he falls quiet, and I don't know whether he's upset, thinking, or a million miles away. I don't want to interrupt him, but I can't keep him in pain, and at this rate it'll be at least two-and-a-half hours getting through what we need to. On the frenetic daily news cycle this would be impossible, spending this amount of time teasing out what will probably amount to less than five minutes of useable audio. But I'll sit here all day if it means I can show him I'm taking him seriously.

Sometimes when it gets all too hard, I stop the tape, and we chat about footy. I tell him my dad used to coach the Essendon under-19s when I was little, so I had no choice but to barrack for the Bombers. It's the days of the doping saga, and he tells me he feels sorry for James Hird, that he thinks the Essendon captain was somewhat of a scapegoat. Adam tells me he's a Brisbane man—formerly Fitzroy before they merged—and one of his favourite matches was a 1986 VFL final with his dad, when Fitzroy beat Essendon by a point. It was Micky Conlan who kicked the decider with about a minute to go, he tells me. 'Condan?' I ask. 'No, ConLan'. He makes me repeat it. When I fact-check this later, sure enough, he's spot on. Mark James says his little brother is somewhat of a savant. Take the 1978 sci-fi movie *Battlestar Galactica*. As boys, after they'd watched the movie just once, Mark says Adam could recite the closing credits with his back to the screen. There's nothing wrong with his memory—his intellect is just betrayed by his condition and a stutter. I get the feeling that Mark is the only person who has never underestimated Adam. Apart from his mother, of course.

'As me and Mum were walking down the street back home, she said to me, "Adam, are you okay?" And I said, "No, no, Mum." She said to me, "Adam, did Father Bongiorno do anything to you?" And I said to her, "Yes, mum" ... so I pointed down, that meant ... I could tell something wasn't right, I could see it in her eyes she wasn't very happy, she was a little bit mad about it, you know what I mean?'

When I ask follow-up questions, at some points, Adam drops into the third person—I'm guessing he does this when it gets all too hard—whereby he's 'the boy', Maria is 'the girl who is the mother of the boy', and I'm 'the girl in the green top and pencil skirt'. It takes a while for me to figure out this system, but once I do, it flows easier. It just takes a while to get there.

For example, when I ask Adam, 'Do you remember how many days it was before your mum died?' he changes the question to, 'Would the boy remember how long after it was, until the girl, who was the mother of the boy, was killed?' And it has to be asked in a very specific manner: he says a word, and then I have to repeat it.

'It was one day before. Good going, Rach.'

This tick of approval he gives me is often comical. Then I have to pull him back into hell. I ask him if his mum had said anything after he'd had pointed to his crotch.

'She said to me, "Adam, tomorrow I'm going to ask Father Bongiorno to come and have a chat with me."' That's all she said.'

The next morning, Adam says his mum told him she had to make a call to the parish. What he overheard was muffled, but he sensed she was upset. When she finished the call, she walked him, like always, to the bus stop. As she waved goodbye, he could see in her eyes that same mix of fear and anger.

That day, around midday, Maria James was murdered.

I ask Adam who he thinks killed his mum. His answer is about to spin this whole case on its head.

Adam James is 47 now. It's been nearly 36 years since everything changed, since he lost the woman who helped his world make sense. He wakes in a residential-care unit run by Villa Maria. They're good people, there are always other residents to chat to over breakfast, and then on weekdays he heads off to Knoxbrooke. It started as a Rotary initiative to provide services to children in the area with intellectual impairments; now it also has an adult support centre that runs activities and promotes independence. Adam gets a lot out of it: there are cooking classes, a men's group, yoga, and drama lessons. And he's pretty proud of all the kilometres he's been clocking up at Bootcamp. At nights, it's home for TV time and then dinner. His favourite is spaghetti bolognese.

But this past month there's been a bit of a change to the

program. A journalist has spoken with him about those times with Father Bongiorno. It's uncomfortable and embarrassing to talk about. For so long he's been too terrified to say anything. Those priests were supposed to be good people, and in the end they weren't good at all. But it does help getting it out, releasing some of the pain.

Most days, he can push it down. When he was sent to live with his dad and stepmother after his mum died, they looked after him. And since then, he's done a lot of public speaking with a group called Valid. He's grown braver at speaking about issues affecting people with disabilities, and he's met the nation's leaders, like Bill Shorten and Julia Gillard, in his travels. Public speaking lifts him up, because it can be a voice, and encouragement, for young people who don't have a voice. He's just won the Supreme Court's Funds in Court Award for 'Speaking Out', and his booming cheer echoed through a city law office as he held his trophy aloft like he'd won an Olympic event. Yeah, he's doing well. There are monthly excursions with his mates from Christian Youth Camps, and catch-ups with his brother Mark, stepmum Patricia, and his half-sister Sam. And he relishes any chance to holiday in America. He thinks visiting Disneyland as a kid kicked off that love for him.

But it often creeps in, the memory of that day. Patricia, instead of Mum, was at the bus stop to pick him up. His dad broke the news at home. There were police there—Brian Ritchie and Paul Delianis, he thinks. He must've gone into shock, because he can't remember much more after that. The journalist has asked him whether he wrongly worries if his mum's death was punishment for spilling the priest's secret. This might sound strange, but he never really made the connection between his abuse and his mum's murder. Not until 2013 anyway, when he told his brother and Ron. But since then, in realising certain suspects were overlooked, he feels a real hatred for Father Bongiorno and others, for what they put him through, for what should have become of them.

1996

In 1981, the year after Maria James was murdered, Father Anthony Bongiorno was transferred twice, in quick succession. The Australian Catholic Directory, available on microfiche at the Victorian State Library, records the priest's moves: to Reservoir North, and then on to St Ambrose in Brunswick, where he's promoted to parish priest. Oddly, there's no record on microfiche of his time at St Mary's Thornbury. It's at St Ambrose where Father Bongiorno allegedly abuses three other boys. But it takes another 15 years before the now young men summon the nerve to face the priest in court.

The police informant, Detective Sergeant Sol Solomon, charges Father Bongiorno with four counts of indecent assault, and arrests him. The detective tries to do it respectfully, referring to him as Father, so the priest insists that he be handcuffed, thinking it will bring shame on Sol. It's just the start of the power play. In the Melbourne Magistrates Court, Sol watches Father Bongiorno's accusers, who trusted the priest and looked to him for guidance, and paid for it in personal anguish that would last their lifetimes.

First there's 'Rex', who was 11 years old when Father

Bongiorno asked him to stay overnight at the Brunswick presbytery, then touched his genitals in the shower and in bed. A social worker, Bernie Geary, gives evidence he once had to kick the priest's door down to rescue the boy. Rex can remember precise details from the two years of abuse. He recalls Father Bongiorno's family home, where he'd be brought along for gatherings, and he remembers things about the priest's body, including an unusual feature on Father Bongiorno's genitals—maybe a wart—and a scar at the base of the priest's bum, where he'd had an ingrown hair removed. *Spot on*, thinks Sol.

As for the second victim, 'Fred', he was younger than Rex. The court hears when Fred soiled himself as an eight-year-old, the priest showered him, then touched his genitals and performed oral sex on him. Fred had been traumatised making his statement, which included an account of penetration; it had taken a lot of coaxing. *Poor little Fred*, thinks Sol, glancing across to the former altar boy. *He's terrified of Bongiorno, the Church, what his family will think of him, all of it*. The court hears that the third case, of 'Adrian', also an altar boy, involved inappropriate touching over six years.

Father Anthony Bongiorno denies all the charges, says they're from the mouths of mixed-up youths from broken homes, and his defence team swoops into ruthless and demeaning cross-examination that upsets Sol to watch. *Any means possible to rattle or discredit them*, thinks Sol. Rex, for example. How else could he have known about the priest's scar? The defence paints Rex as a pest, someone desperate to hang around Father Bongiorno, so that's how he knew so much about him. Despite all this, Magistrate Barbara Cottrell is satisfied there is enough evidence to direct

Father Bongiorno to stand trial. Magistrate Cottrell even comments that the boys' evidence is credible and compelling. Sol wonders if this is a dig, if she's been moved by the boys' stories and was unimpressed with defence counsel's vicious cross-examination.

But at trial, the cases are severed on presentment, split into three. Each jury is only told about one set of allegations, and Sol's case becomes a house of cards. The first to fall is Rex. The priest is acquitted, and Rex thinks the answer might be to contemplate a leap from Melbourne's popular suicide spot, the Westgate Bridge. The prosecution rolls straight on to Fred's trial. Again, Father Bongiorno is acquitted. So, not liking its chances, the Director of Public Prosecutions abandons Adrian's case. The victims have and are lost, traumatised all over again, wondering why they let themselves dare to believe this would end any other way. It's been a painful, demeaning waste of time

Not all ears are deaf, however. The next year, the Victorian government's Crimes Compensation Tribunal rules that Father Bongiorno *had* committed child sex-crimes, and awards compensation to the men. The payout is the equivalent of a second-hand car, but it's something. Given all the bad publicity, the Melbourne Archdiocese keeps Father Bongiorno 'on leave', and in 2002, after he suffers heart problems, he ends up in an unmarked grave, his name forever sullied. Two of his three victims try to rest themselves in early graves, making numerous suicide attempts over the years to come.

March 2016

As Adam rocks opposite me, and runs his hand over his face and up though his hair again and again, I wonder if he kept quiet for 33 years because of guilt. Because of what happened when he blabbed to his mum. Or was it because the hush order came from a priest? And a priest's word was gospel. Or maybe Adam's silence was born of shame? Or perhaps a toxic cocktail of all these things? The Royal Commission into Institutional Responses to Child Sexual Abuse has found 33 years is actually the average time it takes victims to come forward.

When I ask Mark James about this a little later, he feels the answer is a simple one: sheer fear. 'Adam said he'd been terrified for years of what would happen to him if anyone ever found out.' By the last decade or so of his brother lugging around this cross, the priest was dead, and Adam didn't even know it. The secret was finally breathed just by chance.

In 2013, a family friend, Margaret Quill, reached out to Mark James, and told him she'd been following his mum's murder investigation. She thought Father Bongiorno should be looked at closely. And she asked Mark if he or Adam had ever been sexually abused by the priest. Mark tells me this sounded unbelievable, so he initially dismissed it. But after one of the brothers' Saturday lunches at the pizza place that Adam loves for its half Capricciosa and half The Lot, Mark asked the question. Just because he'd promised Ms Quill he would. Just to rule a line under it.

'And I am sitting in that car expecting Adam to say, "No, no, everything's fine." And I tell you, when he told me that something happened, that Father Bongiorno, he said, "had been touching me down there", and he pointed to his private parts, I tell you it was like a bomb had gone off. He was very uncomfortable and he pointed down to his private parts, and I was just silent for a while. And then I started to cry.'

In all my chats with Mark, this is the first time I've heard his voice waver, talking about the man who will forever be his little brother.

'I tried to get a little bit more information out of Adam as to what happened, and it was difficult because Adam didn't want to talk about it. But he told me of two or three times when Father Bongiorno had sexually abused him. These were times when Mum had dropped Adam off to be in the care of Father Bongiorno, supposedly to receive religious or spiritual counselling.'

Mark spits out the last two words like they're venom. He says after Adam dropped this bombshell, he called the police officer he trusts the most. Ron Iddles.

The veteran detective is one of the few people Mark's leaned on who haven't betrayed him or his family. First it was the priest. Not that Mark knew, but until recently the smarmy bastard had terrified Adam into submission. Then someone cut his life out from under him with a blade, tipping the 13-year-old into an introverted daze. His family and friends tried to help, of course, but they were struggling with their own trauma. And they weren't his mum, whose antennae were so sharp she always knew when something was off with him or Adam without them even saying anything. After her funeral, he really struggled. He felt like he was held in a fog, and wondered if it would always feel that way, his life permanently interrupted.

Mark thinks predators must be able to smell vulnerability. They must gravitate towards weakness. Because after taking time off school, he wasn't long back when a Marist Brother teacher pounced, abusing him for several months. Next, and this cut deeper, was his godfather, Frank Todd, who abused him over the next couple of years. He felt confused and trapped. He quietly told a school friend and his cousin about the sexual abuse, but back then it was taboo, so he didn't tell any adults, as he was fearful of the consequences. His personal development, his climb towards maturity, stagnated. When he turned 16, he still felt 13, in the glare of those flashing sirens and press cameras. None of this would've happened if his mum had still been around. Funny how absence can weigh a tonne.

He adored her. Honest, ethical, hard working—everyone said so. She and his dad were proud of their bright kid, and encouraged his hobbies. Mark liked making transistor radios and remote-controlled cars and aeroplanes. Although one invention didn't go down too well: his home-made hang-glider. He did a fair bit of damage when it collapsed during his jump from the roof.

Mark thinks it wasn't really until his twenties that he got back on track, felt a little more normal, and started doing the things he used to dream about. He got his pilot's licence and flew regularly, just like Biggles. He's been scuba diving and has travelled overseas. Life's not easy, mind you. There've been other misfortunes he'd rather not talk about: maybe they're manifestations of trauma, or maybe they're just plain bad luck, but he battles on. He's a firm believer that you've just got to play the cards you've been dealt.

Mark has held a range of jobs in the public and private sector. Lately, he's been running his own business dealing with quality control in the resources industry. He's not doing too badly, all things considered. The questions are always there, though, of course, scratching away. Ever since Margaret Quill asked if his brother had ever been abused, he sees everything in a different light. Thank God he can trust Ron. The veteran detective has kept in touch over the years, keeping him updated and his hopes up. And the police have been incredible—dedicated and persistent. The media, too, have been great. The *Herald Sun*'s Keith Moor has helped keep the story alive over the years. And now this ABC podcast. Mark sees it as his final shot for an answer. If this podcast doesn't succeed, his mother's murder will never be solved.

1981

Father Anthony Bongiorno's reputation arrives at St Ambrose, Brunswick, before he does. Parishioners in the largely ethnic congregation are bracing themselves for an obnoxious priest who wears shorts, sometimes staggers into church, and screams at everyone. The church's organist, Enrico Constantini, and his partner, Rita, gently tell the new appointee that unless things are done a certain way at St Ambrose, parishioners will get a shock. The parish gets a rude awakening anyway. Father Bongiorno, with his throaty cackle, shouts the good news, literally, from the rooftops through exterior amplifiers that broadcast his masses outside, whether locals like it or not. Some think he's a larrikin; others just wish he'd shut up. He fills the church with holy statues, so sometimes the frozen deities outnumber the churchgoers. He has no shame, walking over to collect the morning newspaper in his dressing gown. He likes his booze. And he calls a spade a spade. But despite their apprehension, the Constantinis can't help but love him.

St Ambrose's revenues have been flagging, so the priest—a former market boy who used to work in his dad's fruit business—is in his element. Father Bongiorno sets up potato and soft-drink stands to entice parishioners after masses. 'Spud and spa,' he yells. It's a hit. He even makes the papers. 'Cut-price priest faces ban' yells the headline. He mocks up a theatre and shows Italian films, and while it's illegal to sell tickets, he reverses the transaction. 'Can't charge 'em to get in, but we can charge 'em to get out,' Father Bongiorno tells a team making a documentary on the parish. 'They [the government] don't want you to operate with any degree of success, they think that Jesus somehow or another made a virtue of being miserable and being a failure. Well, I think he also expected you to succeed in what you were doing,' he muses. 'I suppose with us Bongiornos, it's crash or crash through.'

The Constantinis have the priest around every week for a Sunday roast. It's their way of giving back, for the priest's generosity in bringing in the sick, the lonely, and the hungry. And they can see through his bluster. But he can be an exasperating jester. He even jokes about whether anyone has said anything to him, in the confessional, about that poor bookshop lady who was murdered in his other parish.

'Do I know? Don't I know? Do I know? Don't I know?'

'Stop playing up on it,' Enrico tells the priest, 'or they'll end up blaming you.'

It bugs Rita, too, but more because she's worried her friend might be shouldering something heavy. 'Do you know?' she's asked him, more than once.

'In the confession, if anyone confesses to me, Rita, I cannot tell what was said.' This is the unpardonable sin, punishable by instant ex-communication.

'You know, but you can't say anything?' she presses.

'I can't say anything,' is always the obtuse reply.

Is this a game? She can never decipher whether he can't talk about it because something did happen, or that he just won't talk about it. One time she's adamant.

'Bonj, would you *like* to tell me?

The priest doesn't budge. 'I've just finished telling you, I can't.'

Rita points out, 'Bonj, what if someone is wrongly put in jail? If you tell me, I can tell.'

It doesn't make a scrap of difference in the priest's eyes. 'That's the same as me telling. Let's not talk about it again.'

Rita wishes he never mentioned it in the first place.

January 2017

___ [a former detective] had Mrs Rennie's daughter written as Joan Biggs, when we know from the inquest statement it was Joan Gibbs

— Text from Rachael Brown to Andy Burns, 13 January 2017

Given our six-month wild-goose chase of the wrong Peter, I wonder whether police also recorded the neighbour's surname wrongly. The coroner's finding states that when John James raced into a house across the back laneway to use a phone, the woman he spoke to was 'Joan Gibbs'. But in a detective's notebook, she was recorded as 'Joan Biggs'. *Should we scour Victoria* for *Biggses?* It's worth a shot, I tell Kerri Ritchie.

'No,' comes the answer to one of Kerri's cold calls, 'no Joan here.' But just as she's about to hang up, Mr Biggs adds, 'I did know John James, though, worked with him at the town hall, used to go to the footy with him, too.' You couldn't write this stuff.

Armed with cake, Kerri and I visit Bert Biggs, his wife, Lorna, and their daughter, Maureen. He's been here 70 years, and the house shows it. It's packed with memories and knick-knacks jostling for space. A Fabergé-inspired egg collection greets us on entry. In the kitchen, Maureen shuts the fridge door at one end, and a glass topples off the microwave at the other. Bert proudly shows us his newest treasure: a medal for his efforts as an aircraft mechanic in France during the war.

His eyes crinkle at the corners as he discusses his other former life. 'I knew Johnny at the town hall—he was the town clerk, he was the youngest town clerk there was.' He and Lorna attended the mayoral ball a couple of times with John and Maria James. 'Childhood sweethearts,' says Bert. He grew fond of Maria; he'd wander down and visit her even after her split with John James. 'Full of battlers, this place was,' he says of Thornbury in 1980, 'but she'd always talk to you, very patient. Actually, that was Maria's style—patience. She was a real nice person. Every now and then you think about it, or you see a paperback book, or go into a bookshop and think of Maria.'

Bert also knew someone else I've been curious about: John James's mate and Mark's godfather, Frank Todd. Bert knew Frank from his days as a council traffic officer, and saw his funeral notice in the paper a few years back. 'To be honest, I was surprised when I heard about Frank and his misdemeanours, because he seemed not that person.'

'What misdemeanours did you hear of?'

'There were a couple. One was that he did time for paedophilia. Another was that when they put in machines, parking machines, I understand Frank put the money in his pocket as well.'

'Is it disconcerting, years later, learning things about paedophiles now? Can you reconcile that with the people you knew then?'

'Going out with Frank and being with him, I never had a clue.'

Lorna Biggs pipes up, 'He was engaged to be married.'

'Yeah, with—I forget her name—the secretary.'

Maureen remembers him, too. 'We always went in Frank's car to the football, a V-Dub Beetle—no one else had a car. He was always the first one to stand up for you.'

'Frank was always friendly, no aggression or anything,' says Bert. Whereas another man he's also recently discovered was a paedophile had a history of slapping back when challenged. Bert says, all these years on, he's still furious about Father Bongiorno's funeral mass for Maria.

'It was a shocking day—really, really bad, shook me the rest of the day and rest of my life, really. You wouldn't have even known it was Maria's funeral, because her name wasn't mentioned. His service, it was religious, but it wasn't a caring funeral, that's for sure. He was a shocker. I'd had words with him before that, actually, because he was undermining the shopkeepers around the place by his sales in the church—soft drinks, vegetables, you name it. All those shops around the place were selling the same, but he was undercutting the whole lot. And at that particular time I was acting for town planning, and it was against town-planning regulations, what he was doing. So I visited him and told him he had to stop, and he said he wouldn't, and I said, "Well, if you don't, you're off to court," and he wasn't very happy about that.'

I ask, what if it was a woman taking him on? A woman defending her sons?

'I don't know what she [Maria] would've done, but she would've been pretty feisty, I tell you.'

Maureen has no doubt. 'Oh, she'd defend them to the end.'

Maybe she did.

Would Maria the Catholic have agonised over accusing a man of the cloth of sexual abuse? Or would Maria the mother trust Adam implicitly? I ask this of Patricia James, that day in the Barbantes' lounge-room.

'My thought would be that she would take the priest on. Wouldn't matter what robe they were wearing. Maria was fiery, and literally went on the attack—that was her personality.'

There's one thing, though, that Patricia can't reconcile. That Maria would be calm enough to have such a conversation.

'As I said, she and John were friends. They had one very serious common element, their kids. It wouldn't have been a case of Maria unilaterally just acting without seeking John's counsel. I just can't envisage that.'

'But that earlier call to him at the council,' I say, 'maybe that's what she *was* doing. Calling him to say, "Look, the priest is about to come over because Adam said this." And then he [John] called five minutes later, and the priest was there, and that's when she said, "I can't talk right now, someone's here."'

Pat Barbante jumps in. 'But she would have said, "The priest is here."'

'Even with the priest in the room?'

'Yeah, she wouldn't have cared.'

So I float another theory. I drop the name of Frank Todd.

'His name was throughout a police diary. Certain allegations have come out about him. I'm wondering whether there was a reason he was talking to police?'

Rapid glances volley between the three old friends. They're wondering if I know. And, sadly, I do. It was another dirty secret kept by one of the James boys, until its 1996 release over John James's deathbed. Mark had learned that his godfather, Frank Todd, who'd sexually abused him, had also abused his cousin. Mark was torn; he didn't want to further hurt his dad, who was busy fighting Non-Hodgkin lymphoma, but he was worried that Frank Todd might target other children. So Mark says he told his dad the secret he'd carried for 15 years.

Patricia James sighs. 'When the allegations came out in terms of Mark and his cousin Tony, John was very sick at the time. That is literally his son and one of his long-term mates.'

'If you look at the motive that was applied to Father Bongiorno in terms of molesting Adam, and Maria confronting him, maybe we need to look into Frank Todd as well?' I venture.

'If John were sitting here and we were having this conversation, he would find it very hard to think that Frank would have had anything to do with it.'

I know I'm in awkward territory. Frank Todd was best man at Santo and Pat Barbante's wedding. I've seen the photos—him in his tux, holding white gloves.

But Santo graciously obliges. 'What about the description [of the killer] they had?'

'Police were looking for a man in his late thirties to early forties. One hundred and sixty-six centimetres. Dark receding or brushed-back hair. Stockily built.'

'Frank was about five foot four,' says Santo. So that fits. But in 1980 Frank Todd was 50 years old. And he got along well with Maria. In fact, Pat adds, it ate away at him that he wasn't there to stop her killer.

'Frank used to go to Santo's mum's place, in Mansfield Street, for lunch all the time,' says Pat. 'Frank used to go past there nearly every day, have a coffee with Maria, and then go home, or go back to work.'

But not *that* day.

'That's what I heard,' says Pat. 'That's what Frank used to always say, 'Why didn't I call in that day?''

'Did it haunt him?'

'I think he always thought, *Why didn't I?*'

March 2013

Never in a million years did Ron Iddles suspect the priest. None of them did. Ron remembers Father Bongiorno being in the bookshop while detectives were working. He remembers a fight between his boss, Brian Ritchie, and the priest over the sanctity of the confessional. He remembers the priest presiding over Maria James's funeral. But they never looked at him as a *suspect*. They couldn't see past the clerical collar and robes, a veil now known to have hidden a litany of sins. Now here's Adam James, who he remembers as an 11-year-old kid, telling him that Father Bongiorno molested him three times in the months leading up to his mother's murder. For Ron, this is the thing that's eluded him for 33 years—a potential motive.

Adam's revelation is a gravitational shift. Ron thinks that being exposed as a paedophile is a reasonably strong motive for murder. This might explain Father Bongiorno's bizarre character assassination of Maria James at her own funeral. Maybe, like a magician's trick, it was all about misdirection: he drew the crowd's attention to where he wanted it so they'd miss his sleight of hand. Defence is the best form of offence, Ron thinks. Perhaps the priest was trying to discredit Maria and her children, in case they ever said anything. And the priest does fit the description of a man seen going into the shop before the murder.

Ron thinks back to the priest's alibi that day. Father Bongiorno said he'd been at a church meeting in Coburg, a nearby suburb, with his friend Father Sean O'Connell. Ron remembers Father O'Connell verifying this, adding that he dropped Father Bongiorno back around 4.00pm. And that was that. No reason for doubt. Nowadays you'd speak to someone else who was at the meeting, check CCTV footage maybe, or phone records. You'd go to the nth degree to corroborate an alibi. Sadly, Ron thinks, that wasn't done.

Adam sits opposite Ron Iddles, in a small interview room at the Rowville Police Station, ready to give his police statement. This is the first time that Ron has had a lengthy conversation with him. And if Ron has one regret about the handling of the James case, it's this. In those early days, Adam was ignored. Perhaps it was a fatal flaw in the whole investigation. Yep, he has a disability, and is often hard to understand, but he has a brilliant brain. And Ron and his colleagues dismissed Adam back then, put him in a certain category, presumed he wouldn't know anything, when maybe he's held the answer all along.

Ron appreciates what a big deal it is for Adam to come forward. He's extremely nervous, and embarrassed, and has brought along his brother, Mark, and a social worker, for support. In Adam's agitated state, he says a couple of words, falls into stammers, and then, after a minute or so, controls his delivery and gets a sentence out. It's clear he wants to tell his story. He tells Ron that, some time ago, when his brother, Mark, asked him some questions about Father Bongiorno, he decided to tell him what the priest had done. 'I had never told anyone this, other than my mother. I wanted to tell Mark the truth, as I felt it was important for you to know, Ron.' Adam says he doesn't remember why he was left at the church in the priest's care, but, until it was broken by the sound of Maria's footsteps, the last episode of abuse lasted around ten minutes.

'I don't know if Mum actually went and spoke to him or not. The day of the murder, Mum took me to the bus stop to go to my special school. I was at the bus stop about 8.45am, and Mum waved me goodbye. I looked around, and as Mum walked away I saw a man walking behind her. He was wearing a knitted jumper, and had light-coloured slacks on. I only saw the man from behind, but I thought it might have been Father Bongiorno.'

From what he remembers about the timings of things

that day, Ron thinks this man could have also been Mario Falcucci. It fits with the story of him trying to sell Maria his comics. But Ron lets Adam continue.

'I've been asked why I have never disclosed this information. I did tell my mother, but have never told anyone else, as I have always been frightened that Father Bongiorno would find out I told Mum. It is something I have kept to myself, and I have never felt I could speak about it.'

Ron feels for Adam having to relive all this, and is grappling with the news of Father Bongiorno's ultimate betrayal of the trust that Maria placed in him. What a different path this investigation would have taken had they known this from the start. But they didn't ask the question. As Ron has since learned over his career, a child can often be the bearer of invaluable clues.

In a later statement, to the Melbourne Response, Adam elaborates a little on the toll:

Over the years, when I've been at church, and saw someone that looked and dressed like Father Bongiorno, I was terrified that I could be left alone and it could happen to me again ... Sometimes I have had nightmares. I don't understand all of these nightmares. In some of them, I get these images of me in that room near the church altar and he is there doing it to me and I keep on saying to him, 'Stop, stop,' and then I wake up and realise that it was just a dream.

Sadly, though, it wasn't.

When I said that he had been touching me on and around my penis there was more to it than that. It was more than just touching. But I feel that I can't talk about it to explain exactly what he was doing to me. I just can't bring myself to speak about it because I am so upset, uncomfortable and ashamed about it.

Adam writes he was nervous, terrified and couldn't understand why Father Bongiorno was doing those things:

I was glad that my mum was going to do something about this, but at the same time frightened because I didn't want to see him ever again, and was scared that he might get angry or do something to mum or me. I didn't want any trouble. One of the last memories I have of my mother before she died was that she was going to confront him about what he had been doing to me. I felt, and feel betrayed by Father Bongiorno. He said that I could trust him. He didn't have any right to do those things to me. It was very wrong. I was a kid and he was an adult; and he was my priest. His job was to talk about Jesus and not to do those things to me.'

January–February 2017

Doing AEC [Australian Electoral Commission] run now, any last minute inclusions? Speak now bc hopefully this is my last visit

— Text from Rachael Brown to the *Trace* team, 30 January 2017

To establish whether Father Bongiorno had a pattern of offending, the small team of myself, Kerri Ritchie, and Jeremy Story Carter decide to find three alleged victims of

Father Bongiorno, and also find his friends and family, to get a rounded picture. So first up on our 'to do' list is Bernie Geary. The former social worker, and Victoria's first child-safety commissioner, treads towards Kerri and me across the wooden floorboards of the Fairfield Boathouse. And as rowboats bob on the Yarra River, this man, who's seen many things he wishes he hadn't, tells us about one time he feels he failed.

It all has to do with a boy called 'Rex'. Bernie Geary tells us that one morning, when he was working at the Brosnan Centre in Brunswick, beside the St Ambrose church, Rex's sister ran in, screaming for help. Bernie followed her into the presbytery to Father Bongiorno's bedroom, which was locked. Bernie says he kicked the door in and found Rex in the priest's bed. The priest was in an open dressing gown and underpants. Bernie dragged the boy out of bed, screaming at Father Bongiorno the whole time. He'd heard the rumours—they all had—but this was the first time he had proof. He can't remember what he yelled at the indignant priest, only that it wasn't pleasant. 'It was just about getting this vulnerable, blameless young bloke out of there.'

In the past few years, as I've watched the royal commission play out, I've been staggered by the number of people guilty of wilful ignorance when it came to the abuse of children—whether they were in denial, or just chose not to ask the right questions. And here's Bernie, who did step in, who did speak up, who's now rubbing tears from his eyes while recalling how the court case fell over. He says it was a sad example of how the system can inadvertently protect bad people.

Bernie says he'll try to find him for us, that he sometimes sees Rex hanging around a local shopping centre. As we leave the boathouse to climb up to the road, Bernie's shoulders are hunching into the hill, carrying a load others should have shared. He turns slightly to deliver us a parting gift: 'I'm glad someone still gives a shit.'

Kerri and I have tracked down Rita and Enrico Constantini from the 1994 documentary *No Death in Brunswick* about the St Ambrose parish. Gone are their 1990s hairstyles, but their faith remains, as does their conviction that their late friend Father Bongiorno was not a paedophile. They were with Bonj, as they called him, on his deathbed, his face puffy from the medication for his heart problems. We're very keen to learn whether he said anything to them. Whether he sought absolution.

'Help yourself,' Rita says, pointing to the little tray of Turkish delights sitting in the middle of their kitchen table.

'That's where Bonj used to sit'—Enrico looks at the chair next to me—'every Sunday.'

Rita doesn't waste any time defending her friend's legacy. 'I'm just angry, because all he wanted was his parish back.' Bongiorno died in 2002 while he was, it seems, still at a loss as to what to do with himself while the Melbourne Archdiocese kept him 'on leave'. She reminds us, 'He *was* acquitted, after all. No one knew the real Bonj.' She sighs. 'He played the violin, he read poetry, he was very cultured, no one saw that part, they just saw this big, rough guy. Rah rah rah,' she bellows, mimicking his bluster. 'He was loud and he was rude sometimes, and he had a little drink, and that would make him more obnoxious.'

From what I can gather, I say, people either loved or hated him. There was no in-between.

'But his church was open for everybody, any denomination, anything. He was there when I lost my biological children, and he was very kind, very gentle, he was so saddened by it. He was there when I needed to talk about things, he was really very sensitive, not at all the brash, bombastic person he came across with other people … and I think, you all talk about him, but none of you knew him.'

I ask about Rex, how she rationalises all that. Why, for example, would Rex have been in the priest's bed?

'If he could've adopted Rex, he would've. This is a guy he loved in a very different way, not like they tried to paint it. Rex was very clingy with him and demonstrative sometimes; when he'd see him, he would kiss him. I don't know if Rex sometimes in his mind thought Bonj was his dad, priest, his friend. I'm not sure.'

As for the other two boys, Rita and Enrico say their stories didn't stack up. They say one got dates wrong, and the other mentioned dubious details. So the couple wondered whether the boys concocted their stories for money. Enrico thinks one of the church's various factions might have been behind it. 'Certain groups, whether they be the six o'clock group or Broken Rites or whoever, had their own agenda and dangled the carrot on the boys and said, "Well, you know, you're going to get money out of this." The kids would've thought, *Ooh, we'll get money*. They tried to manipulate them for their own reasons.'

'We'd known him for a long time, and through these cases, through these allegations, he was gentle with the boys. He even tried to protect them in the courts.' Then Rita throws in an odd rationale. She used to work at an East Melbourne café, where some of the waiters were former St Ambrose boys. When they found out about the sex-abuse allegations, they were shocked. 'These were very handsome young guys who would've been extremely good looking when they were young. One said to me, "Not once when we were left alone with him did he ever lay a hand on any of us."'

But that's not how it works, is it? I think. The prey are not necessarily the pretty ones. They're the troubled. The vulnerable. The damaged. The outcasts. I can only think of Adam James.

'A couple of years ago,' I say, 'long after Father Bongiorno had passed away, came the allegation that Adam James had been molested by Father Bongiorno. How did you feel hearing that news?'

Rita pales. 'Sick. Absolutely sick. I thought, *Oh my God. Could he ever have done something like that?* I couldn't come to terms with that, you know? The part of him that was good, was great, but then I think, *My goodness. Could that ever have happened with this man? Could I have been mistaken?* I would then have to close off from Father Bongiorno completely.'

'So you're not willing to close your mind off to that possibility completely?' Kerri asks.

'No. Not with anyone. No. I've counselled a lot of sexual-abuse children.'

What Rita *won't* bend on is the idea her friend could have possibly been a murderer.

'Why would that [Adam's accusation] make him kill the mother?'

'Well, if he was trying to hide that,' I say.

Rita can't see it. 'They went to the police, the others [Rex, Fred, and Adrian], and he didn't go killing their parents.'

'But that didn't come out until long after Maria James died,' I remind her. 'That came out in '95.'

Rita says she never saw a violent streak. And the idea he could snap, and kill a person? Definitely not. 'He's just not that type. I've seen him a little intoxicated. That time, maybe he'd been a little bombastic, but I've never ever seen him aggressive ever in any way, or angry, or talking in any way of getting anyone back or doing anyone harm.'

Enrico checks, 'When did the murder happen? What year?'

'Nineteen-eighty. She was stabbed 68 times.'

'Oh, my God.' Rita shakes her head furiously, 'That's someone nuts. No. I could never see Bonj, he'd never lose it to that extent. Sixty-eight times.'

'Nonsense,' spits Sol Solomon, when Kerri and I relay the Constantinis' 'grab for cash' idea. We've nabbed a table at the back of Bourke Street's Mail Exchange Hotel, as far as possible from the trill of poker machines and the sports commentary spilling from big screens. Given its proximity to Victoria Police headquarters, I'm guessing this a popular watering-hole for the boys in blue. I'm surprised Sol has time for us, as he's just started on yet another harrowing case, that of a driver who mowed down more than 20 pedestrians just a few blocks up the road in the Bourke Street Mall. Six people died in or after the carnage, and Sol is the lead investigator. But as I'm finding with some of the finest police, if a case has hit a nerve, they make time.

'I thought it was worth taking on,' Sol says of Rex's case, which was referred to him by a victims' advocate in 1995, when he was with the Child Exploitation Squad. 'I will always remember their anguish. And the evidence was compelling.' Sol paints a picture of the perfect target. Rex was a runaway from a troubled family with nowhere to go. So Father Bongiorno would take the boy in. 'Rex was putty in his hands. He [Father Bongiorno] was a predator'. The detective says he worked hard to corroborate the allegations against Father Bongiorno. So he finds any suggestion of collusion deeply offensive. 'The first victim who came forward ['Rex'] with his allegations of sexual assault, I remember him being so traumatised and emotionally fragile that I was only able to obtain his statement with the assistance of his counsellor at the time. The other two victims ['Fred' and 'Adrian'], I didn't even know about. I actually had to track them down. They were both very reluctant to make any disclosures to me. It wasn't until after a lot of support and encouragement that they finally worked up the courage to disclose what had happened to them. There's no hint of any motive there of a grab for cash. There is no doubt in my mind what the boys told us was true … they were too traumatised.'

Sol remembers the trial, and the priest's behaviour, bitterly. 'I don't want to sound vindictive or unprofessional in any way. But he was not co-operative, he didn't show any remorse for the victims, or any empathy with them or the impact that his actions had upon them. Quite obstructive throughout the whole process. It was terrible to watch. They [the victims] were forced to relive their ordeals, which in the end brought only further disappointment and rejection. Such an unjust outcome for those boys. I wondered if it was worth me putting them through the ordeal of a prosecution.'

It hit Rex the hardest. 'We had to go and find him,' Sol said. 'He'd caught public transport, then walked to the Westgate [Bridge]. I found out that he was going there with the intention of jumping off the bridge, so I drove there with another detective and found him in a street nearby and took him to a safe location for support. I was sorry for Rex. It was another case of 'them' not believing him. I kept in touch for a long time. I could see the pain he was going through.'

I ask if, like Bernie Geary, Sol feels he let the boys down. 'If I got hurt by every loss, I wouldn't last very long in this job.' But he does blame the legal machine. 'It was just the weakness in the system, which allowed the defence to weaken a strong case against the perpetrator by separating the trials. If you fast-forward to now, he'd be in jail. He would have been convicted.'

As he heads back to his mountain of files, Sol asks something of us, if we ever manage to find Rex. 'Tell him I still think of him. I've never forgotten him.'

June 2015

Maria James would have been 73 this year. Her boys would have grown up with a mum. Ron Iddles wouldn't have this nagging sense that something is wrong.

As secretary of the Police Union, Ron can't do as much as he'd like in an operational sense, but he's passed Adam James's statement to the crew who are looking after the cold case. He's also heard that an electrician has come forward who apparently saw Father Bongiorno acting suspiciously near the crime scene straight after the murder. From the whispers he's heard, this electrician has a pretty explosive story to tell. He thinks the electrician gave his police statement in late 2013, but nothing's come of it yet. Perhaps the detectives are biding their time for a reason.

He knows a detective has made inquiries with the Coroners Court about exhuming Father Bongiorno. But Ron has a back-up idea. To get DNA, why couldn't they just apply for a search warrant under the Crimes Act? A warrant that just happens to apply to the dead priest's plot number at Springvale Cemetery. 'Search Row _ Grave Number _ for the body of Bongiorno to prove or disprove his involvement in the crime'. He's not sure a magistrate will share his creative enthusiasm, but it's a novel idea. *Regardless, we're in business,* thinks Ron. With the testimonies of Adam and the electrician, there's a strong case for exhumation. The James brothers are closer than ever before to real answers.

Then, come mid-2015, there's movement from the Homicide Squad. It rules Father Bongiorno out as a suspect. Out. The Squad's Detective Senior Sergeant Stuart Bailey says Father Bongiorno has been 'eliminated as a suspect through a variety of investigative techniques. The investigation has produced other avenues of inquiry which are currently being pursued.'

Father Bongiorno is never exhumed. The electrician's statement is never made public. This sits uneasily with Ron Iddles.

And it guts Mark and Adam James. Mark's not convinced. He wants to know the steps the police took, and just *how* they ruled out the priest. Also, Mark thinks, if only the cops would talk to Adam, gently, patiently, maybe with a psychologist, he might have some things locked away that could be vital. Mark can't let go of the idea that the Church was involved.

March 2016

'Hey, Rach, watch this!' Adam James proudly shows me the Superman cape that Mark bought him. Press a button, and little lights flash around the red-and-yellow 'S' insignia. He's got a thing for superheroes. At his last party, he dressed up as Batman and belted out some karaoke.

'Adam, turn the light off, you'll waste the batteries,' Mark says. Once an older brother, always an older brother.

I'm still hoping that Adam somehow turns out to be the hero in this story. Because there's so much locked away in his head that investigators still haven't tapped into. Now that Adam has managed to claw his way through his mum's murder, and his abuse by Father Bongiorno, I have just one more question before I can end what's been one of the hardest interviews of my career.

'Adam, who do you think killed your mum?'

'With me,' he instructs, dropping back into the third person. I again parrot him, repeating each word as he reformulates my question: 'Who — does — the — boy — think — killed — the — girl — who — was — his — mother?' His answer blindsides me.

'I think it could've been the other man who was working with him.'

Who? I'm confused now. What other man? Adam names another priest who was working at St Mary's with Father Bongiorno.

'This other man, O'Keeffe, well, I believe he could've done it.'

Father Thomas O'Keeffe. Apparently, despite Father

Bongiorno *acting* as though he ran the show, it was actually Father O'Keeffe who was the parish priest. I think to myself, *What in the world would give him a motive stronger than Father Bongiorno's?*

'He was being friendly, friendly to me but not to my mum, you know what I mean?'

I hold my breath, scared to even ask. 'Adam, did Father O'Keeffe ever touch you?'

In a tumble of stutters and third-person distancing, it falls out. Adam says that after one of the occasions Father Bongiorno had abused him, the priest left the room, and soon after, Father O'Keeffe walked in.

'I remember walking out of the room with O'Keeffe, and I remember going up to a table in the parish where all the other kids used to do their Communion, and I was standing around looking at all the pictures [stained-glass windows], and O'Keeffe asked me, he said to me, "Adam, would you remember coming into our parish with your mum and Mark to do your Communion?" And then he asked me to look around, and I remember my pants were only halfway up, and then he put his hand down my pants and touched me. And he said to me, "Adam, you can trust me," then he said something to me like, "Adam, you can do them up now," then he went.'

Same day, assaulted twice, by two people he was supposed to be able to trust.

'Did you tell your mum about O'Keeffe, Adam? Did you tell your mum about O'Keeffe as well? Or just Bongiorno?'

'With me, did — the — boy — tell — the — girl — who — was — the — boy's — mum — about — what — the — other — man — did — to — him?' ... I parrot again, word by painful word.

'No, Rach, at the time I was a bit scared, you know what I mean?'

'Why did the boy wait so long to tell police?'

'At the time, I was really a bit scared. I'm sorry, Rach.'

'Don't be sorry. Anyone would be scared. I'd be scared.'

'The girl in the green top and the pencil skirt would be scared?'

'She'd be very scared.'

As I am now, given what this could all mean. When Maria James called the presbytery on the morning of her murder, wanting answers about Adam's abuse claim, what if it was Father O'Keeffe who responded? Because it sounds like he had just as much to answer for. I look to Mark. He's only recently learned of this second abuse allegation, and he's revolted.

'What's going on here? Is Adam some kind of a smorgasbord, is that how some of these bad priests view these vulnerable people—what, as a buffet for them?'

The journo in me knows I should nail down a clearer chronology of the abuse: where, when, and how each event occurred. The human being in me knows I need to leave it. For now, at least. The basics have to be enough. The basics have taken Adam more than two hours. I wonder how police are going to rake through this. It could take days to draw out a complete statement. The James brothers have given up for the moment, though. Earlier this year they called the police officer who'd let them know that Father Bongiorno had been eliminated as a suspect. Mark says Adam tried to tell the officer about Father O'Keeffe, but felt it was met with cool scepticism. 'The reaction I had was, "Well, it's been noted, but first of all you said it was Father Bongiorno. Now you're saying it's Father Bongiorno and Father O'Keeffe. Do you want us to dig up everyone?" Which was quite unusual, because Victoria Police in the past have been absolutely excellent with Mum's case, they've left no stone unturned, but this particular reaction I got was a little bit unusual. It's almost like it was in the too-hard basket.'

Maybe the officer was just busy. Or maybe she doubted Adam. I can't say. But I can understand why so many victims are too scared to come forward. They feel ashamed. Then their honesty is called into question. And this, as adults. I get upset thinking about Adam as a little kid. Had he decided to speak up after his mum's death, would anyone have believed him? As an 11-year-old? An intellectually impaired one at that?

I feel furious about how much has been taken from the two brothers. As I leave them, Adam yells, 'See ya, Rach', and gives me a high five. 'Say hi to your dad for me. Go Essendon!' I'm spent, a migraine is rolling in, and tears follow. I just hope this all works.

1998

As usual, Max Schiavon's desk is buried under files of armed robberies, fraud, serious assaults and sex offences. There's always at least 15 files sitting in the 'corro' tray, waiting to be picked at between the inevitable new and pressing jobs that arrive daily. It's his first year with the Geelong Criminal Investigation Unit in this, his eleventh year in the force.

The office is messy but functional, and he's learned fast

that he'll need a thick skin to handle his colleagues' ribbing, rough play, and offensive banter. But this work family is actually what makes it all bearable: all the stressful shifts, and the violence and misery that victims drag through the door every day. He'd be lost without these guys.

The phone rings. It's someone called James Shanahan. He wants to report sexual abuse by a priest. A Father Thomas O'Keeffe. This is a new one for Detective Schiavon. Victoria Police doesn't get many of these. A couple of years ago, Australia's Catholic leaders published a document on the management of child-abuse cases, called *Towards Healing*, but the full extent of the depravity is not yet known. And it'll be another few years before the Boston Globe's 'Spotlight' investigative team publishes a series of reports on Catholic Church sex abuse in the United States and Ireland, which helps crack open the international scandal.

Mr Shanahan tells him that Father O'Keeffe abused him in the 1960s, when the priest was based at Sandringham. But there's more. He says he was inducted into some type of a cult, a satanic one, by the sounds of it. And at certain rituals he watched the murders of four people. Mr Shanahan is lucky it was Max who picked up the phone. Some of his colleagues would've joked it must be a full moon. Dismissed it. He knows if he follows this up, he'll be ridiculed by co-workers. But Max listens intently, as he always does, because if he's learned anything in this gig, it's that anything is possible. Humans can be strange creatures, capable of extreme cruelty.

Max chases it. He tracks down a woman in Bendigo, in regional Victoria, who might be able to shed some light on all this. The word is she's a white witch. It comes to nothing. This woman says she doesn't have a clue what James Shanahan is on about. Max checks Victoria Police's missing persons' register, and its homicide records for the 1960s, but finds nothing. Also, historical cases are notoriously hard to firm up: people's memories fade, witnesses move interstate. So he has to let it go. With no leads, he can't afford to spend any more time on it when he's got a dozen cases on his plate, with more coming in every day. But he will always wonder.

May 2016

> I see no reason why I shouldn't accept what you say ... Amazing as it is, I accept it.

— Comment of Peter Callaghan QC to James Shanahan, 9 October 2000

It's 11.00pm during yet another nightshift with me as the last person left in the newsroom. The only visitor will be the overnight cameraman if he pops in between jobs. A phone rings on the chief of staff's desk, but experience has taught me that it's safer not to answer the colourful callers who reach out at this hour. Recent nightshifts have felt lonelier than usual. ABC Southbank is in the middle of a major expansion, so that its other site at Elsternwick (for TV production) can also be based here at Southbank. This newsroom is being packed up: many of the cubicle partitions are already down; cabinets and desks have been moved, revealing stray notebooks, coffee stains in the carpet, accreditation lanyards, and other marks of the ghosts of journos past.

Tomorrow's *AM* bulletin is looking in good shape. There's the NSW Premier's Literary Awards, and an update on the futile search for MH370. Melbourne's pretty quiet news-wise, so it's a good opportunity to look into the comment from Adam James that's been gnawing at me. '*I think it could've been the other man who was working with him*'. The thing is, Adam's been the only person to utter Father O'Keeffe's name so far. This priest was never on the police's radar—not even just as someone they should have a friendly chat with, in case Maria James or her killer had dropped a clue in the confessional. But back then, Ron Iddles and his crew had no idea about Adam's abuse allegations. So Father O'Keeffe is worth a look.

Most of my research grunt-work so far has been manual. Tediously so. Checking federal rolls for addresses, and then landing on people's doorsteps with a Boston bun and a smile, hoping they're holding on to one of the missing puzzle-pieces in this cold case. The internet hasn't been as helpful tracking people down as it usually is with the daily news churn. That's what you get trying to solve a mystery that's nearly four decades old. So I'm not holding my breath. I type in 'Thomas O'Keeffe'. The only result that seems relevant is an article from Broken Rites, a site that documents Catholic Church sex abuse. The article lists three victims, 'Percival', 'Liam', and 'Peter'. It also mentions that O'Keeffe has an alternate spelling: O'Keefe. Short snapshots of these three victims detail the abuse they suffered in the 1970s when Father O'Keeffe was the priest at Holy Family parish, in Doveton, a suburb around a 45 minutes' drive south-east of central Melbourne. This parish is now notorious for having harboured a string of paedophile priests. Fathers Wilfred Baker, Peter Searson, and Victor Rubeo were also channelled through Doveton, leaving behind them a string of damaged lives.

The Broken Rites article says that Father O'Keeffe

sodomised Percival, who later had to be referred to a
psychiatric centre. Liam describes how the priest would
drive boys to the beach, then later make them shower
together, where he'd rub soap on them 'to get the sand off'.
Peter, a former altar boy, talks about boys being invited to
the presbytery, where Father O'Keeffe would show them
pornographic magazines. There's a list of six parishes where
Father O'Keeffe worked, and a note at the bottom that he
died in 1984—four years after Maria James was murdered.
For argument's sake, I assume he died of old age, when he
was around 80 years old. This doesn't sound like Maria's
frenzied killer. I can't see an 80-year-old having the energy
to stab anyone that many times, to wrestle with his victim
and hold her down. I know what they say about the folly
of making assumptions, but if the murderer's motive was to
prevent being exposed as a paedophile, Father Bongiorno
would be my more likely bet.

It's late, I'm tired, and I should stop faffing about and
go home. But just before I do, I search for the name of
O'Keeffe, using the alternate spelling with one 'f'. Thank.
You. Google. Halfway down the list of search results is a link
to a submission to a 2013 Victorian parliamentary inquiry.
The writer is a Mr James Shanahan. His submission begins
with a criticism of the Church's response to paedophilia
allegations—that it shuffled the priests who had been named
into new parishes, instead of blocking their access to children.
The submission then bemoans low compensation payouts
under The Church's 'Melbourne Response'. Mr Shanahan
writes, 'The strategy was to take the allegations out of the
public arena and out of the hands of the legal system. It
was meant to silence victims.' To illustrate this, he cites his
$33,000 payout, explaining, 'In 2001, Peter O'Callaghan,

the church's investigator, accepted my claim that I had been abused by a satanic cult which included at least one priest, Father Thomas O'Keefe'.

Attached to this submission, is text cited as a 2006 blog by Gary Hughes, a journalist at *The Australian*. It begins: 'The most extraordinary thing about today's allegations of murder during satanic rituals involving a Melbourne priest is not that they've been made, but that the Catholic Church admitted in writing that it accepted they were substantially true.'

I have to read this twice, and am still confused. Murder? Mr Shanahan's submission mentions a satanic cult—nothing about murder. The blog goes on: 'Indeed "extraordinary" was the word used by the Melbourne Archdiocese's experienced sexual abuse investigator Peter O'Callaghan QC to describe the allegations when they were put to him in 2000.' According to the blog, Mr Shanahan claims he was forced to take part in satanic rituals, in which he was sexually abused. During these rituals, he says, he witnessed at least three murders: of a young girl, a youth and a child. 'He says the victims were mostly drugged and appeared to be in a daze before having their throats cut ...' What the hell? I again read back '... before having their throats cut or being hacked with an axe.'

Is this for real? This is the stuff of the big screen, of *The Da Vinci Code*, not of beige suburbia. I've covered some horrific stories in my time, but never anything like this. I click on the hyperlink to Gary Hughes's blog. I get an error message, 'The requested URL could not be retrieved.' I sign up for a trial account with newspapers.com and try the keywords 'O'Keeffe', 'O'Keefe', 'Shanahan', and 'cult' for articles published around the same time as the blog, 26 May 2006. The search result suggests that articles exist, but when

I click on the links, again I get error messages. This is getting strange now. I whip back to Hughes's blog:

> 'I see no reason why I shouldn't accept what you say,' Mr O'Callaghan told the victim during a formal interview on October 9, 2000. 'Amazing as it is, I accept it.'

I google 'James Shanahan' and 'O'Keefe', land on a blog written by James, and find myself in a rabbit hole I was in no way prepared for. It's 1961, James is 11, at a Christian Brothers School in East St Kilda. Thomas O'Keeffe is the school chaplain, and also the assistant parish priest at Sandringham where James is an altar boy. James remembers Father O'Keeffe calling him out of class for the purposes of sex education. James does what he's told, and goes to the brother's quarters. It's here that James is sexually abused:

> It was a large dim room. There were tall windows at the end and I could see trees outside bathed in bright summer light. O'Keefe sat next to me and began to fondle me. I focussed on the trees through the window and lost awareness of everything else. I had dissociated. It was something I had learned to do to cope with the violent nature of my home life. This fact was not lost on O'Keefe.

James says the sexual abuse became regular, and that Father O'Keeffe inducted him into a satanic cult, led by another paedophile priest, Kevin O'Donnell. First, he says, he was terrorised with dogs and guns, and sometimes raped with a loaded gun. Next, he says, came the electroshock treatment. James says he was strapped in a chair and made to hold two batons through which the shocks were administered. He remembers being subjected to a high-pitched noise in his right ear, while Father O'Donnell would yell nonsensicalities: 'God is evil, Satan is good', and 'Good is evil and evil is good'. James says he witnessed four murders, in which he was involved in various ways. 'The most direct demonstration of power over others is the stealing of their lives.'

It's chilling reading. James writes of the murders of a young man, a teenage girl, an infant, and a woman he'd fallen in love with, within the cult. He details beheadings, throats cut, cannibalism, and the drinking of blood. This is a crassly brief summary, because once you see it, you can't unsee it. James acknowledges that, 'What happened is beyond most people's imaginations and it would be a burden, to say the least, having those images in your mind.'

It's boiling hot in this newsroom — the heaters are overcompensating for the chilly Melbourne autumn night — but my skin prickles all over with icy goose bumps. I get up, do a lap of the office, a little dazed, and sit back down. It's still all there on the screen.

The knife was pressed against …

… threatened to kill me if I didn't eat …

…'You killed her' …

How can four people be murdered, in a satanic cult, and there are no online media articles about it? No mentions in the current royal commission? The next morning, I visit the Victorian State Library to dig into its microfiche collection. I'm embarrassed to admit that someone has to teach me how to use the machine. The fast-and-furious world of daily

journalism rarely allows such luxuries. 'Just loop it through
there,' the librarian instructs me. 'It's like threading a sewing
machine.' Once the film is under the lamp, the machine starts
happily spooling away. After a blur of newsprint, there it is,
in black and white:

> The Catholic Church has accepted as substantially true
> allegations that a Melbourne priest took part in ritualised
> sexual abuse in which a number of deaths occurred … .the
> statement details three deaths … gang rapes and other
> forms of sexual abuse … animals were also killed during the
> ceremonies … the police advised that inquiries had been
> made with the homicide squad and their missing persons
> records and intelligence was unable to confirm the allegations
> … (*Herald Sun*, 26 May 2006)

> Melbourne's Catholic Church has paid $33,000 to a man
> who says he was abused by a Melbourne priest who took
> part in satanic rituals in which three people were killed …
> the independent sexual abuse investigator for the Melbourne
> Archdiocese, barrister Peter O'Callaghan QC, 'substantially
> accepted' the victim's claim … (*Age*, 27 May 2006)

'Holy shit,' I breathe. I should call the podcast this. At
the moment, that's the only direction this investigation is
careering into.

> A man compensated by the Catholic Church after claiming
> to have witnessed three murders by a priest during bloody
> satanic rituals yesterday criticised the Church's handling of
> his complaint … 'I have no reason or justification for doubting
> his credibility,' Mr O'Callaghan wrote to the victim's lawyers

in 2000 ... but the man who wishes to remain anonymous, said: 'I was dismayed that there seemed to be no follow up.' (*Australian*, 27 May 2006)

You and me both, buddy.

I print copies, and head outside, feeling a little fuzzy. The trademarks of the library's forecourt—its fluttering pigeons, a busker's love song, the rapid ticking of a pedestrian crossing, and the smell of roasting chestnuts—jar with the images in my head.

Could Father O'Keeffe have murdered Maria James? Both he and Father Bongiorno have been accused of molesting Adam James, so both had a strong motive. Either could have answered Maria's call when she phoned the presbytery, ready for a confrontation. It could feasibly be either of these priests. Or *both* of them.

This won't be the only time I think, *What the hell have I got myself into?* I have to find James Shanahan.

October 2000

He feels trapped. *They always win in the end,* he thinks. That's how the structure's designed. He's avoided this process for years, the so-called Melbourne Response. It's not compensation—it's a cover-up. It's effectively signing away your right to sue the Catholic Church, in exchange for a paltry sum that won't even make a dent in the psychologist's bills.

But James Shanahan has been backed into a corner because of a fire in his workshop, with which his livelihood also went up in flames. It's suspicious, he thinks. It could've been an electrical fault, but he'd had the whole shed re-wired with trip relays. He doesn't think it was theft, because he's sifted through the ashes, and all his tools still seem to be there. The workshop is charred and useless now, though. And given that he owes more on his house than what it's worth, he's staring down a future of bankruptcy and homelessness. So he slinks back, cap in hand, to the very people who caused all this mess. *The Church'll bloody love this,* he thinks bitterly.

The meeting with his lawyer, Paul Holdway, and the Church's independent commissioner, Peter O'Callaghan QC, is in the QC's city office. There's a lot of talking. He wonders why the tape recorder sitting in front of him hasn't been switched on yet. When it finally is, it's all formalities.

Mr O'Callaghan says, 'I have read a statement that you made ... could you just look at that, please? I don't want you necessarily to read through it, but do you remember making that statement?'

'Yes,' James replies. 'This was written up from material, and it's correct.'

'All right, well, look, the position is that I am an independent commissioner, and if I am satisfied that a person has been the victim of sexual abuse by a priest of the Archdiocese, then I can refer that person to Care Link, which you know about. I can also refer that person to the compensation panel and make an application for compensation, which I take it that you're desirous of doing, are you?'

'Yes.'

'Well, what that entitles you to is an award of

compensation up to a limit of $50,000. What I will do is to indicate that I am satisfied that you were the victim of sexual abuse. I see no reason why I shouldn't accept what you say, and it's certainly supported by what you told Dr Driscoll and indeed what you've told a number of people over many years. Amazing as it is, I accept it. And if on that basis, what I will do is I'll send out ... an application for compensation, and you can fill that in ...'

James Shanahan thinks there will not be any justice. Mr O'Callaghan's subsequent letter to his lawyer offers 66 per cent of the possible amount: $33,000. That's it. Once lawyers' fees bleed out of this, it'll be nothing. They've won. Again. Even despite the astonishing acknowledgement made by Peter O'Callaghan in a letter to Paul Holdway:

I refer to our conference with Mr Shanahan and yourself on 9 October 2000 and confirm that I am satisfied that Mr Shanahan was a victim of sexual abuse inter alia by Father Thomas O'Keefe deceased substantially in the circumstances described by Mr Shanahan in the statement he made to you in November 1999, and which statement he verified at the conference today.

I confirm that the events which Mr Shanahan describes are extraordinary, but I have no reason or justification for doubting his credibility. In that context I note that an experienced psychiatrist Dr Helen Driscoll accepts what Mr Shanahan has described was the fact.

This validation will be useless, because he can't use it in court. James Shanahan thinks he should have kept hiding in his cave.

July 2016

Hello Rachael, [name redacted] phoned me and said you would like to talk with me about Thomas O'Keefe and his time at Thornbury.

— Email from James Shanahan to Rachael Brown, 18 May 2016

It worked. I'd put out some feelers, asking people who liaise with sex-abuse survivors if they know James Shanahan, and if so could they please pass on my contact details. It was a long shot. My appeal to his lawyer, Paul Holdway, had gone nowhere. And then this email arrives, from James, to set up a meeting.

But sitting in this café in Thornbury, just down the road from Maria James's old bookshop, I'm still not sure he'll show up. I don't know whether *I* would. What a scab to pick at. But the café door tinkles open as I'm on my second coffee, and he scans the room for a face similar to the photo I've sent him. The 11-year-old who was terrorised within an inch of his life is now 67. Behind his glasses, the corners of his eyes dip into soft wrinkles when he smiles, and he has grey in his hair, moustache, and beard. He's wearing a check shirt, and reminds me of one of my high school science teachers. When James Shanahan takes a seat, he angles his left side towards me, telling me that's his better ear. I remember a line from his blog: *I was subjected to a high pitched noise in my right ear.* James is polite but guarded.

Over coffee and soup, I explain what I'm doing and how he might be able to help. But only if he's comfortable, and he can be anonymous if he wishes. Because I remember neither he nor Father O'Keeffe were named in the 2006 blog by Gary Hughes, nor in the newspaper articles I found at the State Library. I've always viewed anonymity as a shield for tentative interviewees. Many important stories would never be told if it wasn't for this armour. But in the first of what will be many such times, James shifts my mindset. He thinks his name will protect him. 'Because then it raises too many questions if you suddenly disappear, because people know of you and you've put yourself at risk, so you're safer, ironically.'

It's a strange transaction, journalism. A crass description, I know, but that's exactly what it is. In the famous opening paragraph of her book *The Journalist and the Murderer*, Janet Malcolm ruminates:

> Every journalist who is not too stupid or too full of himself to notice what is going on knows that what he does is morally indefensible. He is a kind of confidence man, preying on people's vanity, ignorance, or loneliness, gaining their trust and betraying them without remorse.

I don't entirely agree with this. I don't think betrayal is inevitable. That depends on the journalist. Nonetheless, I do sometimes wonder why anyone talks to us when there's so much at stake. Maybe it's cathartic; maybe it's for a desperate snatch at justice; maybe it's just because a friendly ear is willing to listen. Regardless, interviewees unwittingly place a great amount of faith in us, complete strangers, in handing over their story. It's like a blind date with potentially far more damaging consequences.

I wonder what James's motivation is. I'd tracked him down, granted. My former colleague and investigative-journalism great, Chris Masters, says the whistle-blowers who approach *you* are the ones you have to be more wary of. So what's in it for James? It'll mean reliving abuse, detailing events that I'm guessing a lot of people will find unbelievable, and possibly pissing off the Church. But his answer is simple—painfully so. I'd made the point in my email that his story might help the James brothers, so he'd agreed.

'I think it was Tuesdays,' James tells me a couple of days later at the ABC's Southbank studios. After that first time, when Father O'Keeffe called him out of class for 'sex education', he was abused twice a week, on Tuesday and Friday afternoons. 'The arrangement was he'd drive me home, and we stopped along the way and he would abuse me.' Through all of it, he disassociated, his mind taking him away from the hell. James thinks this is why he was picked. 'I had a traumatic home life, so I learned to dissociate. O'Keeffe noticed that the first time he abused me, I'm presuming, and so I was intelligent and I'd be a good candidate to draw into the cult, into the ritual and training side of it.' He speaks of around eight or ten people being involved in the rituals. Most wore robes with full hoods. Not Father O'Keeffe, though. 'I suppose O'Keeffe had nothing to hide from me.' James says the rituals took place in an old vacant house that was attached to Sandringham's Sacred Heart church. The house was later demolished, and a new church built on the site. James thinks there wasn't enough holy water in the world to purify that site before the new church was built. He also remembers being driven to another location for ceremonies—he thinks it might have been in Dandenong.

And then he tells me about the murders, just like I've read in his blog. A man in his early to mid-twenties, and a teenage girl: both appeared to be drugged. An infant. James says he was ordered to choose who would die, the infant or a young boy. He was told if he didn't choose, both would be killed. He says the boy's terrified eyes made his decision for him. Woven through his memories are knives, an axe, a hatchet, blood-drinking, cannibalism. I ask about the fourth murder. Maramar, a woman in the cult James was in love with. He begins, then says he's not sure I want to hear the rest. It's way too late for that. My stomach's been doing slow rolls for the past ten minutes. So he continues in his low, measured voice, his eyes fixed somewhere a million miles away. And it's beyond horrific. There's a hot prickle on my neck that usually flags nausea, and I wonder whether I should stop the tape so we can both have a break.

It was this murder that broke him. When Maramar was killed, that was it—he was done.

'There was nothing else to hold me there. I didn't care who they were going to threaten to kill, or me, I just couldn't do it anymore. And next year was Form 3 for me, Year 9, and they had cadets, which were compulsory, and O'Keeffe was mixed up with the cadets. He was right into guns, and there's no way I was going to do it, so I just refused to go back to the college, and my parents finally put me in a high school. I avoided the church, and I'd keep an eye out the front window all the time through the lounge waiting for O'Keeffe to come in. And he did turn up. He'd drive in the driveway, and the boy's bedroom had a side door on it, so I'd go out the back, round through the garage, onto my bike, and pedal off. I managed to avoid him.'

I ask James why the hell he kept going back before this.

'Good question. A lot of it's to do with dissociation and programming. Repressed memories from your conscious mind. That's part of it. Another part of it is that they condition you to respond to signals—they can bring up that part of you, and that part's been traumatised, and it's often very obedient and so on. That's part of the reason.'

But he says he did try to escape the cult a couple of times, before the end.

'I don't want to go into the exact details. I'll just say that he caught me at home one time. And I think my mother wanted to go to the shops and he said, "I'll look after Jim", as I was known then. And he comes into the bedroom, and his hand's under the blanket, he's trying to molest me, and I'm fighting him off, and he turns around and storms out of the room. I thought I had a reprieve, but he came back in. He'd obviously gone to the kitchen, and he got the carving knife and threatened me with it. He threatened to run me through with this carving knife, and he was out of his mind with rage. I'd never seen him anywhere near that, actually, but he was just demonic.'

The bit about Father O'Keeffe grabbing a knife from James's own kitchen turns my skin cold. He says he was told he'd be killed if he ever spoke about what he'd seen, or the abuse.

'He'd threatened to kill my mother as well. I'd seen them, and they were very friendly, and I'd think, well, I wondered, how much she was part of it. I certainly don't think she was, but she'd been groomed by O'Keeffe, so there was that.'

James says that telling his mother was never an option. 'She wasn't demonstrative or emotional or empathetic in any way, and I'd always been encouraged, whatever it was, to just grin and bear it—she wouldn't give any time to any complaints or anything. It was not an option. I just didn't do it.'

So James fumbled through on his own. From 1964 he was in a new high school, in year 9, free of the priest but not of his shadow. James says he'd grown too good at dissociation.

'I couldn't concentrate, didn't want to concentrate. I used to wag school a lot, go off with friends. Finally in year 11, I failed. I never did any homework. And I started drinking at 14, started getting thrown out of pubs, which was, looking back, extraordinarily cheeky. At 14 I was all of five foot. I was just wild, and I used to get into fights in pubs. I functioned by using alcohol to socialise, so I had a wide group of friends who were great mates, and I used to be a bit crazy, and sometimes look back on it and think, *Why did they put up with me?*'

Into adulthood, nothing would stick. Not the two university courses he started and never finished. Not one of his three marriages. His one joy is building sports cars.

'For years, I wouldn't buy a house because it wouldn't move. There's no safety in a house for me. Safety is being able to move. When I got away from O'Keeffe, it was because I could get on my bike. So I like motorcycles, fast cars—that's what got me into sports cars.' It seems the only think that has stuck is the urge to run. And a decision to leave the past buried.

It was more than four decades before James Shanahan decided to speak up. Because something had happened in the US that he thought fortified his experience. Something that made him feel less alone. In early 2006, a Catholic priest called Gerald Robinson was convicted for the ritualistic murder of a nun, Sister Margaret Ann Pahl. The nun was stabbed 31 times, including nine times in the shape of an inverted cross, the day before Easter, in 1980. This was a couple of months before Maria James was murdered. Police questioned Robinson at the time, but no charges were laid, and a cover-up was later alleged. The case wasn't revived until 2003, when a woman came forward claiming she'd been abused by Robinson as a child during a series of satanic rituals that also involved human sacrifice. Robinson's conviction emboldened James. Maybe society was ready for his story? He believed there were other victims of ritualised abuse in Australia who were too afraid or embarrassed to speak out. So he told Gary Hughes his story, the newspapers followed it up the next day, and that was it. As far as he's aware, no authorities or journalists followed up the murder allegations.

I ask the question I've been putting off: 'Have you ever considered that they might not be real, these memories?'

'Yeah, well, a reaction to it—it's common with people who've been through this—is that you don't want to believe it's real. And I remember remarking to a lawyer who was supposedly representing me, saying, "I find it hard to believe, too", and he was kinda shocked, and I think he thought I wasn't sure if it was true or not. And it was certainly true. But it's so surreal against everyday waking life, and so that sort of does your head in, too.'

I'm acutely aware that my credibility will soon also be on the line. And even if I can shore up these claims enough to report them, I'm fearful of their reception. James nods.

'People go missing all the time. Children go missing all the time. They don't end up in the papers—a couple do. People think they live in one world, but they don't. If they start to think about it, they don't want to believe it, because what you're dealing with here is from inside one of the major institutions in the world, which has more than a billion members. You're basically telling them that they're not following Christ, they're following Satan, and that's distressing for a lot of people—it turns their world upside down. And as shocking as SRA [satanic ritual abuse] is, I've asked a couple of people,

"Well, what aspect of it can't you believe?", and they've said a couple of things after some thought, and I've said, "But you know it goes on. You know cannibalism goes on, you know people get killed and people drink blood — this terrorist in Syria cuts the guy up and eats his liver, for goodness sake. It goes on. All of it." And the torture, well, the CIA has been exposed in one of the congressional Senate inquiries of doing just that. Exactly the same thing that was happening to me. At the same time. If you break it down into its constituent parts, you know that they're all practised elsewhere, and it's acknowledged. Put it all together, though, and people find it hard to handle. The guideline here is, I say to people, if you can imagine something, somebody out there is doing it.'

I'm grappling with all this. But I also find it hard to believe someone would stab a mother 68 times. Or molest a child. So through this lens, why would satanic ritual abuse be outside the realm of possibility? I know from sad experience that survivors of sexual abuse often seek a permanent escape, so I ask the other question I've been putting off. Has James had to battle suicidal thoughts?

'Oh, I came very close to doing exactly that when I was young. There is a chronic level of suicidality going on. Sometimes it gets quite intense, but it's pretty much a constant companion. Although one part of me desperately wants to die, another part of me is ferocious in hanging onto life. But I've got a larger context these days, and I have an understanding of what love is and what evil is, and why we're here.'

I guess this larger context is why he's sitting here with me, telling me all this.

'I hope it's helpful for people who've been similarly abused. I hope to shine a light on the nature of part of the

Catholic Church which has an inordinate amount of control, because these are public institutions—they run schools, and they've got this image, which is undeserved. They're scamming everybody—people need to be aware of that. Any bureaucracy, given enough time, is going to be run by and for the psychopaths, and the Catholic Church is the oldest bureaucracy on earth.'

James tells me that Father O'Keeffe was your classic psychopath. I show him a photo from *The Catholic Advocate* I've managed to find on microfiche in the Victorian State Library.

'Yeah, that's him. He looks rather angelic in that picture. The images I have of his facial expressions are generally more focused and intense. But he had the ability to charm people. In public, he was a mellow guy, like so many psychopaths are—charming, got their act together, attractive people. In the cult settings, again, for the most part, he was even and measured; he only got upset when I wouldn't do what he wanted. It's bizarre how normal they can behave in these extraordinary situations.'

The story of Father O'Keeffe using James's own knife against him bothers me. And I'm wondering whether the priest had other traits that mirrored the MO of Maria James's killer.

'Did he ever bind you?' I ask.

'I don't have a memory of him binding me up. However, I don't like things around my ankles, and I don't like them around my wrists. I don't wear a wristwatch or do my cuffs up, but I've just got this one [mental] picture of my wrists being bound with cord or a rope.'

And then there's this: 'A friend of mine used to call him [Father O'Keeffe] "Creeping Jesus", because he would sneak around. He had these rubber ripple-soled shoes which were in vogue at the time, and he would sneak around. He'd love coming up behind you, and he'd walk into the family home and he'd scare my mother because she'd be in the kitchen at the sink, and he'd be standing there behind her. He'd walked in, hadn't made a sound. He just delighted in doing it.'

Ron Iddles' observation about John James rings like a cymbal crash. *That can only mean that the time he viewed his ex-wife on the floor, the killer was standing behind the door.*

Once I save the interview—five times, just to be safe—I take James across the road for a coffee. We both need one. The satanic images that my mind is swimming in haven't left much room to watch the traffic. James is kind and patient. He knows this is a lot to take in. He describes it like the red pill in the sci-fi movie *The Matrix*—the pill that frees Neo from the dream world, but means a harsher existence. James thinks most people are quite content living under an illusion, ignorant of the world's ugly mechanics. For a girl who grew up in a happy, middle-class family, maybe I've been blissfully naive as well?

So I think this through. We have a priest with a motive, with a propensity to snap when things aren't going his way, and who's known for creeping up on people. His age at death, though, is still bothering me. Could an elderly man be capable of a furious stabbing? 'Oh no,' James corrects me, and confirms something he'd flagged during our first phone conversation. 'My mother told me he died in his sleep at the age of 51.'

And I'd thought he must have been around 80. This changes everything.

Stomp, stomp, stomp, stomp. *Don't stop running until you're exhausted,* I tell myself. *You need to be so tired that even the nightmares won't wake you.* They've been horrendous. In the first one, I was about to be raped after the attackers jumped over the backyard fence of the house I grew up in. In the next, I watched four people gunned down in a car, their blood splattering across the windows. In another, I was administered general anaesthetic for brain surgery, and I remembered crucial questions I'd forgotten to ask. 'Wait, wait, wa ... ,' I mumbled, as the anaesthesia took me away. I've been hugging a pillow because, for some reason, I feel safer with my vital organs covered.

Drinking hasn't helped the situation. It's been two straight weeks of dying a cruel death in my dreams, and then jerking awake with a racing heart and damp sheets. Which is why I think, while someone needs to investigate satanic ritual abuse further, I'm not sure I'm that person. Once you swallow that red pill, there's no going back.

Stomp, stomp, stomp, stomp over a cigarette butt. Did cops find any butts near the crime scene? Father O'Keeffe used to smoke Kents, apparently. Certain elements of my investigation are starting to outpace the original police one. Father O'Keeffe was never questioned, let alone suspected. So James Shanahan's story, along with Adam James's allegation, could mean a seismic shift. But can I really have been the first to make this connection? Have others discovered and then abandoned this lead, either because something smelt fishy, or because they were leaned on? Am I in dangerous territory? Either in terms of my credibility or personal safety?

Stomp, stomp. Pass a smug couple discussing their dinner plans. Stomp, stomp. Lucky for some. Stomp, stomp. What am I even doing? All this stolen sleep, all my spare time spent shouldering stories of child sex abuse and satanic rituals, for what? So far, two newspapers have produced successful true-crime podcasts: *The Australian* with 'Bowraville, and *The Age* with 'Phoebe's Fall'. Meanwhile, I'm struggling getting mine commissioned. Granted, it's a new idea, so it's uncharted territory in terms of where it'll live within the ABC. Also, it'll take brave bosses to back a big project like this. I knew this podcast was never going to be a cakewalk, but the current inertia is exhausting.

At least it's amusing John Clarke. Every Wednesday, during his meander around the newsroom before taping his *7.30* politics segment with Bryan Dawe, the withering satirist leans over my desk partition and raises his eyebrows in a look that asks, *What's the latest?* He listens to every update with his wry, crooked smile. This is his kind of story, where truth is stranger than fiction. Stomp, stomp, nearly there. Stomp, stomp, just hold on.

1972

'Bill' trudges back to Doveton's Holy Family Church, covered in mud. He'd slipped in a puddle during his footy match, so Father O'Keeffe, who'd been umpiring, had pointed him towards the presbytery to get cleaned up. Oddly, the priest joins Bill in the shower, with no clothes on, saying he'll wash the mud off. Bill's uncomfortable—he doesn't know where to look or what to do as the priest pays particular attention to washing his genitals. Bill keeps his eyes shut, because the priest's penis is close to his face. 'You're lucky,' Father O'Keeffe says. 'You're a special child of the Lord.' Then he adds that Bill shouldn't tell anyone about the shower, or he'll go to hell.

Bill wishes that the showers and the priest 'adjusting' boys' cricket protectors were the worst of it. One day, he's in the school office area doing some printing when the priest says he has a job for him. Father O'Keeffe walks Bill into the presbytery office, tells him to face the desk, then pushes his chest down onto it. The priest pulls down the 11-year-old's pants. Bill, expecting to be smacked, is confused—he doesn't remember doing anything wrong. Instead, he feels a sharp pain in his anus. He thinks it's the priest's finger. Three times it goes in. Searing pain. When the priest lets him turn around, Father O'Keeffe's penis is in his hand, which he's moving back and forth. Then the priest makes some noises, and a liquid comes out of his penis onto a white cloth on the desk. Bill thinks the priest's penis must've been sick. Bill is asked to hold it, as Father O'Keeffe blesses his forehead, saying, 'This is our secret.'

This secret plays out three more times. Maybe he's been chosen, Bill thinks, because the priest always says he's a special child from the Lord. But Bill understands that the second he tells anyone, he won't be special anymore, and he'll have to go to hell.

The final time the priest shares their secret, Bill cries, but he knows he just has to wait it out. Like always, he'll be asked to kiss Father O'Keeffe's penis, the priest will bless his forehead, and then it'll all be over. Not this time. After Father O'Keeffe takes his finger out, Bill feels something else in his anus. He thinks it's the priest's penis. The pain is like nothing he's ever felt. It seems to go on forever, and he squeals in pain. Bill doesn't remember Father O'Keeffe ever being this rough before.

Bill fights back one day, releasing the pain by throwing a stone through the presbytery's front window. *Let him who*

is without sin cast the first stone. But when the priest storms
out, he hits Bill so hard across the head that he falls to the
ground. Next, Father O'Keeffe is squeezing his genitals,
saying if he ever does anything like this again, or rats him
out, Bill will be in trouble. His own father is no solace, either.
Bill skirts around the abuses, just tells his old man that Father
O'Keeffe had punished him. 'Must've been your fault,' his
dad tells him. 'If you'd done as you were told, you wouldn't
be in trouble.' So Bill never brings it up again.

Father O'Keeffe's sex-education lessons continue. 'Keith'
is invited on trips to the beach. Father O'Keeffe makes all the
boys shower naked afterwards, and makes fun of those too
embarrassed to undress in front of them. 'Peter' is introduced
to pornographic magazines. He's never seen an erection
before, and thinks, *What happened to his dick? And why is
he putting it in there? And there? And there?'* He used to
think that only urine came from a penis. He's eight, and is
usually only allowed to play with matchbox cars and read Dr.
Seuss.

As for the teachers who work with Father O'Keeffe,
they admire his wonderful command of the scriptures and
the fine liturgy he's introduced into masses in the wake of
changes since the Second Vatican Council. They also think
he has a great ability to communicate with the young. But
his secrets will remain so until long after Thomas O'Keeffe
dies in 1984. And the young—the victims of similar patterns
of abuse, sometimes identical, in at least three parishes, over
two decades—they might get money, if they're lucky.

Money for pain, Bill will think bitterly in 44 years' time
when he's awarded compensation. When he can't remember a
time when he's been happy to be alive. When he's taken all his
anger out on his wife and kids. When he's had a breakdown

and been admitted to a psychiatric hospital. When he's attempted suicide three times. When his story has become horrific in its commonness.

August 2016

> Wednesday is good for me if you can make it down to Geelong.

— Text from Max Schiavon to Rachael Brown, 8 August 2016

'It was an unusual call, not the sort of thing you get every day,' says the former detective above the din of crashing cutlery and a hissing espresso machine. Thankfully, Max Schiavon was easy to find. While scouring the internet for documents about James Shanahan and his allegations about Father O'Keeffe, I found a reply to Mr Shanahan's submission to the 2013 Victorian Parliamentary Inquiry by the Church's independent commissioner, Peter O'Callaghan QC. In it is mentioned the name of the detective that James Shanahan reached out to, all those many moons ago:

> Our client, (i.e. Mr Shanahan) has contacted Detective Max Schiavon at the Geelong or Werribee CIB. The contact was made in the latter part of 1998.

For one of the first times in this investigation, finding him didn't involve protracted ancestry or federal-roll searches—just a little database called LinkedIn. The business social-networking site lists a Max Schiavon as an occupational health and safety investigator with WorkSafe Victoria. It mentions that he used to be a detective with Victoria Police up until 2008. He's our man.

'I mean, a lot of people wouldn't waste their time with something like that, because of how long ago it's alleged to have occurred, and secondly because it is bizarre and a lot of these callers might be classed as being loopy.'

Max remembers James's phone call well. And Max did something he suspects some of his colleagues mightn't have. He listened.

'I had no reason to disbelieve what he said. Anything is possible, so you've just got to make an assessment on what basis they have to it, and other evidence that could corroborate what they're saying.'

'How hard are these things to look into?' I ask him.

'Really difficult, because of the time span that's elapsed, the loss of evidence along the way, memory loss, locations—I mean, you can't just go to that location and search for evidence. And tracking down people where the caller might've been a young person at the time, how accurately they can recall names of people.'

Max's inquiries led him to a woman in Bendigo, in regional Victoria.

'There were suggestions she was a white witch. I can't remember if she told me that, or somebody else did'

He apologises. He doesn't have the information report he wrote up on the matter. Victoria Police has that. He suggests I apply for it under Freedom of Information. *Hmmm, Vic Pol will love that*, I think. It's still yet to respond to my April email suggesting a collaboration. The assistant commissioner, Stephen Fontana, has kindly given the podcast his blessing; Homicide, on the other hand, seems quite cool on the idea.

'What did she say to you?' I ask Max.

'Without remembering the specifics of the conversation, I think she put herself in that area at that time — but she really couldn't elaborate any further, and disputed that she ever witnessed sexual abuse, or a child being sacrificed, or anything like that.'

Max strikes me as a man who's seen and heard it all, because he doesn't raise an eyebrow while talking about witches and warlocks.

'Does that stuff go on?'

'Oh, I've heard that it does, yes. I haven't seen it personally,' he says, chuckling. He probably didn't think his day was going to go this way. 'But I've heard. So I don't think it's unusual even in this day and age that people are involved in that sort of — well, it doesn't need to be a satanic cult, but some type of cult activity, yeah. We've all heard stories over the last 15 to 20 years about sadistic and violent trends that have occurred over various periods of time through the Church, or through schools or other institutions, so it doesn't surprise me. I think times were very different back then. I think we've just got to accept that these things could've occurred, and we have to look into them a bit further.'

Max says he did as much as he could. But with not much to go on, and with no help from the white witch, he typed up the little he knew, and left the rest to the Homicide Squad. 'I didn't know at the time what more they could do with it, but I left that in their hands.'

I put something to Max that's bugging me: the fact that the cult victims reported by James Shanahan didn't match up against any missing persons or homicide records.

'I don't think it's possible in this day and age for four people to be murdered and no one to follow up on that. Back then, do you think it would be possible for four deaths to go uninvestigated?'

'Well, depending on the circumstances, the ages, a young person or a baby, I believe that could be possible. Because if you're born into a cult where there are no records kept, or depending on where it is, if it's out in a regional area, babies are born in those societies and situations, and they're not registered, so, yeah, it's possible. As for other people, there's always people that go missing and they may not have family—family don't bother chasing them up, they might've been runaways. We don't know how good the record-keeping was back in the sixties or earlier.'

This one will have to be chalked up like faith. Just because it might be impossible to prove doesn't mean it's not real.

'This case is just extremely unusual and unsavoury for a lot of people,' Max says, 'and people perhaps don't want to believe just because of the bizarre nature of it. Doesn't mean it didn't happen. I think we have to go in there with our eyes wide open and look for more information rather than just discount it.'

Sometime before 2001

In the bowels of a Victoria Police exhibits-storage unit, a bloodstained pillow sitting on a shelf is transferred into a neighbouring exhibits bag marked 'Maria James'. This action, whether misguided or callously strategic, will forever change the course of this woman's story, and inflame the scars of those who mourn her—including some who never even met her.

February 2017

It is a story that needs to be told ... in the interests of justice ... for a mother and her sons ... and the ugly underbelly ... I think that is where James is coming from too.

— Text message from Helen Driscoll to Rachael Brown, 14 February 2017

'I have no doubt James has been sexually, sadistically, and ritualistically abused.'

It's Valentine's Day, and Kerri Ritchie and I are talking about satanic ritual abuse with James Shanahan's psychiatrist. In a year when I've avoided dating because all I'd have to talk about is exhumation protocols, this all feels pretty fitting, really. But this morning, the *Trace* team was also not feeling the love.

At the end of last year, ABC News got sick of my nagging, commissioned a little idea called *Trace*, and partnered me with Radio National because of its experience in producing podcasts. But now, some bosses are frustrated that the team is not further down its to-do list, so we've been told to tie things up. If only it was that easy. This mess gets murkier and more complicated the more people we talk to.

Helen Driscoll's practice is in a weatherboard Edwardian cottage in Northcote. She specialises in sexual abuse, trauma, and post-traumatic stress disorder. Sun filters through the front window above her desk, catching some dust in its beams. Helen's interest in trauma was aroused by working as a doctor in a post-Pol Pot Cambodian refugee camp. Helen has kindly squeezed me in between patients, but I may as well be one. I'm in desperate need of reassurance. I'm nervous about what people are going to make of James's story and how he is going to cope once it's all laid bare.

'I can understand why some aspects of what James says seem bizarre,' she says.

'In the 1980s, police didn't believe priests were paedophiles, and that's all been proven to be horribly untrue,' I say. 'Back then, there would've been journos who thought, *Nup, this sounds crazy, they must be lying.* I'm not going to be that person.'

'The royal commission has had lots put to it about children being killed,' Helen says, 'and I think that happens, and it happens with organised paedophile groups, and the Adelaide Family, and so on. I'm not sure some of it is simulated to the young person, so that they *think* some things have happened to terrify [them], so I don't know whether everything is factual.'

'There have been murders, I've seen and worked with people who as children had pregnancies, and things were done to the babies—they were never registered or they were aborted. I have no doubt about that. Think about the Third Reich, right under people's noses. So the fact that there are sadistic human beings who think they can do something and get away with it, they will and they do. I think he [James] was totally terrorised, and bad things happened. I've talked with some people who I've no doubt were ritually abused, who eventually, in a safer place, have wondered whether some of it was simulated to terrorise them, to silence them about the things that did happen, so they don't know whether in a drugged, deeply traumatised state whether they were told this has happened, and whether it did or didn't. I mean, the terror was happening, so I don't know.'

But Helen says you only have to look at the larger world order and at history. If perverts feel they can get away with something, they'll do it.

'After the money from illicit-drug-trafficking, the biggest money-maker in the world is child sexual-abuse porn.'

'Really?'

'Yes, it is—huge money. It's just that it's so ugly we don't really want to know about it, so I think that the things James has come out with are consistent with the order of what does go on.'

'Is it possible that he's taken lots of facts, and formed a narrative that's not true, but it's one that fits all the facts?'

'No. When someone has been abused to the degree James has—ritual abuse—their tendency is to minimise, not to exaggerate, because it's too difficult. It's never altered, his story; it's never been embellished. I mean, he can say it more easily now, but when he first was coming out, he was really a mess. And what is very interesting is that people who are fabricating, and believe their fabrications, often don't get better, because the underlying agenda for the fabrication, like Munchausen, is to get attention and secondary gain. What I've found is that those who have actually been sadistically abused as children, if you work with them, eventually they improve. They don't want to embellish—they don't want to be there.'

'One of the things O'Keeffe did to James was very sadistic. James has neurological damage. I had the nerve injuries verified by a physician. You will have noticed he has a slight limp, a gait, there's nerve damage, and it fits with what he says happened, and his mother says he didn't have that before.'

I wonder whether this happened during a particularly gruesome abuse episode that James has told me about, and then I think, *Actually, I don't want to know*.

Helen tells us that several of her current clients are seeing her because of satanic ritual abuse.

'Some are too ill to be giving information to the royal commission. Some have. The stuff I know, they [the commissioners] are very delicately working with at present. I have two others who've given me information that completely fits with some of what James has said, even down to stuff on the floor. But they're just so traumatised. One who was an alcoholic, and has stopped drinking and has just started some part-time work, I go and see her in her home, because if she has flashbacks I'm worried about her getting home. And we've made so many gains. But Professor Bessel van der Kolk [an American trauma specialist] says, "Sometimes the truth can never be fully told, because it breaks your heart forever."'

'Look, I've had survivors of ritual abuse who've had to have colostomy bags because their rectum is so damaged ... I've had others where [medical] records have disappeared. And I think an issue for the royal commission has been that police records have disappeared, because some officers were involved in a cover up to protect the Church. And I wish I didn't know it, but we got on a revolting learning curve in the 1980s, when I became a child psychologist. To quote one woman I've worked with, 'For those who believe these bad things can happen, no proof is necessary. As for those who do *not* want to believe, no proof will ever be enough.''

And this is what I'm most worried about—what James's

reaction will be if his experience isn't received how he hopes. Like art, you can put stories out into the world with the best of intentions, but you can't control their interpretation.

Helen softly but surely reminds me I'm not responsible for others' reactions. 'It's a risk—if he says yes, to doing it—that you just have to take.'

I confess my fears are less to do with James than my own scar tissue. He's highly intelligent, he's patient, he wears a dark sense of humour that serves him well, and he's done the work—he can talk about his nightmares now without them dragging him under. My nerves, when it comes to suicide, are still fairly shot. I tell Helen about an incident in 2009 when I had to report on a doctor accused of sexually assaulting his patients. The allegations were solid. But when I called the doctor for his right of reply, he was so calm: he explained that he dealt with troubled kids, and sometimes this was how they lashed out. He added, 'The very large number of young people whom I have been able to help more than compensates for the current distress and hardship that inevitably goes with this process.' He was so convincing, I nearly spiked the story. But it ran on *AM* on a Friday, leading with an 18-year-old's allegation he was raped while the doctor was treating him for drug and alcohol problems. This teenager added that there were others who'd lodged sexual-abuse complaints with the Medical Practitioners Board of Victoria. The *Herald Sun* newspaper also ran the story that weekend. On Monday, the police informant called to tell me he'd killed himself.

I just remember confusion, and my pulse in my ears. *But, no, that can't be … I was so careful, there was nothing in that story to identify those boys, nothing, I was so careful.*

'No, Rach,' the cop said gently. 'The *doctor* killed himself.'

I spent the next half hour crumpled in the staff toilets,

my head hanging over porcelain, tasting bile. My work had contributed to his death. I was sure of it. The poor excuse for a counsellor I was referred to had the nerve to ask me, 'But *why* do you think it's your fault?' I remember staring her down with red eyes, and saying bitchily, 'You're going to have to do a hell of a lot better than that.'

In the end, those who picked me up were veterans of this often all-consuming profession who've had to dig themselves out of their own dark holes, and the cop who for an hour was a nurse. He took me for coffee, and told me that, on that fatal weekend, detectives had convinced another victim to turn against the doctor. One of the doctor's trusted weapons for the defence was now working for the prosecution. 'That pushed him over the edge, Rach, not you—this is not your fault.' And while those last five words bestowed a gushing relief I still can't describe, the fear remains, of the damage that we as journalists can wreak if we're careless with our power—the power of words.

Helen is nodding kindly and knowingly, and is probably thinking she should be billing me for this after all. But she's been here before.

'I've had people suicide. I skid around suicide all the time in my work. The case you mentioned, the paedophile, there's a high incidence of suicide amongst those. It's like a narcissistic wound. They're happy to tolerate what they've done behind closed doors, and they know what they've done is wrong, but they don't want it exposed. When some of it is exposed, it's an irreversible narcissistic wound.'

This makes me think of Father O'Keeffe. Would the possibility of being outed as a paedophile by a furiously protective mother constitute a narcissistic wound? Most definitely, says Helen.

'This young man's mother believed him, and he [Father O'Keeffe] picked up that she believed him, and she was not going to let this lie. So he was meeting not a fragile mother, not an alcoholic parent—he was meeting his match and her righteous indignation, and he had to deal with her.'

Back to James, though. How much do I have to protect him?

'I think there comes a time when we can't make those decisions for someone. Society is very patriarchal, so what's made a difference is the number of men who've come forward about sexual abuse. Generally speaking, those who are victims have already been through the worst. What drives them to keep going is to have the truth told. James, he'd be relieved about the truth coming out.'

When Kerri and I stand, to let Helen get back to nursing others through their demons, I tell her I don't know how she does it.

'There are times I actually had to leave it for a long time. But I have a very good support group, and I guess it's just the rage, revolution against cruelty, so it's my way of also …'

'It fuels you?'

'Yes.'

'This is my counsellor,' I say pointing at Kerri.

'Well, you can't do it on your own. It's overwhelming at times—you get a vicarious traumatisation if you really connect up with it. On some level I have a shield, but sometimes something really gets under it, and I think, *Oh God*.'

'You're right about the revolting learning curve,' says Kerri.

'Your innocence is gone, shattered.'

But Helen's a firm believer that a little red pill needs to be swallowed regardless.

'I was listening the other day to CNN and Christiane Amanpour [a CNN journalist]. There was a segment of hers in Bosnia, and very eloquently she said something like, "When you've witnessed such violations by human beings against others, you can't be neutral." She said, "I have to tell the truth." I think that's right. It's about, *What's the truth? Break the silence.*'

After we've left Helen on that Valentine's Day, I can't stop thinking about her lamentation, which I suspect will long stick with me.

'Sometimes the truth can never be fully told, because it breaks your heart forever.'

February 2017

We've had a win. Hand-written cards work. The electrician phoned and we are meeting 10:30 tomorrow.

— Text from Kerri Ritchie to the *Trace* team, 8 February 2017

In *Trace*'s investigation, we've been lost down countless rabbit holes. We've asked people to relive their nightmares and brought on tears, many of them our own. While mates have been posting Facebook photos of amazing dinners and getaways, I've been transcribing accounts of sexual abuse and researching which Italian town hall one would need to visit to access certain birth certificates. I've had to teach myself about mitochondrial DNA, how dissociation can affect the hippocampus, and the prerequisites for exhumation. It's a slog, depleting on every level. I get why cops have to do their cold-case work around current jobs—it's taxing, sometimes for only microscopic gain. But then there are days, those rare, gloriously golden days, when things just fall into place.

The last snatch at our Holy Grail, Allan Hircoe, was via a greeting card that had galahs perched on the cover. Maybe that's what Kerri thought *we* were, having chased this elusive electrician for a stupid amount of months. Although she *said* she'd hoped it would remind him of his house by the beach. He was the niggle that started all this, the reason *Trace* was born. I'd heard that the electrician had seen a man acting suspiciously in the St Mary's churchyard soon after Maria James's murder, and that this man was Father Bongiorno. And here's the clincher: rumour has it that the priest had blood on him.

Allan had apparently given a statement to detectives in late 2013, but nothing had ever come of it. Maybe his story hadn't checked out. Or were there darker forces at play here? Could the Church have leaned on Victoria Police to keep this quiet? Kerri had tracked down Mr Hircoe's son through a local footy club, and made an approach. His son told Kerri, 'You wait till you hear his memory—it's impeccable. He's not a bullshit artist. He used to work for the council: he can tell you about that lane that connects to the street, he'll tell you street from street, the colour of the fence—he's got that type of memory. When you meet him, he's like an old-school copper.' He'd added a kind warning, for us to move gently: 'I'll ring Mum in a minute, but it will take a day or two for him to think about it; he'll ho and hum for a while, walk around for a day. I don't see any reason why he wouldn't speak to you, but he'll go into his shell if you put pressure on him.' Good tip. So we wait. And wait some more. And then, holding our breath, we pin our last hopes on a galah greeting-card, asking if we can show Allan some photos to clarify who he saw in the churchyard that day.

And he *calls*. Kerri's looking out her front window, thinking it needs a clean, when her mobile starts flashing with an unknown number. It's Allan and, yes, he'll meet with us. 'But it's Allan with a double 'l',' he says. 'You wrote A-l-a-n'. *Stickler for accuracy,* Kerri thinks, laughing. *Love him already.* Kerri says she nearly cried with sheer relief. She's spent, too, working huge hours making little progress, on top of wrangling two boisterous young daughters. We're all too quick to tears these days. You know you're frayed when you tear up at a pathetically tacky airline ad. But we've found him, and this investigation is going somewhere, and all this heartache—for people like Mark, Adam, and James—might actually have a payoff.

A blustery northerly whips around us as we wait on Allan's doorstep. I spot a gnome in an Essendon Football Club guernsey through the window. After all this time spent looking for him, it turns out that Allan lives where I grew up. Typical. He ushers us in warmly, but a tad apprehensive. His wife, Rhonda, is a straight shooter, 'Hello, you're the one he's been trying to avoid.' *Yep, that'd be me.* As she tells me her golf's been called off because of this crazy wind, Allan starts rummaging through an old wooden chest of drawers. There's a video he's keen to show us, a taped statement he gave police, which, he's surprised, hasn't amounted to anything. He pulls out all manner of DVDs—some in plastic covers, and others in paper pockets with scrawled writing. He clicks his tongue. 'When we shifted, we chucked a heap of things out.'

All good, Allan, we have the real thing right in front of us.
'It won't be there. I'm sure you threw it out,' Rhonda

interrupts, in that tender chastisement only a wife can nail. 'Who's coffee and who's tea?' She puts out a plate of dry biscuits, with cheese and salami perfectly apportioned on each.

They've recently downsized, but this light-filled house is already home. The walls are covered with photos of their travels around the world, and of their grandkids. Allan sits down beside an old rocking horse he's just managed to find a new mane for. He reaches for a biscuit, and I notice two Band-Aids on his arm. 'Melanoma,' he explains. He's just turned 70, the age when all that time in the sun catches up with you. But otherwise he's clean-cut, in a maroon Quiksilver polo shirt, with brushed-back short, grey hair and a freshly shaven face.

He remembers back to when he was 33. He'd been called out to work on an electricity box on the wraparound porch of St Mary's presbytery. He chuckles, remembering being given short shrift by a woman who answered the door. She was European-looking, he says, short, neatly dressed with a freshly pressed pinafore. 'I said, "I'm going to have the electricity off, will that be all right?" and she slammed the door. But then another person came around the side, on my right-hand side. He was a priest, he had black trousers on, and a flannelette shirt with braces over the shirt, and he was an Australian. Looked a bit like John Cain [junior], the premier. "What do you want?" he asked. I told him and he said, "Yeah, go ahead," then he left.'

Allan had been working for around 15 minutes when he noticed something odd. 'A chap came on the left-hand side, and I looked at him from about eight metres away. He had blood on one side of his face, and one of his sleeves was rolled up, and he had blood on that arm.' He can't remember which arm it was, and whether the splatter was on the same side as the one on the priest's face. But he remembers there was a lot of blood. 'Looked like a reasonable sort of cut. I said, "What have you done?" and he said, "I cut my face on the wire fence near the roses," or "I cut my face on the roses near the wire fence." Long time ago—I'm not sure which way he had that.'

'I just want to show you a photo, if that's okay, just to double-check. So this is a picture of Father Bongiorno.'

'Yep, that's him. He's a lot older.'

'Is this the man you saw in the presbytery garden that day?'

'Yeah, but the one in the paper [the *Herald Sun*], the photo's younger. So he's older here.'

'I think this was at his next parish—St. Ambrose in Brunswick.'

'Not that much older. Yeah, but that's him.'

I ask about the blood. Was it a spray? A splatter?

'No, it wasn't a smattering. Where it was, he could have smeared it. I don't know. It was only a fleeting glance. Well, not a fleeting glance—you can see a lot in five or six seconds.'

'And what can you tell us about his voice?'

'Well, I thought he had a European accent, like an Italian accent.'

'Did he sound distressed or was he just blasé, "Oh, I just scratched my face …"?'

'No, he sounded distressed. Anyway, I said, "I've got a first-aid kit," which we carry in the vehicles. I said, "I'll be back in a second," and I said, "Don't go away," and I walked off, and then I turned around … gone. Completely gone.'

'He moved pretty fast?'

'Well, he only had a couple of metres to go. He was round one side of the property. It had a return veranda. Apparently there was a house out the back, and a laneway down there.'

'I might just show you a map, Allan, here on my phone. This is High Street, Thornbury. Number 736 was the bookshop, and there's Mansfield Street. Now the school and parish are in this block.'

'Doesn't show the lane,' he says.

Stuff this iPhone nonsense. Allan reaches for a piece of paper to draw a mud map.

'The church entrance is there. That's High Street. Now there's the property there. That's the beautiful old house, the return veranda.' Allan draws an X for where he was standing on the verandah.

'And where were the roses?'

'Looking at the presbytery, on the left-hand side, there was a garden there. So the roses are here'—he draws a square (representing the garden) next to the house, and puts a small circle in the middle—'and then the lane there.' He adds short double lines linking the square to Mansfield Street. These lines are parallel to the ones he's drawn running behind Maria's bookshop.

'So the lane looks to be the extension of the lane that runs behind the bookshop?'

'Yeah, went right through. But now, detectives tell me, the lane's gone, the house is gone, the roses are gone (he puts a cross through the square), the fence is gone, and it's now a car park for the church.'

'Would he [Father Bongiorno] have run in from here?' I point to the lane that cuts into the presbytery from Mansfield Street.

'No, I couldn't tell you that at all, no. He came from that direction, down towards the bookshop, but he could have been standing in the roses for an hour and a half, just doing exactly what he said he was doing.'

Allan's sighting was for about six seconds, from eight metres away, and then the priest disappeared.

So the electrician went back to his business until another peculiarity pierced the churchyard. A muffled female scream came from inside the presbytery, and then an argument in what Allan thinks was Italian. 'She was completely distressed and screaming, and I thought, *Boy, fancy getting that much in trouble for getting a bit of blood on your shirt*. I just assumed it was the woman who opened the door. I did what I had to do: I finished the job, I got the power back on, and I left.'

Allan thinks he remembers hearing something about a disturbance on High Street on that night's radio bulletin, but it didn't call to mind the rose-bush story. He never joined the bloodied dots. He only made this connection more than three decades later, when he was flicking through a newspaper while on holidays in Torquay.

'Never thought one iota about it [until then]. I opened the [Herald] *Sun*, and they had a whole lot of cold cases, and it [Father Bongiorno's photo] jumped at me. I said, "That's the bloke I saw with the blood on him." I was with another bloke, Ray Potter, and Ray said, "Go to the police." He kept at me, and at me, and at me.'

Then his detective mate, Howard Beer, provided the successful last prod in November 2013. Otherwise, it sounds like it would have been one of those items that keeps sliding down a man's to-do list. 'We were having a few beers in my backyard in Strathmore, and I just said, "Howard, there's something on my mind," And Howard said, "Why didn't you come out with that a year ago?" He said, "Could be something, could be nothing—probably nothing. I'm going out tonight with some detective friends, and I'll give you a call in a few days." He rang at eleven o'clock that night, from the restaurant, and he said, "They've made a few phone calls, and they want to have a yarn to you." And they were here the next day, the *next* day.'

'Something you said obviously got their attention.'

'Yeah, I was surprised that they moved so quick.'

'And on that, why did it take you that long?'

'I just didn't think much of it, and I thought it could be a waste of time for the police to investigate it. Because there was no proof. It was only what I saw—a bloke who said he'd cut himself on a fence or on the roses.'

I had wondered about this. But maybe Allan was like those heart-attack patients who delay calling an ambulance. They don't want to be a bother, in case it turns out they're wrong. So that clears up why it took him so long to report his rose-bush story, but why didn't his eventual police statement amount to anything? And why didn't Allan subsequently pursue it further, or tell the media?

'I thought, *I've done my bit, and it didn't work out.* Simple as that.' Fair enough. He just trusted the cops to get it right. Well, Allan certainly clears the Chris Masters whistleblower bar. We really had to work to find him. So there are no alarm bells ringing for me. As for the cops, 'Howard told me not to look it up, not to go to the internet, don't do anything, because what you'll do is start putting what you know and what other people know all together, and you'll mess it all up. That's what Howard said, so I've never looked it up. So I'm telling you exactly what I saw.'

Sage advice, Howard.

'They came out and interviewed me in my lounge, and then they said, "I'd like you to come over to Brunswick, and we'll really make it formal." I went in there, and they had all cameras and that set up, and they asked basically the same questions. We were in there for a good hour.'

'Did they seem to think your information could be valuable?'

'Well, they did. They said, "We have now got enough information from what you've told us to exhume the body." She [the detective] told me that. She kept me in the loop, and then she said, "We're waiting for the right coroner. Not someone from the Church." That almost floored me. I said, "What's the Church got to do with a coroner?" She said, "It's old-boy stuff." She asked me the same question as you did, "Are you a Catholic?" I said no. She said, "I am, but we've got to put it before the right coroner." All she said was, "Just old boys," and then I twigged what she was talking about. Well, I think I know what she was talking about. Incredible, eh?'

So then, while both Allan Hircoe and Adam James were waiting, expecting any day to learn that their testimony had prompted the exhumation of Father Bongiorno, the priest was *eliminated* as a suspect. 'For some reason or somehow, they said it wasn't his DNA, that "the DNA we found at the crime scene is not his". They had the DNA of the woman [Maria James] and another [man's] DNA, and they said it's not his. I waited and waited, and they never got back to me, and I just left it at that. But it's always been in the back of my mind.'

'Did they say to you why they thought it wasn't his DNA on Maria's pillow?'

'No, and I'm wondering how they got it [a sample of Fr Bongiorno's DNA], because the sister wouldn't give them any DNA, I believe.'

'Did they mention another way that they might have got it?'

'No, but Howard told me they can get it out of her feminine things in a rubbish tin, toothbrush, feminine napkins … I almost fell over.'

'Do you think this is a situation where the police might've thought this is just too hard? If it was looking like it might be Father Bongiorno? *Too hard, we don't want to go there, we don't want to take on the Church. If it is him, he's dead, he's not going to hurt anyone else?*'

'No, they never gave me that impression. Never gave me that impression at all. They'd come into a bit of a roadblock, but they were determined as ever.'

Something else sticks in Allan's mind. According to detectives, for Maria James to go to the Church about Adam's allegation, if that's indeed what happened, 'would have been the worst thing she could ever do'.

'They said, "She should have come to us." I assumed they meant Maria would get nowhere with the Church, and that, from what's going on there in Ballarat, all that business, that they [the Church] would just push it under the carpet, so to speak. They [the detectives] already had trouble getting the records of the Catholic Church, of who was working that day. I thought the police would get that in ten seconds, but obviously not.'

'You asked me if I just dismissed it, but I haven't. I haven't. It's going to go on and on, and I'll take that to my grave. One way or the other. But I've done as much as I can do. And even talking to you, what exactly is the purpose of your visit? What are you going to do? Are you going to shelve it?'

'We're going to try to solve it.'

'But how can you solve it when the best brains in the Victorian police force haven't? It's not run by idiots.'

I offer Tammy Mills as an example of just where tenacity, and perhaps harassing police officers, can get you. Kerri tells

Allan, 'Ron Iddles says if she hadn't done those stories, on a girl in Shepparton, the Buckingham case, it would have sat in a box on a shelf for another 20 years. And then he went and arrested the guy. He [Stephen Bradley] lived in a hostel up in Brisbane, and Ron says, "Ringing that mum to tell her we got him was the best thing that's ever happened to me."'

Allan rubs his non-bandaged arm. 'Ah, it's giving me goose bumps.'

'And you know what,' I say, 'some things like this, it might be something you say, it might be something someone else says, which might tug on the heartstrings or conscience of someone police have never spoken to before.'

Kerri adds, 'Because some people are dead, and people say things on their deathbeds, and who knows … We're hoping someone will come in with some information, like you did. There's tonnes of people sitting on secrets.'

Tonnes of people maybe sitting on their own rose-bush story.

'What do you think?' I ask Ron Iddles. I thought he'd be excited to learn we've found the electrician, and that his account is solid. But he's never doubted its veracity.

'There is absolutely no reason for that electrician to come forward and fabricate a story. He is 100 per cent confident that the day that he saw Bongiorno is the day of the murder, and it's around the right time when he sees him covered in blood. I would think that is credible evidence which you could put in a brief and say ultimately, sadly, Bongiorno is not alive, but if he *was*, that person [the electrician] would give evidence against him. There is probably sufficient evidence to exhume the body.'

In Ron's mind, the priest is still the strongest suspect.

'Yes, if you put the DNA to one side. Oh, look, Mario Falcucci was a good suspect, but he's eliminated because of the DNA—that was done prior to the electrician coming forward. Mario Falcucci said he went in [to the bookshop] at 9.10am. This may be so, but it also could have been Bongiorno, because priests often wore grey trousers and a blue reefer jacket. You've got the evidence of Adam, who says, "I was sexually assaulted." He says Maria was going to challenge him [Bongiorno] about it. You've got the electrician saying, "I was working at the church that day, I saw Bongiorno covered in blood," and we know that the killer would be covered in blood because of the amount of blood that was in the bedroom. As I sit here now, if I was to reinvestigate it, I would say Bongiorno is the strongest suspect, based upon the evidence of the electrician. I think that the whole DNA issue needs to be re-looked at.'

This is what I'm struggling with the most. Reconciling these two things: the electrician's testimony and then Father Bongiorno mysteriously dropping off the suspect list. The rose bush story, granted, could be true, but it's sounding a bit like 'The dog ate my homework', especially when the priest was supposed to be at a church meeting two suburbs away.

'DNA is a mathematical equation,' says Ron. 'It's a good investigative tool, but it's not absolute. It helps you to eliminate people, it's a great way forward, but it's not what everyone thinks, which is, *Oh well, if you've got the DNA, that's it*. Because if it comes back as a lower—you see, there's about 22 bars—if it comes back only three bars [three DNA regions], then there's probably going to be five people in every thousand who would have that same profile. The higher the statistic [the less chance someone at random will fit the profile], the better it is.

'I know historically, from doing homicides for 25 years, there have been mistakes made in DNA. If we go to America, Barry Shack, who is a defence barrister, an expert in DNA, looks often at the chain of custody ...'

This chain that Ron is referring to is a documentation trail that tracks the custody, transfer, analysis, and storage of evidence. If there's a break or weakness anywhere in the chain, the strength of the evidence can be challenged in court.

' ... and quite often there's been a mistake. All I'm suggesting here is there's a possibility something is wrong with the actual sample, or where it came from. I'd like to know where the DNA came from to eliminate him. Yes, you've got a sample from the crime scene, but what's the comparison? We know they didn't exhume Bongiorno, so how confident are you that the DNA that you got to check against the sample is actually Bongiorno's relative? Because it must have come from a relative. How confident are you that it's a brother or sister, a true relative?'

'Something's not right here, and I don't have access to the file, but I think a great idea would be if the coroner reopened it. Adam and Mark could make an application for the inquest to be reopened. You could call the electrician to give evidence, you could call evidence that would discredit the original alibi, and you could call the evidence of the forensic biologist who has done the DNA, and ask questions in relation to how Bongiorno was eliminated. If it came from a relative, can you prove that relative has a linear relationship to Bongiorno? The next thing is, let's look at the sample from the scene. Is the chain of continuity intact?'

This is another possibility I hadn't thought of—that the primary sample might also need checking.

'I don't know how strong the DNA sample was that was taken from a bloodied pillow,' Ron says. 'Maybe it's a case of going back over, to make sure that the exhibits we have from 1980 are actually identified, that the chain of evidence and the custody of it is thorough. Because a defence barrister could say, "I want to call for the records to check that bloodied pillow has been secured and no one could tamper with it."'

It's an incredible science, DNA, says Ron, but it's not foolproof. He cites the Tapp case. A 35-year-old nurse, Margaret Tapp, and her nine-year-old daughter, Seana, were murdered in their Melbourne home in 1984. Semen was found on Seana's nightgown. Two-and a-half decades later, Russell John Gesah was charged—not because he did it, but because a DNA sample from an unrelated case just happened to be sitting in the Victoria Police forensics lab on the same day that the Tapp exhibits were being tested, and became mixed up. Cross-contamination is a constant risk in forensics laboratories.

Then, in late 2014, *The Age* newspaper broke the story of another almighty forensics stuff-up, in which cold-case evidence was destroyed. 'In 1980, we had a property office which was in Russell Street, and then in around 1994 the property office was closed down, and all the exhibits of unsolved cases were taken to Collingwood.' Ron says that, in this relocation, Homicide crews were asked to review their cases, to determine which evidence was no longer needed. Detectives estimate that the destruction of evidence in up to 40 cold cases was signed-off on—maybe because they'd been through the inquest stage, or maybe because some blood stains were considered a biohazard. But it meant that evidence was destroyed at a time when the possibilities of burgeoning DNA technology were only just being realised. It affected

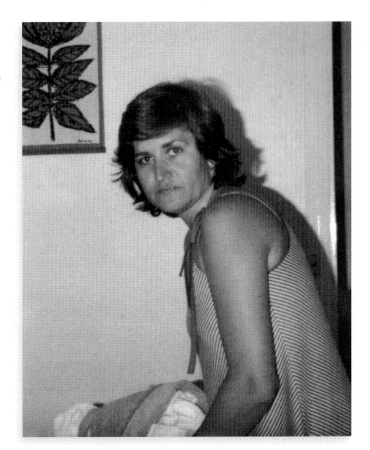

Mark (five years old), Maria, and Adam (three years old) James at the Silverbird Hotel, Las Vegas [*Mark James*]

Maria James's bookshop at 736 High Street, Thornbury [*Coroners Court of Victoria*]

Maria James's kitchen, with open cutlery drawer [*Coroners Court of Victoria*]

Adam James's bedroom, with the phone still off the hook after Maria James answered her ex-husband's call [*Coroners Court of Victoria*]

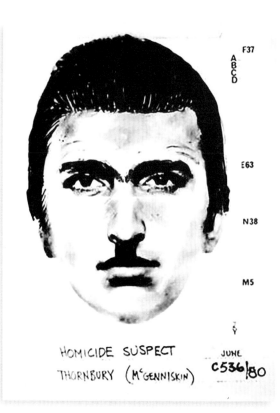

5.00am man photofit
[*Victoria Police*]

HOMICIDE SUSPECT
THORNBURY (M^cGENNISKIN)
JUNE
C536/80

9.10am man photofit
[*Victoria Police*]

C778/80

Mark and Adam James [*Jeremy Story Carter / ABC Commercial*]

Ron Iddles [*Jeremy Story Carter / ABC Commercial*]

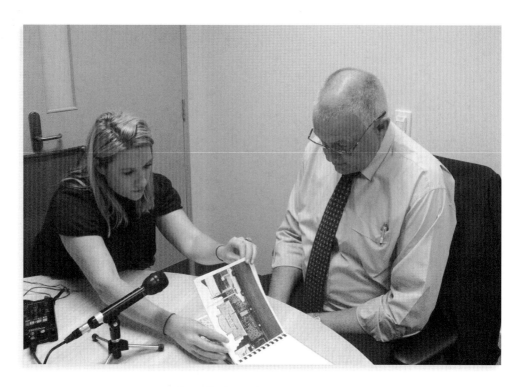

ABOVE: Ron Iddles and Rachael Brown review the crime scene photos [*Kerri Ritchie*]

LEFT: Father Bongiorno, 1980 [*Peter Cox / Newspix*]

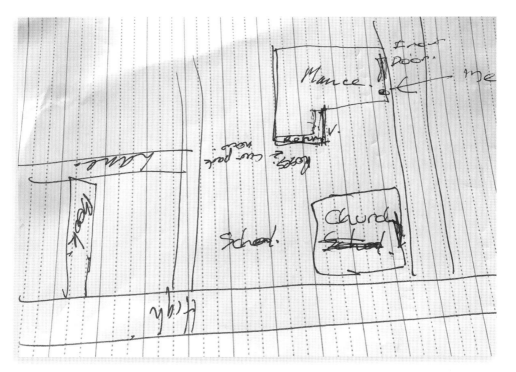

Allan Hircoe's map of where he saw Father Bongiorno covered in blood [*Rachael Brown*]

Kerri Ritchie (left) and Rachael Brown reading victim statements [*Nicholas Brown*]

RIGHT: Mark James's Confirmation (with Father O'Keeffe in the background, in white) [*Mark James*]

BELOW: Jesse Cox (left), Rachael Brown, and Jeremy Story Carter (right) collect the 2017 Walkley Award for Innovation [*Adam Hollingworth / Walkley Foundation*]

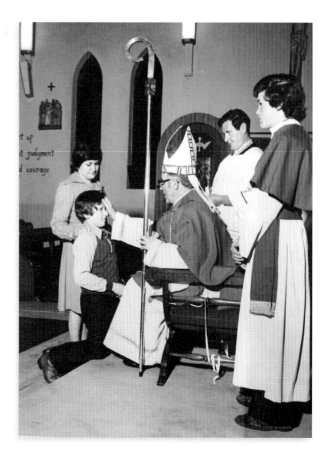

Ron's second-oldest cold case, that of Michelle Buckingham. 'When I went to get all the exhibits, they'd been destroyed, so I was asked a question in the witness box, "Is there any DNA to link my client [Stephen Bradley]?" "Well, sadly, no, because someone authorised the destruction of all exhibits in an unsolved case." So there can be times when, whilst people are eliminated on DNA, there's always a slight possibility that something's not right. And with this case, because the electrician is so strong about what he saw, I've got to ask the question, or you've got to ask the question of someone, "Is it possible there's been a mistake?"'

A mistake or a cover-up? Society is only now too well aware of the lengths those in the Catholic Church, and supporters of it, went to in order to hide a multitude of sins. After meeting the electrician, I wonder whether someone helped Father Bongiorno's name drop off the suspect list, be it out of protectionism or just pragmatism.

'Did it ever cross your mind,' I ask Ron, 'that Victoria Police might've decided this is one for the too-hard basket? Or do you think we're past those days?'

'Oh no, I think we're past those days. I don't think Vic Pol would ever stop you from looking at the Church. Times have definitely changed.'

But something is off. Mark James and Ron Iddles have felt it for years, and now I feel it, too. There's a strong possibility that a priest from St Mary's murdered Maria James. There's also a strong possibility that someone else knew, or knows, about this, and is ensuring that the secret stays buried.

Not long after the electrician's interview, I'm called into a meeting with two of my bosses, and *Trace*'s launch is, for now, called off.

Dash, dash, dash, dash. That's it. Done. All over. Dash. All this work. Dash. All their pain. Dash. Poured out, for what? Dash. The Yarra's banks blur by through my tears of fury. It's a monster of a project. The to-do list of sources needing to be tracked down is like a serpent's head. Strike one off, and three new targets rise up in its place. But bosses need to see words on paper. Dash, dash, dash, dash. Cops have had 37 years, and still not solved it.

The rape victims are fragile, and I can't rush them. They usually go under pseudonyms, so we have to rely on advocates or counsellors to reach out on our behalf. Then we wait. Sometimes victims take weeks to mull over whether they can bring themselves to be involved. Some decline. Others agree, and then pull out later. For some, their interview day arrives, and they or their social worker ask for a postponement because they're not ready, or they're having a bad day.

This can't be hurried. This needs to be more than just a polished podcast. It needs to be a genuine investigation — otherwise, what's the point? It'll just be a rehash of the same details that have been trotted out for years. It won't inspire new leads from the public. 'Sorry, Rach, it's not there yet, we need to put this on ice.' They're right — it's not there yet, but we're very close. I know how this 'icing' is going to go down. Victims will hear 'You don't matter.' James Shanahan will think the Church is somehow involved. As for the James brothers, I can't even begin to imagine how crushed they'll be.

Plod, plod, plod, plod. My mates have been falling in love and having babies. I've invested my past year in a dead woman, missed two overseas weddings, and it's fairly likely I'll end up a spinster with eight cats. And I hate cats.

Butterflies filter through a willow. One hovers at my right cheek, where my nan used to kiss me. Then a stunned blink that shifts a teardrop sends it off. Yes, I tell myself, shitty things have happened in your career, Rach, but you know what other slice of history keeps repeating? You getting back up. So quit your whinging. Keep moving. Murakami says that in long-distance running, the only opponent you have to beat is yourself, the way you used to be. One foot in front of the other. Plod, plod, plod, plod.

March 2017

It won't always feel this raw and bad Rach, but just remember, you are going to get through this, we all will together. We will have chicken pasta dinner ready for you. And lots of wine ... lots. xx

— Text from Kerri Ritchie to Rachael Brown, 28 February 2017

After the crying and the swearing, Kerri bundles me into her home, insisting I not return to an empty apartment. Her partner, Pete, force-feeds me pasta, and I watch their girls dance in front of the telly. My pathetic contribution to their concert is catatonia. 'Can you take *Trace* somewhere else?' Pete asks. Even if I could find it another home, it won't have the reach of the national broadcaster. I need *Trace* pumped out on all the ABC's platforms—radio, TV, online, social media—to give the James boys their best shot at answers. I'm stuck. How can I just sit on this story, when it promises such an illumination of crimes within the Catholic Church, and possibly other institutions?

Surprise, surprise, the answer wasn't sitting at the bottom of the bottle of red, but it did manage to prod through the hangover. We just have to get this story out, as powerfully and as soon as possible. So I devise a compromise. I suggest condensing *Trace* into a two- or three-part series for the *Law Report*. It means letting go of the podcast idea I've clung to so tightly because of the audience interactivity I was hoping for and the new leads I thought it would inspire, but it'll mean that all the stories—from Adam, Mark, James, Rex, Bill, and all those caught in the wake—will see daylight.

So our little *Trace* team—Kerri Ritchie, Jeremy Story Carter, and I—ploughs on. As part of the massive job of digging into the pasts of Fathers Bongiorno and O'Keeffe, we have been trying to find three victims of each. Where possible, we've tried to quarantine the different elements of this investigation—the murder, Father Bongiorno, and Father O'Keeffe—so that victims of each are unaware we're also looking into the others, ensuring untainted accounts. I don't want them telling us what they *think* we want to hear.

Today is our interview with 'Rex'. Bernie Geary had made a couple of visits for us to the local shopping square where Rex usually hangs out, but hadn't spotted him, so we'd found an address for him and left a hand-written card. Rex called Kerri that very afternoon. But it's taken him a long time to feel ready for this, so there's no time for a meltdown from our end. A little battered, but with our game faces on, Kerri and I arrive at Rex's favourite café in Fitzroy, trying to convince ourselves that this won't be just another exercise in pouring good intentions down the drain.

Rex is already here, chatting to his social worker, his large frame nestled into a back corner of the café. He shakes my hand. This is such a common and inadequate seal, I always think, for the bestowing of deepest secrets to a stranger. He has a big, round face, and often a hint of a phlegmy rattle that rounds off his sentences. I know abuse survivors often feel they've been robbed of power, so I hand it over to him straightaway.

'What would *you* like us to hear about you growing up, and your relationship with Father Bongiorno?'

You steer, Rex.

'Things weren't good at home with my dad and my mum. My dad used to drink a lot and used to get violent, and that's when I used to run away from home. That's how I met Father Bongiorno. I used to go to school at St Ambrose, and I was sitting outside on the seat and he saw me one morning, and he invited me in, and he showed me around his place and said I could use his shower and his bathroom, and that's how it all started. I needed a father figure, and I classed him as that ... then he molested me.' Rex reminds me a lot of Adam James, eleven at the time, lost and vulnerable, with a mental impairment making the world even more mystifying.

Rex says the abuse continued for two years. 'I was confused. I didn't know if what he was doing was right or wrong.' It's a sick Catch 22 when the person you run to for comfort is the very same who metes out the need for it. 'Yes, and I tried to get him back for what he did, like break his windows, and steal from him, and sort of hit him, and stuff like that, and he used to call the police. And the police used to charge me and ask why I'd done it, and I used to say that was my way of getting him back for what he did.'

I confess to Rex that I've heard stories of him setting fires, and once trying to tie up the priest. There's a sound, a guttural heaving. *Oh God, I've made him cry.* Rex's shoulders are shaking, and he gasps for some air. It's only when I see his eyes shining that I realise he's laughing. And he can't stop, each guttural chuckle tripping into another.

'Where did you hear that?' he asks incredulously, a little

embarrassed but secretly proud. 'Where you getting your information from?'

'We've done a lot of work on this,' I tell him.

Rex spits it out in blurts. 'I tried a lot of times actually. I tried to, pardon me ...' He tumbles into paroxysms of laughter again. It defuses the moment beautifully, and it's infectious. Soon Kerri is wiping her eyes and doing her trademark leg slap, which only comes out on special occasions. The belly laugh—Rex's is jiggling all over the place—feels good for all of us. It's been a while. When he finally calms down, Rex explains the plan. 'I wanted to put handcuffs on him, and strip him naked and call the police, and say they can find him naked—that's what I wanted to do.'

As payback?

'Yes, as payback.'

'Didn't work?'

'No, because he called out for help, and someone came out from the next room.'

He implies that Father Bongiorno's paedophilia was one of the suburb's worst-kept secrets. 'They were in denial. He used to have a lot of boarders, and all the boarders were on his side, and I used to steal from them as well—that was my way of saying how he was. And then towards the end, the boarders knew how he was, there were rumours going out that he touched little kids and that he touched me.'

Rex says he gave the police a statement when he was 15, but the priest didn't seem fazed by it. '[He acted like] nothing could touch him. I used to ask him why he'd done it, and he used to say because he loved me.'

'That's a confusing thing for a 15-year-old to hear.'

'Yes, it is.'

'Did you think it was love?'

'I know it wasn't. It was a different kind of love, what he done.'

I ask why the abuse eventually stopped.

'I suppose I was getting older, and that's why he stopped touching me, I think he wanted other boys.'

A decade later, Rex's confused way of reclaiming some power was to put himself right back in that vulnerable position. 'When I was about 25, I used to ask him if he could touch me, and he used to, and then I used to stop him because I never used to stop him when I was younger.'

'So that was your way of rewriting the past, in a sense?'

'Ah, yes, that was my way of getting him back as well.'

And then he cracked. 'I thought it was destroying my life, just going there every time, and I said to myself *Enough's enough*, and I was afraid that he was going to do it to someone else. I decided to write a letter to the archbishop, Frank Little it was back then, and that's how it came about. I was in Royal Park hospital, a psychiatric hospital, and these two ladies came to see me. One lady's boyfriend used to be a boarder at Bongiorno's place, and they came to see me about the letter and spoke to me, and next minute I find out that the Vicar General wanted to see me about it, and that's how it happened.'

I tell him we know how the trial unfolded. He doesn't have to wade back through that swamp. He says it took a lot to drag himself to that courtroom every day. 'A lot of courage, actually. My sister, my older sister, was a witness, too—they threw most of her evidence out.'

'What had your sister seen?'

'She used to come to Father Bongiorno's to try to get me home, and he used to scream in the middle of the street, saying that he loved me.'

'How often would that happen?'

'Quite a few times, actually.'

'Your case fell over. How did that make you feel?'

'Angry and hurt. I was heading towards the Westgate Bridge. I got stopped by the police. I feel like the justice system let me down—they should've had the trials all together. Hopefully, one day they can improve the justice system.'

It's a part of the job I hate, being a parrot for other peoples' slurs, but I have to put to Rex the claim that he was playing the system. 'A friend of Father Bongiorno said to us, "We didn't believe the boys. He was a good guy, so these boys must've made up the story for money."'

Rex recoils like I've slapped him. 'Whoever said that is wrong. Can I guess? Rita?'

Kerri tries to soften the blow. 'In Rita's defence, Rita's weighing everything up. She was with him when he died. She genuinely is sorry for a lot of things and, I would say, is now not convinced about anything.'

'It's not about money. Money doesn't bring your childhood back, like what happened to me. At the same time, I must admit, I got paid twice—once from victims of crime, they believed it did happen, and once from the Catholic Church hierarchy, their processes. But it wasn't about money; it was about justice.'

I'm sure he'd return that money in a heartbeat if he could get his innocence back. I stop the tape, and we start chatting about trivialities: footy, cafés, the things you *think* matter until you meet people like Rex. I mention that we tried to speak to Father Sean O'Connell, the person who provided Father Bongiorno with an alibi on the day of the murder, but, sadly, we were a month too late. He passed away in December. Rex's 'humph' suggests a history, and disdain. He tells me he'd never trust what Father O'Connell said anyway.

'He gave me a thousand dollars one time. He said [to the archdiocese] he'd asked me about the abuse and that I said to him that nothing happened, but that's not true. I never said that to him. And he gave me a thousand dollars.'

I don't even have to look at Kerri to know our cynical journo minds are asking the same thing. Hush money? I remember reading a Broken Rites article on Father Bongiorno and his transgressions, and it mentioned that when the Catholic diocesan office learned of Rex's complaint in 1985, it asked another priest to look into it:

It asked another priest, Father O (who was a close friend of Bongiorno from seminary days), to 'investigate'. Bongiorno denied the allegation, and Father O reported this orally to the archdiocese, which dropped the matter.

So, according to Rex, this redacted Father O was Father Sean O'Connell. And instead of interviewing Rex about Father Bongiorno's abuse, he never did. He simply told the Church that Rex had said that nothing had happened.

'What did he say the thousand dollars was for?' I ask.

'He didn't say—he just gave me a thousand dollars. I think it was just to keep quiet.'

'You'd asked him for a bit of money?'

'Just a couple of hundred, but he gave me a thousand.'

What did you need the money for?'

'I'll be honest, I used to go to brothels.'

'Was it in the same conversation that you asked for the money and he asked about the abuse? He didn't actually use any words as in, "This is to be quiet"? What makes you put the two things together?'

'I believed that he gave it to me so I could be quiet, that's my belief.'

I don't think Rex realises what a bombshell he's dropped in between taking gulps of his milkshake. If this *was* hush money, if Father O'Connell was the type of person prepared to lie for his mate, was he also lying five years earlier when he told police that they were together at a church meeting at the time of Maria James's murder? Couple this with the evidence of the electrician—who says he saw Father Bongiorno covered in blood around lunch-time—and the 'church meeting' alibi seems more and more threadbare. I ask Rex what he makes of it.

'I believe that Father Sean O'Connell was lying.' He surprises me by saying he actually asked Father Bongiorno about Maria James's murder one day. 'He went into shock, sort of, that I found out about it.' Rex does, however, admit that he never saw a violent streak in Father Bongiorno, just an icy one.

'He didn't give a damn. He was just cold-hearted. I believe he had something to do with it, and they should dig up his body for DNA. And I mean, if his sister's got nothing to hide, she should give her DNA to the police.'

Out on Smith Street, Rex towers above me. I come up to his chest, so his hug is more of a headlock. I thank him for the laugh, and his low chuckle starts whirring away again. When I tell Rex I'm grateful for his bravery, he says it's his way of giving the James brothers a hug. And in his perfect crystallisation, this gentle giant with a pretty dark sense of humour has reminded us why we're here, and why we need to keep pushing.

April 2017

There is a McDonalds across the road from Bunnings on the highway.

— Text from 'Dave' to Rachael Brown, 19 April 2017

'Dave' strolls in, decked out in khaki. Camouflaged shorts, shirt, and cap. *Tad unnecessary for Cranbourne McDonalds,* I think, *but, hey, whatever makes him feel safer.* 'Laundry day,' Dave apologises, shaking my hand. 'These were the last things clean.' He places a tattered orange envelope on one of the small McCafé tables. His younger self's proof of misery. As if he needs any, the weight's in each step of his loping walk. But the orange envelope is the paper trail—his sick almanac from his time at Doveton's Holy Family Primary School in the 1970s. Like James Shanahan, Dave is a little guarded, and he chooses his words slowly and carefully. Like James, it all started when he was an altar boy for Father Thomas O'Keeffe.

'Most altar boys would've termed him as a bit of a bloke's bloke. He liked to play cricket, and he'd talk about his altar boys being "in the slips". He was fascinated by military history and violence. He had a cap-badge collection and war figurines, and he was into his knives and guns. A gun was left in the presbytery when Searson [Father Peter Searson] got there. And he would often use quite bad language, which as boys you thought was OK, you know, and I guess that was part of his persona for grooming.'

Even as an eight-year-old, Dave found Father O'Keeffe odd.

'One minute you'd be in the back of the presbytery, and

you'd be talking about anal sex and necrophilia, and then next minute they [Father O'Keeffe and Father Wilfred Baker] would be talking about 'Don't stone a lady to death for adultery' and that type of thing. So even as a child I knew there were very conflicting views being given to me or being shown to me.'

This now makes four people—three abuse survivors and a teacher—who've told me that the priest had a habit of talking about necrophilia. It's not a conversation to be having over the din of Big Mac orders, so we move to his old station wagon to chat. I clear papers and food wrappers from the worn upholstery, turn on the recorder, and stories from Dave's vault are poured into this little black box.

'On occasion, I heard him talk about how it would be possible to have relationships with a dead person, even a dead male. He claimed they would be erect when they were dead. I don't know whether that's true or not, but he claimed it would be possible. As kids, we obviously didn't know much about anything. Also, the priests were also the ones who taught sex ed in the schools back then too, so who were you to argue with them?'

'Looking back now, is that weird that priests were the ones teaching sex ed?'

'It is now, but at that stage, since they sat at God's right, they were considered his intermediaries, so why wouldn't they know something about everything? I didn't even know what sex was. I was eight. "Bloody" was a swear word.'

Father O'Keeffe meted out Dave's sex education, more than once a month.

'I was in grade three or four. Think of the worst things you can, they probably happened. You'd be pulled out of class, on holy days of obligation, then you'd fall behind in your work.'

'Funerals, you'd go and do funerals, Saturdays, you'd be there doing the morning service; sometimes you'd do the Saturday and Sunday. It seemed like forever. And you're getting a sense that this probably isn't going to stop. At that stage, you're just hoping, *I'm not going to be at the school forever*. I hated school. I hated going there. I wished the damn place had burnt down.'

He tells me he's not sure it was ever about sex. It was about power.

'I don't want you to go into detail because it's painful, but did the abuse veer into torturous abuse?'

The silence is so long and heavy I stop the tape. To leave Dave be, wherever he just ran to.

Sometimes the truth can never be fully told, because it breaks your heart forever.

When he finally speaks, it's about being robbed. 'Surprisingly enough, disassociation is a skill that stays with you.' Dave used to dissociate during the abuse, and can't remember leaving after each assault. 'I just remember being home with gifts like models, badges, and pocket knives.' He became so adept at dissociation that he's broken bones as an adult and not felt all that much. His mind has somehow found a way to file away pain. But this defence mechanism also robbed him of an education. 'I think as a child my neural networks weren't established properly. It's not just laziness. If you do poorly at school, it hits you hard—it's a poverty trap. I didn't learn my alphabet, or the months of the year.'

This is how early scars can map someone's life trajectory.

'Always having to work at the lower level where you're working with younger men that are stronger and faster and able to cope, as you get older you're not. Physically I'm not coping, and I've carried too many injuries from doing very heavy work, you know. Definitely robbed that way. It's not so much the money situation; it's the fact you're just working so damn hard your whole life, because you can't climb the ladder, you just don't have the literacy skills or the education to do it.'

And here are the ripples not many see. The callouses on his hands have also hurt his family. He sounds so ashamed admitting there's no money for braces for his daughter, or new clothes for her, or for fun family holidays. In robbing one childhood, priests rob generations more.

Dave passes me the orange envelope, and I skim through what's in it quickly so he's not marinating in self-loathing. There are dog-eared pages and hand-written scrawls on torn-off squares of paper: counselling reports, Melbourne Response compensation documents, victim statements. There's no order to it—just a mess, in every sense. One comment jumps out on his Melbourne Response submission: 'Penetration was easier to take'. This gives an idea of the horrors.

'Violent rape couldn't be that easily covered up,' Dave tells me, 'because you wouldn't be able to return to school.' He says Father O'Keeffe was into painful sexual acts.

'He was all about inserting things, or encouraging you to do it. He was into things that cause pain. Like tearing a foreskin, or pulling your genitals down hard in opposite directions. You have to think of this as a child would have, not what you've made of it now. If someone sticks a knitting needle down your penis and tells you it's normal, you believe it.'

I have to ask him to repeat this. Not long ago, I'd come across this, in another victim's statement: 'O'Keeffe got me in the lounge room and put a knitting needle down my penis.'

'Did that happen to you, Dave?'

He ducks, 'I'm just saying, that's the kind of thing you have to look at through a child's eyes. I didn't know what would be considered strange for a priest'.

Another striking similarity is how his Melbourne Response interview transcript was typed up.

'Your copy of the conversation isn't complete,' he says. 'When I quoted O'Keeffe saying, "… it is possible to have sex with a cadaver …", this would be marked down as "(inaudible)", so I didn't bother keeping my copy. I threw it out.'

I'm guessing '(inaudible)' would've also been peppered right through a disturbing example that Dave gives me about the reach of the Church. This relates to alleged criminality beyond paedophilia. But he's too terrified to share it.

'If I discuss this bit they'll easily identify me. As you can see, I'm uncomfortable because it's a frightening institution and we're conditioned to be frightened of that institution all our lives. It's a fear that's hard to break, whether it's rational or not. I have no idea how far its tentacles reach.'

Dave says the Melbourne Response process was just an exercise by the Church in trying to trip up victims.

'They play double jeopardy. Them: "Ms Lavery was the headmaster." Me: "No, she wasn't." Them: "What brand of ciggies did O'Keeffe smoke?" Me: "Kent." Them: "You sure it wasn't Camel?" Them: "The pistol was an imitation." Me: "It didn't have a plugged barrel." They were double-checking what I knew, and how sure I was about it.'

I remember a warning Dave gave me during one of our phone-calls: 'Be careful, they will destroy as much as they can. They're a dangerous mob. If they believe in God, I'd be surprised. They believe in money.'

I ask about this, about Dave's conviction that Father O'Keeffe's calling was all about power and money.

'He would use unreasonable force, in reasonable situations.'

Dave remembers coming into the presbytery while Father O'Keeffe was counting money, and there was a loaded rifle on the counter.

'I'd seen him with a rifle to defend fete takings. A firearm was something you hunted with—it's not for house security.'

Then there was the revolver.

'I'd seen him brandish what I believed at the time to be an imitation revolver, but I've been told by others that it was real. I knew he had a couple of 'em. I'd heard him discuss his willingness to use violence. When we were altar-boying, he brought one of the revolvers with him in case the people who were riding their bikes around at church-service time on the Saturday came again. He was going to go and confront them. You would've said, *we think that's a bit of an over-reaction*, but of course he was the priest, he could talk to God, so you figured it would be all squared away, no matter what he did. He'd just have a word with the big fella, and it would be sorted.'

Before I leave Dave, I ask about sweeter things. About how he manages to keep going.

'I've only ever been with one woman. My wife. We met when I was 20. Some people ask me, "Wow, you've never been with another woman?" And I think it's strange *they* think it's strange. It's like a car—if it's a good one, you stick with it.'

For kids who were so betrayed, so many of the survivors I've spoken to have managed to hold onto a precious vulnerability. And, oh, the things they share. They can't have oral sex with their wife because it reminds them of 'him' and makes them feel dirty. Or there's a certain smell about oral sex that propels them back. They're in their fifties and still renting because they haven't managed to hold down a job ... Do I know how they can get their small-business idea off the ground? Or it's feeling all too hard; they're tired of fighting. They confide in me—36-year-old, woefully-unequipped-to-deal-with-all-this me. I call on what should be able to get one through most things in life: heart. I listen, sympathise, and try to offer some solace, but it's pathetically inadequate. A wise cop mate once tried to protect me from approaching this abyss: 'You can back away now and tell them you can't help ... or you can try to help, get their hopes up, fall short, then back away, apologising because you can't help. You can't fix them.'

Part III
The Podcast

17 June 2017

The taster episode of the *Trace* podcast is uploaded to iTunes and the ABC's radio app, asking people to tune in on Wednesday:

> Maria James was murdered at the back of her bookshop on a winter's day in Melbourne. We begin this podcast on the 37th anniversary of her death. Her murderer's never been found. This is Trace. Was it a scorned lover? A random stranger? Or was Maria's murder tied up in the sins of the Catholic Church?

The first eight chords of *Trace*'s theme always makes my skin prickle. The sound designer, Marty Peralta, had sent me his original composition during the week, and I ran for my headphones and perched nervously on the couch. And even with the sun through the window on my closed eyelids, it took me there, to that shrouded world this investigation has been navigating. Green Day was the soundtrack to my final high-school months; Powderfinger, to my uni days and first serious boyfriend. Now Marty's theme somehow manages to encapsulate all the pain and hope of the past year. The theme begins as recognisable nostalgia and melancholy, with piano, cello, and strings becoming the soundtrack to Maria's honest and fragile story. Then in come the drums and synthesiser, a little rough around the edges, which inject a sense of curiosity and determined striving. As it evolves it gets more distorted, dark, and unsettling, evoking horror and mystery, before it hits the climax and promptly crashes down into a void. But even then, the synthesiser keeps prodding away like a heartbeat, tentatively at first, then confident. And under all of this is a wind, brushing things away.

It's really happening. Soon after that meeting in February, when *Trace* was 'put on ice', I was asked to write a page about why this case means so much to me, why I was so distraught to be losing it. And, somehow, it helped stop *Trace* from flatlining:

> This is a story that's crawled under my skin, stayed there, and is screaming to be told. Because of its characters and consequences.

I stressed it would illuminate failings within the Catholic Church, and possibly also Victoria Police, and could give the coroner grounds for reopening the case:

> I set out to find if a priest murdered Maria. If one did, it'll be a first for Australia's modern history. Given the current climate of the Royal Commission, it's a question that must be asked.

I also explained what an important precedent *Trace* could set:

It's an odd synergy, this podcast's reliance on old-school journalism techniques (federal roll checks, microfiche searches, handwritten letters), alongside the innovative element of interactivity, but that's where I think its beauty lies. Subscribers will be able to filter through new information/leads that can be rolled into the next episode … and if this model works, imagine what that could mean for nation's other 1300 cold cases languishing in dusty boxes. In our profession, that's becoming more and more about a quick churn, the chance to drive a project that could help people and effect change is exciting, and why many of us get into journalism in the first place. We're asked all the time to be brave, to do brave journalism. It's time consuming, and often, all consuming. But it's worth it, to give a voice to those who can't speak for themselves.

And whether it was thanks to divine intervention, or just to angels within Aunty, we had a pulse. *Trace* was back. The ABC decided that, yes, the podcast might be taking longer than first thought, but it was worth the investment. I couldn't wait for the next wry arching of the John Clarke eyebrow, but this generous genius, avid bird-watcher, and my friend would suddenly pass away soon before the podcast fought its way to air. He would have loved to learn that *Trace* was finally about to see daylight.

The production grunt started by trying to fashion this monster of an investigation, and all its tendrils, into compelling radio that would not only sing but would get listeners emotionally invested enough to want to contribute new leads. With my editors, Tim Roxburgh, Jesse Cox, and

Sophie Townsend, each draft was a waltz: I'd pour all my research and observations into a first draft, it'd be mercilessly stripped back to its bones, I'd sneak some detail back in, and the editors would strip again, but leave a little colour to humour me. *One, two, three, four.* Write, strip, sneak, strip. Together, the steps were just right.

Then, the voice: how to unlearn 15 years of newsreader speak? 'Don't read the story,' Jesse would say. '*Tell* it'. For the first few run-throughs, he'd make me turn my script facedown. 'Just tell me. Who is Ron? What makes him tick?' And with Jesse, Tim, and Sophie's gentle instruction, we found *Trace*'s voice: soft and close to the microphone, with all the colour and intonation confined within a much tighter space. 'There it is,' Marty Peralta would joke, 'Rach Noir'. Funnily enough, the tone we landed on to relay this horrific murder was my Ollie voice, the one in which I read my three-year-old nephew his bedtime stories. Sorry, Ollie. A bit morbid, I know. I'll explain when you're older.

This time last year I'd only just started emailing James Shanahan about a potential interview, and was still about five months away from getting this damn thing commissioned. Now, a few meltdowns later, here we are, with Episode 1 set to air on 21 June. So there's someone I feel I should meet. I buy some roses, yellow with red fringing, from a florist around the corner from Templestowe Cemetery. She kindly gives me flower food in little test tubes, and asks me to say hi to her dad.

It's sunny, and the birds are oblivious to any solemnity. 'Hi, florist's dad.' There's a heady scent of freshly cut grass. 'Hi, Maria'. I sit beside her plaque on the lawn. *In loving memory of Maria James. 23–8–1941 — 17–6–1980. Beloved mother of Mark and Adam. In God's care.* It's the first time I've visited the grave of someone I've never met. So much is being invested in a stranger. I guess I'd hope that if this were me, or my mother, sister, or friend, that someone would do the same—ask questions, even years on.

The buried cylindrical plastic vase above her plaque is filled with dirt. Clearly, no one's been here in a while, so I start clawing away at the hard, cracked top layer until soft mud seeps under my now-filthy fingernails. I wedge in one of the test tubes and drop in the three roses. For Maria, Mark, and Adam. 'I hope it'll all be enough,' I whisper.

August 2016

DNA Dadna i/v

— Diary note, 12 August 2016

Father O'Keeffe's remains are buried in a stone vault in Melbourne's General Cemetery. Above it sits an impressive bluestone chapel, and etched into a marble plaque is Father O'Keeffe's name, along with those of 30 other Catholic priests. I've only seen photographs. The day I visit, the chapel's iron gates are tied with a thick metal rope and a hefty padlock. Visitors apparently have to first seek permission from the Melbourne Archdiocese. It's a completely different story for Father Bongiorno, whose abuse cases *had* come to light by the time he died. He lies in an unmarked grave in the burbs, in Springvale Cemetery, in the same plot as his father, who had died eight years earlier. No headstone. No plaque. Nothing. You wouldn't even know it was there. Both sites could be crucial, as they hold DNA that could be matched against Maria James's bloodstained pillow.

I feel this investigation needs to keep playing an each-way bet. Yes, Father Bongiorno was ruled out in 2015, and his possible exhumation abandoned, but there *have* been errors with DNA historically, and he *was* seen covered in blood. Father O'Keeffe, on the other hand, had a habit of 'unreasonable force in reasonable situations'; a horrifically and arguably psychopathic dark past; and the same motive as his clerical colleague.

It's been 15 years since Father Bongiorno died, and coming up to 33 years for Father O'Keeffe, and I'm not sure how it works, whether their DNA would still be viable to test against the killer's blood, so I call on one of Australia's top DNA experts to step me through it. Dr Dadna Hartman manages the molecular biology lab at the Victorian Institute of Forensic Medicine (VIFM). Like R.Iddles, her future job was in her name—DaDNA. She's a colleague of pathologist David Ranson, who helped explain Maria James's wounds. I head back down the corridor beside the Coroners Court to meet her. For a place that deals with so much death, she has a refreshing take on her calling.

'I've always had an interest in things that improve life, I guess.'

She means learnings from the institute's extensive investigations and research. She gets my hopes up instantly by telling me that she performed DNA analysis on a skeleton that was more than 130 years old—that of Australia's most infamous bushranger, Ned Kelly. Now there's a good story to pull out at a dinner party. Bones were found at Pentridge Prison more than a century after Kelly's hanging in 1880.

'It was anticipated that one of those were the remains of

Ned Kelly. Obviously, what we wanted to do was work out which one.'

Extensive forensic analysis was done to determine whether these were the bones of a bushranger. A CT scan of a leg bone was used to check for metal fragments, which indicated a shotgun wound, and DNA samples were taken.

'Those bones were quite old, over 100 years old, and we were able to get mitochondrial DNA from those. So it just depends on the condition of those remains, how they've been kept or stored, or the condition they've been found in.'

This DNA was then compared with that of Victorian teacher Leigh Olver, who is the great grandson of Ned Kelly's sister, Ellen. Dadna tells me that mitochondrial DNA is passed through the maternal line, so we all have the same mitochondrial profile as our mothers. All the females in a line will then pass their mitochondrial DNA on to their children, regardless of gender. This time, it just happened to be Ned Kelly, but the same processes could be applied to, say, a missing person. VIFM is doing just that; in 2010, it and Victoria Police set up a Missing Persons DNA database to help match unidentified deceased samples to the state's cold cases. Homicides are actually only a small part of VIFM's work. It does everything from drug testing using hair samples to disaster-victim identification. Its experts have been sent to Iraq, East Timor, and the Asian tsunami, and at home, have been deployed to incidents such as the 2009 Black Saturday bushfires. The fires were so intense that, in many cases, all they had to go on for identification was teeth.

I wonder what it's going to take to help solve a 37-year-old cold case. First, I'm curious about the primary source, the male blood found on Maria James's pillow.

'Can police use the same sample extracted back in 2001?' I ask. 'Or would they have to go back to that pillow and extract a new sample?'

'It depends on the quality of the DNA extract at the time. It may be that the quality of the DNA is quite good, and you don't have to go back and re-extract [from the blood found on Maria's pillow]. What you derive from the DNA is the profile, which I guess is like a code. You can keep that indefinitely; it becomes a record, and it's a code you can bring up time and time again.'

'Like a biological fingerprint?'

'Yeah. Whereas the source from which that profile is generated, the actual DNA extract, that's finite—that, you're consuming as part of the testing. It's not a never-ending well of DNA that sits there.'

Whatever code was derived from this male blood would still be on Victoria Police's system. And Dadna says it's not so much the DNA extraction methods that have improved since Ron Iddles first sent Maria James's exhibits for testing in 2001, but rather the assessment kits, which can analyse more markers.

'Back in 2001, we would've been using DNA profiling kits that looked at nine regions of your DNA. Nowadays, we use kits that look at up to 24 regions.'

So what about a secondary sample? How could police get DNA samples of priests who are long dead?

'Police would need to have a warrant or a strong case as to why a judge would allow these remains to be exhumed. You could exhume those remains and collect samples that may be suitable for DNA analysis—for example, parts of the femur or teeth that would still be present.'

'How do you get a sample from bone? Is it an injection or a scraping?'

'You have to cut through and obtain part of the femur.

Now, we don't need a lot—we are talking about a few centimetres of femur that would be required. That is then sent to the lab for processing. There's a triage: the easiest sample to collect is blood, the next is tissue, and then you sort of go down the list. You may be surprised to learn, for example with decomposed cases, we often used to get a bone sample sent to us. Now, for bones, as I said, it's quite traumatic to collect a sample, because you have to saw ...'

'Are they the hardest?'

'They are, and it's something that needs to be planned for in terms of the-day to-day activities of the mortuary, then it takes us quite some time to process them. Whereas now, for decomposed cases, we can get a toenail clipping. They're quite simple to collect, and that's what we can get DNA profiles from. We're mindful of contamination. We're less likely to ask for fingernails, because if a person has scratched someone, they might have their cellular material underneath their fingernails.'

A toenail. A tooth. Incredible, the stubborn little parts of us that can keep secrets long after we're gone.

'We always try for nuclear DNA first, in the hope that we've got a nuclear profile, because that's more informative. Nuclear, as the name suggests, is recovered from the nucleus, and it's quite large. There's one copy of the nuclear genome; it's inherited from Mum and Dad. But nuclear DNA is quite prone to degradation; so, should that fail, we try mitochondrial DNA. It's a small circular genome, and it tends to survive better, for lack of another word, because it's more compact, and there are more copies of it in the cell.'

Exhuming someone's remains isn't something that's done lightly. The process is expensive, and that's as well as the grief it costs the dead person's family. For argument's sake, let's assume the cops have a good reason for thinking Father Bongiorno's DNA doesn't match the killer's—hence his elimination in 2015. But what about Father O'Keeffe? What if his family holds a clue? His obituary notice mentioned two brothers, one of them deceased, a sister-in-law, and two nieces.

'If the exhumation application is denied,' I ask,' can police go to living relatives and match their DNA profile against the DNA sample from the pillow?'

'If it's for nuclear DNA comparisons, then we would often ask for the closest relative. Are there living children or parents of this individual?'

No, on both counts.

'Or siblings? A sibling would be fine, because siblings share the same mitochondrial profile.'

Please, Father O'Keeffe's brother, please be alive. Or …

'Could you get mitochondrial DNA from his nieces?'

'If they're his sister's daughters, yes, they have to be maternally related.'

'No, by the sounds of it they're his brother's daughters.'

'No, so those daughters will inherit their mum's mitochondrial DNA. It has to be someone who's maternally related.'

So, for any match, we'd be aiming for a brother.

'I guess my question would be, how can you get it? I mean, he would have to consent to give any sample, to check whether there's a familial match.'

Just as I start wondering whether the next chapter in this bizarre year is going to involve me following around a stranger to swipe any discarded glasses or cans, cigarette butts, or, better still, hair follicles, Dadna offers a little gem.

'Was this individual reported to the coroner? As part of people being reported to the coroner, they may undergo an autopsy, samples may be collected—tissue samples. Perhaps samples were collected for toxicology?'

'Sorry, do you mean in suspicious circumstances? He died in his sleep, as far as I'm aware.'

'If you die of natural causes, then you don't get reported to the coroner. But if you die unexpectedly, you may be reported, and perhaps you've undergone some of these testings, which may mean that there's a sample for that individual here at the institute.'

It suddenly occurs to me that dying at 55 years of age might just constitute an 'unexpected' death. News that I might be sitting only metres from a DNA sample of Father O'Keeffe thrills me.

'How would I find out if his name was on that list?'

'You could contact the Coroners Court and ask if this person was reported to the coroner at the time of death. Now, I'm not sure whether that kind of query has to come from the next of kin.'

'Dadna, we need you on our team.'

I'm not going to lie. I run next door to the Coroners Court, and a little too excitedly ask for its operations manager, Lyndal Bugeja, who I've been bugging since I started this investigation. She recently told me that on the day I filed an application to access Maria James's coronial inquest finding, she came home to find a yellow Post-it note on her kitchen bench. On it was scrawled, 'Call Rachael Brown.' My spelling and everything. It turns out it was her husband's reminder to himself, to call a schoolteacher he'd soon be taking the reins from. Just like Mr Real Estate's flier in my letterbox, I took this little scrap of paper that'd floated in from the universe as a sign this project might be getting some higher help.

I relay Dadna's idea, and Lyndal jumps on her computer. She clicks her way through a database of death.

'Looks like it only goes back to 1989.'

'Damn. We need 1984.'

'Let me just work out how to do this.'

'By swiping a cup,' I say half-jokingly, wondering how I can tee up a coffee with one of Father O'Keeffe's relatives to get a saliva sample for DNA testing.

'No, no, let's just try this ...'

'You just don't want me arrested.'

'No. I don't have time to bail you out,' says Lyndal, deadpan. 'What's his middle name?'

'Francis.'

Lyndal lets the internal database whir away for a bit while she does a Google search for Father Thomas Francis O'Keeffe. As the search results pop up, she leans a little closer in, and then whips her head around to face me.

'Is that *him*?' she asks.

'Yep. See where I'm going with this?'

'I do.'

There's no luck on the internal database, no deaths pre-1989, but she has another idea, and reaches for an old plastic folder, red, with comb binding, which lists earlier coronial referrals.

She flicks through to 'O', runs her finger down the list, and there he is: Thomas O'Keeffe.

My jaw drops. I *think* this means a DNA sample that could be matched against the bloodied pillow at the crime scene could be within my reach.

'This man's death was reported for investigation, so in terms of finding out whether we took a sample, we're going to need to recall this file from the Public Records Office, then we'll need to go through the file and see if there's any record in there about whether a sample was taken, whether he had an autopsy and those kind of things, and then we can take it from there.'

Well. Done.

Lyndal now does a chair victory-dance, wriggling her bum in the seat and shaking her arms, her tinkling bracelets providing the sweet soundtrack of progress. I bet that chair dances don't happen too often in this place. It's lovely to see that this place, which concerns itself with writing the final chapter of people's lives, doesn't care if it takes decades to do so.

1997

The book dealer, Chris, quickly scans the old bookshop on High Street for gold. It seems to have been untouched for ages. As a dealer, you know within seconds if people have rifled through. But the place is still packed with books—every shelf, nook, and cranny. Chris knows the history of the place, so he's sad that these literary treasures have been here all this time. But he doesn't have time to feel uneasy about why he's here; he has a removalist to race. He'd slipped them a cheeky $200, as he's taken to doing recently, to be allowed first dibs before they gut the place. And today's a bit of a bun fight. The removalist is going like the clappers, throwing box after box into a tip truck out the front, while Chris grabs whatever he can and fills his Mitsubishi station wagon to the brim.

He wanders into a room off to the right of the main entrance area. There's a wardrobe, no doors, and it's full of books, magazines, and comics; old *Playboy*s, too, stacked sideways, flat-packed. But there's no time for close inspection. Bundles and bundles go into the station wagon.

21 June 2017: Episode 1

Showtime. Four hundred and seventy-four days after floating my *Trace* idea with Kerri Ritchie, over a glass of rosé at a bar beside Flinders Street Station, this is real. Those moody first eight chords of the *Trace* theme chime though Australians' earbuds.

Rachael Brown: Ask any ex-Homicide cop about their biggest regret, and they'll tell you about the one that got away, that case they couldn't quite crack … I heard something on the grapevine that made me suspect something or someone had been overlooked in the original investigation, a piece of evidence, a trace. Turns out I wasn't wrong. There's far more to this story than police ever knew.

The podcast community finally gets to meet the James brothers.

Mark James: She said to me if anything happens to me, I'm to make sure that my brother Adam is looked after.

And Ron Iddles.

Ron Iddles: Some people would say, 'Draw a line in the sand and move on,' but I've always had this view, the answer is always in the file ... There is absolutely no doubt whoever killed Maria told somebody.

Listeners now have a background to the case — its victims and its persons of interest. And they learn *their* role.

Rachael Brown: If you know anything about this case, write to us, at trace@abc.net.au. We still want to talk to anyone who knew the Telecom man, who took his own life, and we'd also like to hear from Jeanette Hodson — she's the driver who nearly hit the suspected killer as he ran across the road in Thornbury, Melbourne, back on the 17th of June 1980. You can follow the investigation, including photos, witness statements, videos, and maps at our website.

And whether it's the compelling story, the window for listeners to also be contributors, or whether the public has caught the scent of the wider issues that will be illuminated, *Trace* hits a nerve and takes off. The early iTunes reviews suggest *Trace* has hit the right note:

RIP Maria James, my heart goes out to Adam and Mark, I hope they get the answers they are searching for.

Anyone who knows anything, even the smallest of detail, needs to come forward.

Deeply moving, you are left feeling the same need for closure as the children and the detective feel.

This was one of the team's utmost priorities, that *Trace* be both a forensic and compassionate investigation. For it to be resonating so early, among audiences who've grown used to media interviewees being chewed up and spat out, is incredibly humbling. And it's not just ABC audiences. Sure, we're pushing it hard, on all Aunty's arms—ABC Radio, TV, online, and social media—so the podcast can feed into and off itself, and so people who don't even have the faintest idea what the hell a podcast is can find their way to the story. But large thanks for the traction that *Trace* is getting also has to go to the commercial media. To be invited onto Channel 10's *The Project*, and have the four hosts who are used to interrupting guests with quips and laughs listen in generous silence while I explain the weight of this case is really quite something.

Carrie Bickmore: Let's talk about this horrible story you're covering here. What was it about Maria's story that's got you, and I guess the whole nation, so involved and so *interested*?

Rachael Brown: For me, personally, a couple of years ago I learned a piece of information, a bit of gold dust, that I thought was the clincher, I thought, *Why hasn't this been followed up*? So I approached Mark James and asked his permission to do a journalistic deep dive. It was important for me to get the family's blessing.

Carrie Bickmore: It must be really interesting for the families of these cases. This is a new medium through which they could possibly find out details about what's happened to someone they love.

Rachael Brown: And that's the positive side of it, that perhaps the whole of Australia will be listening and hopefully emailing in with information. But I do think because audiences are so ravenous for true crime, the danger is that podcasters forget, and treat the crime like a spectator sport, and forget these are real people and real lives.

Carrie Bickmore: Well, all the best with it. If you want to get involved with *Trace*, just head to iTunes or wherever you download your podcasts. Also, anyone with information regarding Maria's death is being asked to call Crime Stoppers. The number is 1800 333 000.

And this starts a shift. This case about a mum and her boys seems to have blurred the traditional battle-lines between competing news organisations. And it becomes more about who can help, as with Hughesy and Kate on the radio station KIIS FM:

Kate Langbroek: Why are people so fascinated by true crime?

Rachael Brown: This happened to a woman, just a couple of suburbs down in Thornbury — she could've been us. You know, you can put yourself in these people's shoes, and she had two young kids …

Dave Hughes: I wanna know what that tidbit was, that got you going.

Rachael Brown: You find that out next week, actually, next Wednesday.

Kate Langbroek: It stays with the detectives, doesn't it, the cases they can't solve?

Rachael Brown: Yeah. He [Ron Iddles] has got a 99 per cent strike rate, Bradmanesqe, but this one still grates.

Kate Langbroek: OK, Rachael Brown, are you going to help him get to 100 per cent?

Rachael Brown: I'm really trying.

Kate Langbroek: Anyone who may know anything …

Producer: Yes, you can go to abc.net.au/trace, and there are contact details there where you can get in touch with Rachael.

Kate Langbroek: And as crazy as that sounds, that's exactly how these cases get solved, by someone going, "Hey, Mum, didn't you used to live near that bookshop?" You know, that sort of thing.

Then there's the culture website *Junkee*:

Serial was a cultural phenomenon like few others. Sarah Koenig and Julie Snyder's radio investigation into Hae Min Lee's murder ranked number one on iTunes before it even technically debuted in 2014, inspired 'five million online detectives', and had a tangible impact on the case of alleged-murderer Adnan Syed. Now *Trace*, a podcast investigation of a 1980 Melbourne cold case, looks set to inspire a similar level of obsession, with the first episode jumping to number one on iTunes Australia's podcast chart within a day of its release on Wednesday.

There'll soon be newspaper articles and write-ups in women's magazines. Me telling *Trace*'s sound engineer, Marty Peralta, whose natural habitat is edit-booth dungeons, that he'd made *Vogue* magazine was a day I bet he never saw coming.

And all this, after just the backgrounder episode, I think. *Wait till they hear what we've got.*

February 2017

> Mark told me today that police don't know if B's sister is a full sibling...we need to visit her. Feel like a drive next week?
>
> — Email from Kerri Ritchie to Rachael Brown, 10 Jan 2017

We'd only intended to leave a card for Father Bongiorno's sister. But now that we're here at this sprawling property in the state's south, we decide that we should at least say hi. Kerri Ritchie starts to fumble around with a gate latch that reminds her of her childhood farm days. 'Just have to line it up right, *and* the right amount of force,' she mumbles. *Please don't crack it*, I think, *I'm not ready*. But of course she does; it's a cinch for the former country girl. Kerri raps on the door. *Don't answer.*

I don't know why I'm being such a chicken. But after a year of wondering about this woman—who refused to give a DNA sample to help clear (or maybe incriminate) her brother—I'm pretty sure she's going to be angry to find us on her doorstep. Kerri swings a gold chain attached to a bell. *Ding Ding.* I can hear the dull hum of a TV. Maybe she can't hear us over the idiot box. Or maybe we're the idiots. *Knock knock*. We should go.

We've stopped here on our way to interview 'Bill', one of Father O'Keeffe's victims, and all my focus is on that at the moment. From the small amount I managed to glean in a phone conversation with him, Bill's abuse was at the darkest end of the spectrum, and involved numerous counts of penetration. In its wake is a history of suicide attempts and admissions to a psychiatric hospital. So this will be one hell of a tough interview. For both of us. I'm keen to shore up claims about Father O'Keeffe's 'unreasonable force in reasonable situations'. I also want to check if whether Bill had heard rumours of the priest's involvement in cult rituals.

'Last try,' says Kerri. *Knock knock*. I hear the pad of footsteps down a hallway. Shit.

And then a wary, 'Hello?' We introduce ourselves while Father Bongiorno's sister slowly opens the door. Let's call her 'Julia'. I'm choosing to give her privacy, because she didn't choose her family. She looks so much like her late brother—the same deep tear troughs, the same drooping cheeks.

'We tried to find your phone number,' I say. 'Apologies for showing up like this'.

'We're journalists working on a project,' Kerri says. 'We know what you've been through.' Julia recoils slightly. 'How could you possibly know?'

Touché, how *could* we really know? I explain that a story I've been working on for a year involves the murder of Maria James. 'We know your brother was once a suspect, and he's been cleared …'

Julia quickly hushes me. 'You better come in—the neighbours …' She turns, and her voice trails off, and the next thing I know we're asking if we should take off our shoes. Julia invites us to sit at a large wooden dining table. For a woman whose brother's alleged misdemeanours have undoubtedly left a shadow over her family, she's extremely gracious, chuckles occasionally, and even offers us a wine. She doesn't want to go on tape; she says it will make her nervous, but she does share some insights. Just like Rita and Enrico Constantini described him, she says her brother was somewhat of a rough diamond within the church.

'He didn't conform to that holier-than-thou book at the time—he'd be up the street to the butcher in a singlet on a hot day. He was intellectually arrogant, he called a spade a spade, and some people didn't like that. Others had the humour to override it, if you could call it humour—they didn't take it personally.' Under all his bluster, she says, he felt people's pain. She suspects he had a lot of his own. 'He drank; he must've been pretty depressed at times.'

I ask what she made of the paedophilia allegations. She says the case was complicated. 'If I told you, it would take a year. The stigma stayed—it could happen to anyone.' She describes the complainants as 'those boys who got him into trouble'. One, she says, was a troublemaker. Another had a problem with his emotions. As for the idea her brother could be tied up in a murder—no way. 'I've never seen him do anything violent in his life, ever. Tony was always angry they never checked on the man that went there regularly—at her bookshop, a fellow with brown trousers used to visit her all the time.' I wonder if this was Frank Todd. I remember Pat Barbante telling me he'd drop in most days for a cuppa. Just not *that* day.

Julia's loyalty is not bottomless, though. 'He didn't live up to expectations,' she says gently. Within their Italian family, she says she was left out of a lot of conversations, and was somewhat stigmatised because of her divorce.

The last big fight she had with him was over inheritance. 'He would never come clean … I deserved an open conversation about things that bugged me, but he made light of it, so I closed the door on him.' She'd been looking after him, on and off through his illness, and enough was enough. But a couple of years before he died, he had an aneurism and called her from hospital, so she picked him up. Because blood runs thick. Julia says she asked him, 'What else would you have done?' He replied, 'I would go to a hotel.' She smiles at this, at his trademark arrogance. 'That's the kind of person he was—he'd always land on his feet somehow.'

I ask if she still feels the need to protect him. Even now. Why did she refuse to give police a sample of her DNA? 'Did you ever think about doing it so it could just be ruled out and you'd never have to hear from anyone again?'

Her answer isn't what I'm expecting. It has nothing to do with being a loyal sister, and everything to do with manners. 'They came, it was dark, the gates were locked, it was around 9.00pm.' She says a police officer yelled over the fence—he obviously hadn't graduated in the Ritchie school of latch-cracking—and she says he scared her. 'He must've then rung me and told me he was out there. I said, "I don't know if you're a policeman or who you are."'

And sitting here in this big empty house, where the air's cut only by a ticking clock, I feel for her. Of course a woman who lives alone would be scared by a stranger yelling over her fence in the dark. 'Rude and intimidating. Fancy being so insensitive—why didn't he call first?' she says. I feel for her, too, for all the letdowns in her life, including her brother's dismissive treatment of her, and here she is, still carrying the can. So she refused to give police a DNA sample. 'I feel like I'd be stooping to their level,' she tells us. Julia believes he didn't do it. That's enough for her, and to hell what anyone else thinks.

All this time I've been sitting rigidly in the wooden dining chair, not daring to move. Through no fault of Julia's, I've felt tense the whole time. I didn't want to do or say anything that would break the flow. Or make us any more of an imposition. So I haven't checked my phone, which is sitting in the bag at my feet. But the conversation seems to be wrapping up, so I reach down. There's a text from Bill: 'Thanks for the no show.' I check the time. Shit. Shit, shit, *shit*. It's 6.30pm. We were supposed to be with Bill half an hour ago. How the hell did we lose more than an hour in here? It's felt like 20 minutes. I can feel blood draining from my face. 'Kerri, it's 6.30.' She quickly makes our apologies to Julia as I race outside to call Bill.

'I'm so sorr—,' but I'm cut off. A barrage of every swear word I've ever heard rolls in. I'm scum. A prick. A c**t. 'You pricks are all the same: you say you care, you don't carrrrre, you don't care at all. You're *scum*.' Bill's guttural screams barrel up from the deepest place reserved for horror times like these. 'You fucking scuuuuum.' I can hear the saliva spraying against his phone. I try to explain that I *do* care—too much, actually, which is why this investigation has consumed the past year of my life and I've only been paid in nightmares.

'You c**t.' He doesn't hear me; he can't hear anything. And you know what, I *am* scum. As a kid, his trust was betrayed again and again and again. And I've gone and done exactly the same thing. 'You pricks are all the same, you don't care'. Yes, being late for an appointment is not the same as abuse, but to Bill it *is*. It's abandonment. It's a message that his story isn't important. He's probably spent the last few days bracing himself for my questions, and I couldn't even rock up on time. 'Leave me a-l-o-n-e.' In trying to help Father Bongiorno's victims, we've lost the trust of one of Father O'Keeffe's.

I feel a hot prickle across the back of my neck as I stop pacing and fold forward. Julia stares at me from her front porch, sympathetically but utterly confused. I'm worried about Bill. Will he lash out at someone? At himself? I'm worried about what this means for the investigation. Could he have shed light on Father O'Keeffe's behaviour, and possibly Maria James's murder, and now we've blown it? For us and the James brothers, I've blown it. *Oh God*, I think, *I'm going to throw up on Julia's flowers.* 'Leave me a-l-o-n-e.'

Kerri grabs my car-keys because my hands have started to shake, and we make it to Bill's local café in record time. But it's too late. It was always going to be too late. We'd lost Bill an hour ago.

The crazy thing is, this isn't me. I'm polite to a fault. Someone can crash into me, spill coffee all down me, and *I'll* apologise. So it scares me that today has gone disastrously wrong. I thought we could run on adrenaline and goodwill, but we're stretched, exhausted, and it's cost us. This interview was crucial. Bill's story deserved to be told. We weren't there, and that's just not good enough. And for that, Bill, I am truly sorry.

28 June 2017: Episode 2

'When Pete flew back today the young couple next to him were listening to Trace!'

— Text from Kerri Ritchie to Rachael Brown

I grin at the text message from Kerri. It's an exciting thing when the work you put out into the world starts getting noticed, and it's not just your mum who's bragging about it, but strangers, students on a tram, or a mate's gym buddies.

Pretty soon after *Trace*'s launch, the podcast starts spreading like wildfire. *Trace* is on its way to becoming one of the most successful podcasts in the national broadcaster's history. It even starts *becoming* the news. As Episode 2 is released, Fran Kelly on RN Breakfast issues a spoiler alert before her 7.00am news bulletin, because one of its stories is about an electrician seeing a murder-suspect priest covered in blood.

The final episode of HBO's documentary mini-series *The Jinx* hit the pages of *The New York Times* when an eccentric millionaire implicated in three murders forgot he was still wearing a lapel microphone from an interview and whispered to himself during a bathroom break that he 'killed them all, of course'. But I'm not sure a podcast has ever prompted a news spoiler-alert. Just as *The New York Times* did, the ABC cops some backlash for its 'spoilers' in its radio, TV, and online stories about Father Bongiorno's bloody hands. My response to this is, *Tough*. This is real life for a family who has been waiting 37 years for answers, and what the electrician saw might be able to shed light on this. So this *is* news. It's not just some juicy tidbit to be enjoyed by listeners who subscribe to *Trace*. But therein lies the quandary: for many listeners, true-crime podcasts are entertainment, whereas I feel we'd be doing *Trace* a disservice if we treated it that way.

Along with the tweets and Facebook posts saying that we'd 'spoiled' Episode 2 for listeners come the messages that we *did* want. Emails start pouring into *Trace*'s special address. I'd dearly hoped that *Trace* would be interactive; but given the traditionally long tail of podcasts, the team had tried to manage its expectations. There was every chance that someone with vital information mightn't hear *Trace* until December, or the following June. But emails keep pouring in and to make sure we don't miss any gold, Jeremy Story Carter swings into triage mode, sifting the genuine leads from the casual armchair-detectives' theories:

The Easey Street murders three and a half years earlier share some things in common with Maria James's murder.

I wonder if the wife of the estate agent, that Maria was seeing initially, has had her alibi checked out?

I knew Anthony Bongiorno as a child. My family went on holidays with him. He was a strange and fearful man.

I think my parents saw someone running away. They're elderly now and in relatively poor health. Can you please pass on my details to the police officer investigating?

My husband and I lived in Thornbury last year and on our walks up and down High Street we noticed so many little Italian and European cafés which have been running for decades with lots of men gathered in there. I wonder if it would be worth you visiting them?

I don't remember any specific Italian housekeepers by name, but Maria ___ who still resides in Thornbury and is involved with the church may remember names.

My husband is from an Italian family and there is one thing for sure. The old Italians love to talk about the business of other people ... I would advise that you place an advertisement for your podcast in *Il Globo*. I expect that this will create a good response from those ageing Italians who still live in the area.

Then we chase up those who've volunteered what look like strong leads. We interview, corroborate, re-script, re-cut. Another waltz. And all of a sudden, we think, *This might just work, you know. That person with the missing puzzle-piece in Thornbury or Cairns or Bunbury might hear this. This might just work!* After each episode drops, I do a live studio chat with Jon Faine on his morning radio program. A lot of his half-a-million listeners mightn't hark from the podcast-savvy generation, but they might have lived in Thornbury at the time of the murder, or know someone who did. And reaching this group of people will be crucial. Jon Faine tells Melbourne:

Evidence has come forward, even since last week. I got to my hockey game last Wednesday, and the guys there, one of them said, 'Oh yeah, my dad knew about that'. It's astonishing how the ripple effect is already taking place since your first and now second episode has aired ... abc.net.au/trace or you can go to our home page, it's right there for you to click on.

You indeed may well be able to provide another piece, the missing piece in the puzzle.

And in what will become the norm after these weekly chats, when I leave Jon's studio, there's a talkback line on hold for me, with the red button flashing. It's a man who says his wife saw a priest standing outside Maria James's bookshop that fateful day.

So the very next night, on a miserable rainy Thursday, I tiptoe wet boots down the hallway of a woman I'll call 'Louise'.

'Sorry, mind those,' she says, edging by a passageway full of photos of family members smiling up from the floor. 'A guy was meant to come and put all my frames up, and he rang at the last minute and said he's not coming.'

The picture of High Street, Thornbury that day in 1980 is still clear in Louise's mind. She was on her way to lunch, but first had to drop by a shoe shop. The traffic was fairly congested, so she and her boyfriend, in his new Torana, came to a stop beside Maria James's bookshop.

'I knew every shop in High Street, yeah, and that shop, it had the polished tiles on the front, and it had a crooked verandah.'

She remembers it being around 11.00am.

'I saw a priest standing in the doorway. He was all in black, he was wearing a hat, and he had a collar, a priest collar. He was short; he was like a Buddha. He had a lot of lines on his forehead, and very bushy eyebrows, like Sir Eric Pearce [a Melbourne newsreader]. I've wondered later if he was coming out, but he was definitely standing in the doorway that day. He appeared to be looking out for something. He had his hands crossed like this ...'

Louise stands up and crosses her arms over her torso, so

each palm is resting on her opposite thigh.

'... you know, how people are put into a coffin. That's a terrible thing to say, isn't it?'

'Is that what you thought?'

'That's what he looked like. The whole thing was, he was freaky. I said, "Oh, look at him", and my boyfriend said, "He's probably donating books", and I said, "Yeah, or he's doing an exorcism."' Louise laughs, embarrassed, 'because it was round about the time of *The Exorcist* [movie].'

'How long would you have spent looking at this priest?'

'Oh, probably 45 seconds.'

'Did you notice any blood on him?'

'No, no. Then I looked away, because he sort of looked at me, so I looked away. And then I've looked back at him, and that's when he's walked, up towards the city.'

So south, from the bookshop back towards his church. I show Louise some photos, just to be sure. I've picked one of the priest and four of random people, compliments of Google Images.

She picks Anthony Bongiorno straightaway.

'And what was he doing before he walked off?'

'Just sort of looking around. Like he was looking out for somebody.'

'As if waiting for someone, or like keeping watch?'

'Not keeping watch, but just like he's ready to walk, but he doesn't want to, in case somebody sees him. It was that sort of look, like he was a bit paranoid, very suspicious.'

I mention that hindsight is a beautiful thing, and wonder whether her memories are coloured by Maria's eventual fate.

'When we were driving back up High St, I saw there were police everywhere, and then, not long after that, they had a caravan there.'

But Louise stresses she did feel uneasy before the murder.

She's fixated on her memory of the priest's forehead wrinkles, and his stance.

'My son, I rang him up the other day, and I said to him what I saw. And he goes, "Oh Ma, it's a known thing that the priest did it, but he was cleared." "Well," I said, "I didn't know that, no one told me about a priest doing that." And he goes, "Oh Ma, you must have known." But I didn't know. The thing is, back then, 1980, I got married that year, I got engaged that year, you don't think for one second that a priest would do anything wrong. To me, priests were like gods. They were. They were perfect. You ever have a problem, you go to a priest.'

Louise tells me that since the podcast she's called Crime Stoppers to report what she saw that day.

'Would you encourage other people to come forward? With things like this?'

'Yeah, of course, because the little things make up the big things. It's like saving money. You tell your kids, "Put away a dollar, and before you know it, you've got $100, $1,000." It's important to come forward with anything, even if it's just the smallest things.'

Soon after meeting Louise, *Trace* gets another dollar for the piggy bank. It's an email from a worried daughter:

This has long been a mystery for my mother. She has long talked of Mrs James and I have grown up knowing my mother is still haunted by this. She says she can still see this man's face running out of the shop so fast he was hit by a car and kept running.

I can't get to 'Laura' fast enough. Her most vivid memory from the 17th of June 1980 is of her bright-green gabardine coat, and then the white blur in front of it. She'd got off the tram, on her way to her dentist appointment, and was just about to pass the bookshop door.

'And this chap comes out of the shop, slammed the door, and he ran straight past, not far from me. He had a white top, but I couldn't tell if there was a pattern on it because he flashed by. And the lady in the car slammed her brakes on. And he actually threw his hand out on the bonnet of her car. And I was watching him. And I virtually said, *What a bloody idiot. What's he doing, dodging all over?* Cars were pulling up, tooting horns. He crossed over, and I walked more towards where the lights were, and I looked down that street [Hutton Street] and I watched him, and he was running like anything.'

All this time, I've been searching for Jeanette Hodson, the driver of the car that nearly hit him. And now we've somehow managed to go one better. The man police think might have been Maria's killer nearly crashed through Laura and her bright-green coat.

'Do you remember his face?'

'Side on, European, couldn't say whether Greek or Italian. His eyes were deep-set. In the paper, I read the car lady said, 'Receding hairline'—I would've called it high forehead, because he had a good thick head of hair. And all brushed back, whether he'd sprayed it, it was so smooth, and brushed back, and it was down to about here.' Laura motions a little bit below her ears, 'Not quite on the shoulders. He's here.' She puts her forefinger to her forehead—the image is seared in there, it seems.

'He was tall bit taller than me. He wasn't fat—slimmish.

He was definitely round about between maybe 40 to 50, maybe 50.'

'You saw him put his hand on the bonnet. Did you notice blood on his hand?'

'No, I didn't, no.'

Laura says she lost sight of the man down Hutton Street as he disappeared beyond a woman loaded up with white shopping bags. Then something else caught her eye.

'I looked up the side street of the shop, because I'm at the lights now, and I've seen this man at the gate, in a suit. And he sort-of kicked the gate and was pushing the gate.'

Was this John James? He arrived at the bookshop to check on his ex-wife between 12.10 and 12.20, by my estimate, give or take ten minutes. And he told the ABC of his anxious laps around the shop, trying to get in the front, and then the back.

'I'm wondering whether you saw John James, her ex-husband, who had come ...'

'It could've been.'

If it *was* John James, this means the police theory that the killer was behind Maria's bedroom door when John found her body could be wrong. Because it sounds like the running man was flying down Hutton Street before John was even in the house. I show Laura a photo of Mr James, but she says it doesn't help—she wasn't close enough.

Now for the big question. Because Laura used to go to St Mary's Church, she knew what Father Bongiorno looked like. I don't need a photo of him.

'An electrician says he saw Father Bongiorno around the time of the murder with blood on his face and hands. Was it Father Bongiorno you saw?'

'Coming out the door?'

'Yeah.'

'No, it definitely wasn't Bongiorno who came out, but I don't know about back entrances of shops and that type of thing.'

I show Laura a series of photos—which, I find out later, Victoria Police privately chide me for. I broke protocol, apparently. It needed to be 12 photos, shown in a very specific way. *Well*, I think to myself when I hear this, *I've been asking for their help with this for over a year now, to no avail.*

'These are the face-fits police did at the time.'

I show her the face-fit of the 5.00am man, the man who regularly chatted to Maria early in the mornings.

'The one I saw didn't have a moustache or a beard—he was clean-shaven.'

Next, the face-fit of the 9.10am man, who I think might have been Mario Falcucci, the local loner who liked comic books.

'He had much more hair than that—not quite as far back as that.'

Then come photos of our other person of interest, Father O'Keeffe. I show her a shot of him when young, and another when he was older.

'No, don't know him at all—don't recognise his face, the hair-do is different. I couldn't say it was him coming out the door'.

Father Bongiorno's alibi, Father Sean O'Connell.

'No, I don't know him.'

Frank Todd, friend of the James's, later jailed for paedophilia.

'The [running man's] eyes seemed to be deeper set; his are more puffy. The hair is definitely different.'

Six strikes so far. I'd love to show Laura pictures of the other men who've niggled at me: Mr Telecom, who committed suicide; and the security guard who a local shopkeeper nominated as dangerous. But I don't even have a name for them, let alone photos. If Victoria Police does, Laura just might be able to rule them in, or out. Victoria Police might do well recruiting her, because she offers up a theory I've been mulling over of late, which could well fit the facts.

'She [Maria] had a couple of friends,' says Laura, 'and I've been thinking, maybe it was one of her friends, and he got such a hell of a fright, he bolted.'

'Maybe he came in and found her, and she was already dead?' I offer.

And maybe hearing John James's frantic attempts to break in, he panicked, and, thinking he might be blamed for the murder, fled.

Laura continues: 'He flashed by that quick. And didgy-dodged over the road, because there was traffic moving. He should've been covered in blood then if he did that—all that stabbing.'

A white shirt would have to show traces of a frenzied stabbing. No witnesses mention anything about the running man carrying a jacket he might have taken off. Or, for that matter, carrying a knife. And had he tossed it before his High Street dash, police would have found it. Around the same time as someone is sprinting away from the bookshop to the west, Father Bongiorno is seen covered in blood around the corner to the south. Both might have been connected to the murder. Or neither.

I ask why Laura never came forward at the time. 'It was in the newspapers. Did you ever think, *Shit, I saw ...*'

'Yeah, I thought that. We were all sitting at the table, and I said, "I saw a man bursting out of there," but of course my husband said, "Oh, you better not get involved—young kids and newspapers and pictures and everything," so I just sort-of sat on it, like a lot of other people have, but it's always been here.'

She presses again on her tortured temple.

'But it might be someone like you with that tiny little crumb, a tiny little piece of information, that solves this thing.'

I now can't shake the idea that there could have been two people present at Maria's murder. Just because Father Bongiorno might have been sprayed with blood doesn't necessarily mean he was the attacker. And the second person I'm thinking of is not the white-shirted sprinter.

February 2017

Full calendar for next two weeks. Tuesday 21 Feb – between 7am to 9am.

— Email from Ron Iddles to Rachael Brown, 8 February 2017

'This Broken Rites article lists his history of paedophilia. There are four boys documented on this form: their stories range from being shown pornography, to being asked to soap up in the shower after cricket practice, through to sodomy and torturous acts.'

I'm handing over a pretty macabre retirement present to Ron Iddles. I've bundled up everything I've found on Father O'Keeffe: his obit, photos, victim statements, and transcripts of interviews with those who had dealings with him. Ron finishes up in three days and should be planning his farewell party, but again he meets me, this time to see if my O'Keeffe scrapbook is enough to clear the bar for an exhumation request to be granted. I've recently heard back from the Coroners Court, and it's unlikely that any histological samples taken after Father O'Keeffe's death in 1984 would still be in storage.

'He died from a myocardial infarction. He died at 55,' I tell Ron.

I steer Ron through the chronicle of Father O'Keeffe's assaults, including Adam James's claim.

'Adam says he was abused by Father O'Keeffe on at least one of the three occasions that Father Bongiorno abused him, between 2 June and 14 June 1980.'

I tell Ron about James Shanahan's claim he was forced to participate in satanic cult rituals.

'He was paid $33,000 compensation by the Church, and its independent commissioner said in a statement, "Your allegations, as bizarre as they are, I accept them." And in those rituals, James says, at least three people were murdered. This was investigated by Victoria Police—a detective called Max Schiavon filed an information report—but police had to let it go because it didn't match missing persons' or homicide records.'

And I mention that the priest's habits seem to fit with the killer's MO.

'James says things like, "He came at me with a carving knife once and threatened to kill me." He threatened his mum at one point ... His friend used to call Father O'Keeffe "creeping Jesus" because he would sneak up on people in rubber-soled shoes ... O'Keeffe used to talk about having sex with dead bodies, and he was into painful torturous acts ... One victim says he was prone to unreasonable force in reasonable situations, and he thinks O'Keeffe would've been willing to use deadly force against someone.'

I speak in rapid fire at Ron Iddles for about 20 minutes. Apart from the occasional 'Hmmm', he doesn't get a word in. When he does, it's a painful full stop, delivered with his trademark economy.

'Interesting.'

That's it, Ron?

'The strongest bit, really, is the fact that he's assaulted Adam and he's at the presbytery or the church next door. It's not enough yet to push it over the line.'

'What would you need?'

'You'd need a stronger connection to Maria, I think, or to the fact that there might've been a threat or something—perhaps Mark knows if O'Keeffe ever visited Maria? Yes, Adam says he was assaulted, he's [O'Keeffe is] next door in the church, and has a history around sexual issues and obviously young boys, but does that then translate to a mother?'

'But Bongiorno was treated as a suspect because paedophilia was a motive ... so why couldn't we apply that theory to O'Keeffe?' I press.

'You would have to have some other evidence, other than the fact that O'Keeffe is a paedophile, a sexual deviant, and all the rest of it.' For Ron, a big sticking point is the other persons of interest who gravitated around Maria's bookshop. 'The question would be, who sent the flowers? Can I eliminate that person? No, I can't, because I don't know who it is ...'

Ron means those flowers sent to Maria by an admirer the week before her murder.

'... so a magistrate might say to you, "Well, maybe *that* person is the killer."'

'So because you can't eliminate everyone else, exhumation is too big a deal?'

'Correct.'

'Just on some flowers?' I ask, annoyed. Surely satanic ritual abuse trumps a mysterious bouquet?

'Who's the Telstra man?'

He's asking about the Telstra worker, the one who committed suicide. Ron's playing devil's advocate, and while I'm feeling like he's fast unpicking six months of my work, he's right. If he sees holes, a magistrate will. 'It's all about exculpatory evidence' he tells me. Falling into this annoyingly large basket of motley characters is the secret admirer; Mr Telecom; the 5.00am man; the potentially dangerous local security guard; and all the other names sitting in that cold-case box that police won't let me anywhere near. Because of all these loose ends, Ron says an exhumation application would fail.

'I'd be reasonably confident that if I was to do an affidavit, I couldn't get him into the suspect category.'

'Even though he's said to have been involved in quite violent cult settings where people were allegedly … '

'Does that mean that he killed her? No. So the magistrate would be saying, "What else have you got which indicates that he might be responsible?"'

'What I was going on was a history of what looks like psychopathic tendencies, and a guy quite able to snap quickly — if Maria confronted him, you know, if he thought he was going to be found out.'

'That's all true. Quite clearly, whoever was in there she knew, and it's a fairly frenzied attack, there's a lot of hatred, a lot of emotion — you don't get stabbed 68 times by an unknown person. So, again, Maria went to the church, Maria would know him, but it's trying to get it a little bit higher than what it is now.'

'He might be responsible,' continues Ron, sensing I'm deflated. 'You wouldn't put him in the suspect category, but you say he's a person of interest, and the only way to eliminate that person of interest, you're probably going to have to get some DNA from a relative, not from an exhumation.'

'Damn.'

'I think someone should go and find the niece, and get the DNA.'

I tell Ron I think the nieces are his brother's daughters, so mitochondrial testing won't help. But maybe I could track down other relatives? I have a vague memory of DNA guru Dadna Hartman mentioning a similar technique that could be applied to any nephews—something called Y-STR, which targets the Y chromosome, which is passed down through the paternal side. So, if Father O'Keeffe's brothers have any sons, they'll share the priest's Y chromosome. But how to get a sample?

'What would it take?' I ask.

'Well, it's not hard. I'd go out there.'

'Could it be me?'

'It could be. You could either get the police to do it, or do it covertly. You go out and have a drink, there's a lab in Fitzroy that would test the DNA ... Ah, but then you don't have the DNA from the scene.'

Whatever DNA profile I might get from somehow swiping saliva from a relative of Father O'Keeffe would be useless, as I don't have the 'code', as Dadna put it, from the primary sample—the bloodied pillow. It would be like playing the card game Snap with only half a deck.

'Is that legally admissible? I'm not saying I will do this,

but is that legally admissible—me swiping someone's glass and giving it to the police?'

'Yes, because it's not covered by any legislation. You'd have to say, "This is a glass which I've preserved, and I've now given it to you." If you swab it and get the DNA off it and compare it, and if it came up, well, then you're there. Then you're in a stronger position to say, *He can't be eliminated, therefore could he be exhumed?*'

Plan B: find a relative. Many of my waking moments become devoted to mapping out Father O'Keeffe's family tree. And on one of these branches is a gift I couldn't possibly have foreseen. A newspaper article about his ordination reads, 'Rev. Thomas O'Keeffe, second and twin son of Mrs H. O'Keeffe and the late Mr O'Keeffe.' He has a *twin*. Surely he'd be the perfect relative to get a sample from? But is this the brother who's mentioned in the obituary, the one who has died, or a different brother?

May 2017

You gave Adam a voice. Adam wants me to say to you, 'Thank you for all your help. You are fantastic at what you do best. If it wasn't for you we wouldn't be here.'

— Text from Mark James to Rachael Brown

The James brothers were completely oblivious of Father O'Keeffe's dark past when he was appointed the parish priest of St Mary's in 1978. Mark James remembers Father

Bongiorno as the PR priest, loud and brash, whereas he says Father O'Keeffe was very different.

'He was the cold, silent one in the background, and he was very methodical with the ritual.'

This is an interesting choice of words. The brothers don't know what I know. So as not to taint their memories of Father O'Keeffe, I'd been waiting until I'd sorted out all the bizarre rumours and sickening victim-reports before I discussed any of the material with them. And now I have to run them through my findings, just as I did with Ron. Mark is with Adam when I call.

'I'd rather hear it and face it, than not hear it and be wondering about it,' says Mark.

I can hear Adam breathing heavily down the phone as I tell the brothers about the other victims, and of eerily similar patterns of abuse. Mark is furious.

'I'm outraged for what these victims have had to go through. It's not just about my brother Adam and me, it's about all the victims, the terror they've been put through … and to learn he's picking up knives, and there's obviously far more out there that hasn't been uncovered yet.'

I fill them in on James Shanahan's cult claims.

'The details are too graphic. I won't go into them, but he says he saw four people murdered.'

Mark takes this in. 'Whilst it is far-fetched, there have been a lot more far-fetched things that have later been found to be true. That's pretty sick stuff. The person who murdered my mother was obviously in some kind of a rage. To hear he [Father O'Keeffe] has been involved in these graphic torture-type abuses makes me think that, well, he may have had something to do with it. At the time, to preserve their own positions, what lengths would they [Fathers O'Keeffe and Bongiorno] have gone to?'

The James brothers have been planning to file an application for the exhumation of Father O'Keeffe. And I can sense that everything I've just told them is only buoying their hopes that a certain stone vault in Melbourne's General Cemetery will soon be prised open. So I take a deep breath and relay Ron Iddles' assessment that any exhumation application would be futile.

But they're not deterred. Mark feels there's enough new evidence, regardless, to warrant more investigation by the authorities.

'I want to make an application to the coroner to reopen the case.'

At this point, that's probably a smarter route. An exhumation application would focus solely on Father O'Keeffe, but given that there are just as many, if not more, unanswered questions about Father Bongiorno, the James brothers would be wiser to request that someone look at the big picture. I explain that they'd need to submit a Form 43 to the Coroners Court, an application to set aside a finding. That way, the state coroner might decide to hold a new inquest, if she agrees that there are 'new facts and circumstances' that weren't considered in the initial 1982 inquest.

'Well, it's completely evident here that there are new facts and circumstances,' says Mark adamantly.

And there are. One: Father Bongiorno had been molesting Adam James. Two: Adam says his mum was set to confront the priest on the day she was murdered. Three: Father Bongiorno had a history of sexual abuse. Four: Father Bongiorno was seen near the murder scene with blood on him.

Mark argues that any of these individual points should warrant a new inquest.

Adam chimes in, 'It should, Rach. I agree. Both of them [the priests] did something, and they both wanted to hide it.'

Five: Father Bongiorno's alibi might be leaky: it came from Father O'Connell who, later, in trying to protect his friend from seminary days, allegedly paid 'Rex' hush money. Six: Adam James says he was abused by Father O'Keeffe. Seven: Father O'Keeffe also had a history of paedophilia, some of it, torturous.

Mark is incredulous that he even has to fill out a Form 43. He says the need for a new inquest is obvious. 'Something very, very strange is going on here between Father Bongiorno, Father O'Keeffe, Adam, and the timing of the murder. It's just all too suss. I think this merits reopening. And Adam needs to be interviewed by somebody that's a professional psychologist, somebody who can calm him. I think he's got a little bit more in there that perhaps a trained professional may be able to get out. Something fishy is going on here, and I'm not going to let it go.'

'No, me either,' Adam cuts in. 'If it doesn't get solved we'll never know.'

5 July 2017: Episode 3

Introducing *Trace* listeners to satanic-cult rituals was always going to be tough.

> He says while other children were sometimes present, he was the only one who participated in the rituals. During them, there

was a group of men; most wore full robes, with hoods over their heads. At the time, he did not recognise anyone except for Father O'Keeffe. Later, he identified another paedophile priest, the notorious Father Kevin O'Donnell, as central to the events. Father O'Donnell died in 1997. At these events, James says he saw four people murdered.

This is the one I thought would most challenge listeners, with its offering of that little red pill. In the end, listeners are fine with it, but James Shanahan is not. He emails, saying I've made it sound like I don't believe him, and that he wants nothing more to do with me. That I can't have one foot on the wharf and one in the boat. Actually, as a journalist, that's precisely the balancing act I have to perform. I reply that if I didn't believe him, he wouldn't have been in the podcast in the first place. And as for my deconstruction of his claims and their acceptance—by the investigating police officer, the Church's independent commissioner, and his psychiatrist—that was due diligence. 'If listeners question my credibility,' I tell James, 'they'll then question yours.' In an approach designed to protect him, and respectfully win ears for his story, I've lost him. It's that day with Bill all over again.

I have to cancel the couple of interview requests that roll in because I can't seem to get out of my PJs. I just feel sick. I keep thinking of Janet Malcolm's blunt summation of every journalist's MO. *Gaining their trust and betraying them without remorse.* Is that what James thinks I've done? They say in journalism that if you keep everyone happy, you're not doing your job properly. But these are the encounters that really sting. The Jameses. The Bills. Give them a little too much of yourself, and they can end up resenting you.

Over the next week, solace—from the nagging doubt of *What the hell are we doing if we're hurting the very people we set out to help?*—comes from listener emails. Many are in support of James: a woman who'd been though something similar; a listener wanting to send him a book of poems; many of the 'good on you for speaking up' flavour. So I pass them all onto him, and while it's clear something has shifted, probably permanently, we're talking again, things are amicable, and that's a start. And I get it; it's this monster that is PTSD—even sufferers often can't predict when it'll rear its head. And, to his credit, despite this millstone, James is one of the few people I know who can be angry with me and still appreciate my underlying intention. Most can't do this because ego gets in the way.

As a court reporter, I'd seen the bad: violence, greed, depravity, you name it. But now *Trace* and its email account are a reminder of the good in people. It's the older generation of abused children, who, despite being shown such little compassion in their youth, are summoning the courage and grace to relive their nightmares in the hope it might somehow help the James family.

It's community members, looking in, reaching out a hand. A police officer who has seen her fair share of family violence, offering to help the James brothers organise a proper memorial service for Maria:

One aspect got me very cross after hearing the 2nd episode. Specifically that Maria was publicly humiliated in life and death by the church, which should have been supporting her. Worse, the church 'victim blamed' her at her own funeral! Maria deserves a dignified funeral, a respectful farewell and at some point soon I think this should happen. It would be very healing

for her family, her community and her extended community
who have come to know her through your podcast.

It's a barrister offering her expertise should the James
brothers want to ask the coroner to reopen their mum's case:

I would be glad to offer my services pro bono and I'm sure
there would be other members of the legal community who
would be able and willing to help.

It's a former detective with fond memories of Ron Iddles:

The bluntest pencil is better than the sharpest mind. Keep up
the great work. It's remarkable you've accomplished what you
have.

All these emails temper the doubters and all the 3.00am
finishes, and remind me why I do this job.

July 2017

Jesse, you're not going to believe this.

Rachael Brown phone-call to *Trace* producer Jesse Cox, 4 July 2017

One call to make a case; one call to break it.

As part of my inquiries into Father Thomas O'Keeffe's
family tree, to try to find nieces or nephews who could
possibly provide a DNA sample, I track down someone

who used to be a friend of his family. I've been putting off calling them, just as I did with Father Bongiorno's sister, as I suspect they won't be impressed by me doing this podcast if they still have an allegiance to the O'Keeffe family. But, again, assumptions can lead to unnecessary self-censorship. This man, who has asked not to be named, invites me over. As we have a cup of tea, with his heater blasting away in the background, he confirms what I'd feared. Both of Father Thomas O'Keeffe's brothers, his older brother and his twin, have died. So that's siblings ruled out. 'Any nephews?' I ask. 'Did the older brother have children?' The family friend thinks there might be a nephew interstate.

'What kinds of things do you need for DNA?' he asks.

'Oh, it could be anything: saliva; hair; blood, of course, is the easiest.'

I tell him they're even using toenails now. A really strange look crosses his face, and he raises his hand as if to say 'Wait' and disappears into another room. He returns, carrying something. 'Would this help?' I keep my distance, utterly confused about what's going on.

'It was ___'s.'

The priest's twin brother's.

'I don't know why I kept it, but now that you're here today, maybe it was meant for you?'

I've been very slow on the uptake, but it finally sinks in, and a chill races down my spine despite this sauna of a lounge room. Here I was asking about nephews, and he's gone one better. The ace card—potential DNA from Father Thomas O'Keeffe's twin brother. *Oh my God, this could solve it*, I think. This man, who I was nearly too scared to call, might have just handed me the missing puzzle piece in the form of a ___. He asks me to be discreet about what this item is; while he wants to help with my investigation, he's equally keen, admirably so, not to open any old wounds of the O'Keeffe family. What the hell do I do with it? This was not part of my journalism course.

I vaguely remember Ron Iddles telling me something about a snap-lock bag when I'd asked—jokingly—about swiping DNA, so we raid the pantry. I carefully lift the ___ into a snap-lock bag with the end of a pen, and seal it. Then I can't help but sit mesmerised by it. As we finish our tea, the little plastic bag sits on a table between us, and it hits me how weird my life's become; I'm about to have a dead guy's ___ in my handbag.

I leave in bewildered gratitude, hopefully on behalf of Maria James. Then there's a frantic volley of calls to make from the road. First, to my producer, Jesse Cox. But I soon realise that my mind is a million miles away from the traffic, so I pull over.

'Guess what's in my handbag?'

Jesse probably thinks I've lost my mind.

'Police could check whether it's similar to the DNA found at the crime scene and if it *is* similar it would support an application to the coroner to have Thomas O'Keeffe exhumed. This is massive.' I'm talking at a hundred words a minute.

All the dirt washes off. The nightmares. Lobbying bosses. Being called the C-bomb by a victim. Missing overseas weddings to keep digging. All of it. For the first time in a long time, I feel a flicker of hope.

'I'm about to call Ron Iddles now and ask his advice about what I should do with this.'

I wait till I'm home for this call.

I tell Ron, 'I think I might have something.'

'Ah, very good.'

'I visited a friend of the O'Keeffe family, and they gave me something that could have familial DNA on it …'

'Ahhhhh …'

'I mean, obviously I should give it to police, but what's …'

'That's the only thing you can do—it will either eliminate him or it won't.'

'Currently it's in a snap-lock bag. Is that right?'

'No, so what I would do is cut the plastic bag open, put it in a paper bag, and reseal the paper bag with the date and the time that you've resealed it. Keep the plastic bag in another bag, because the plastic will actually cause the ___ to sweat, and can sometimes destroy the DNA.'

Rookie error. DNA 101. *Paper* bags. Then the third call, to my DNA guru, Dadna Hartman, to check if Father O'Keeffe's twin brother's DNA could be useful.

'If this item has on it blood, or skin cells, or hair, would any of that be useful for biologists to test for familial DNA?'

'It would. Nuclear DNA profiling would give a more informative match, rather than, for example, mitochondrial DNA analysis.'

'And can nuclear be found in any of those three that I mentioned—blood, skin, or hair?'

'You'd be able to get nuclear DNA material from things like blood stains or other biological material—like semen, for example. Things like hair, unless they've got the root of the hair, you usually can't recover nuclear DNA from, but you could get mitochondrial DNA.'

Not long ago, I'd called Victoria Police's cold-case squad to offer them listener emails containing new leads. This time, my offering is of ___. I organise to drop it off, but just before the arranged time, an officer calls to say something's come

up. *Just hold onto it for now*, he tells me. So I find myself
a reluctant curator of DNA. And having it sitting in my
cluttered and definitely not temperature-controlled wardrobe
is making me slightly nervous.

A mate's mum offered to read my tarot cards recently,
took one look at them and started firing off questions about
my personal security. 'How many people have access to your
apartment? How many people have swipers? And the garage?
Who can get to your car?' So now I'm staring at this little
paper bag sitting above my summer dresses and work shirts,
irrationally wondering if the Church is about to rob my
apartment. I'll have to find it another home. My work locker?
A mate's house in the country? Should I rent a bank vault?
But my fierce protectiveness over my find is about to become
painfully redundant.

An unexpected phone call delivers hope, and then crushing
defeat, in the same microsecond. Father Bongiorno could still
be the killer. Or Father O'Keeffe. Or anyone, for that matter.
But it's unlikely it'll ever be able to be proven. I'm told that
the pillow, which yielded what police *thought* was the killer's
DNA profile, is from an unrelated crime scene.

It has nothing to do with Maria James.

For the past 16 years, police have been chasing a red
herring. They've been eliminating suspects whose DNA didn't
match the male blood left on a pillow ... at a completely
separate murder.

I don't know why this bungle has only now come to
light. I guess it's because whoever's been digging into Maria's
cold-case box—possibly to answer all the questions I've been
emailing over the past year—has found an anomaly. I now

have a million more questions, none of them pleasant, and the most pressing is, *How the hell am I going to tell Mark James?*

I feel like I'm overstepping here. It isn't my job to be breaking this news to the James family. The police should be explaining it, and maybe they will, or maybe they're waiting for a review to be completed. But Episode 4 comes out in three days, so Mark deserves to hear this from me before then.

'I've come across some information to suggest that the [DNA] sample they [the police] got cannot be relied on, because there was a mix-up, and somehow an item from a completely different crime scene was put into your mum's bag of exhibits.'

He takes it better than I did. It's as if a cloud has shifted, and the news, while horrible, validates a long-held nagging feeling that had always been too hazy to put a name to.

'In a way, I'm relieved to know there was a bungle, because I just couldn't figure out in relation to Bongiorno, and what I've learned about him, how he could've been excluded. Now things are starting to make sense to me.'

I originally dived into this project convinced that this cold case was solvable. I'm furious to have to sit in front of Mark James telling him that *Trace*'s answer might be, 'Sorry, there can never be an answer.'

But he waves that negativity away.

'I'm quite devastated by this information, but it's not going to stop me. I'm not ever going to stop trying to find an answer to what's going on. So if it's a bungle-up, perhaps it can be rectified? If there's someone standing in the way of me getting to the truth, well, I'm not going to stop.'

Now there's an elephant that's walked into the room that'll

have to be acknowledged. How the hell did this happen? And was it deliberate?

'There have been bungle-ups with DNA testing in the past, but I find it difficult to accept in these circumstances,' Mark says.

'Given Adam's abuse, do you mean?'

'Yeah, I'm referring to two priests abusing a handicapped person, and the possibility that they have attempted to silence my mother. And that is something that people have to acknowledge is a possibility. And if that is a possibility, it would be something that the Church would definitely not want coming out. What we're talking about is not just a sexual assault, or a series of sexual assaults. We're talking about the possibility that these priests have been involved with the murder of my mother. This brings a whole new order of magnitude to this case. There would be interested parties in this that would very much like it to just go away.'

Shuffle, shuffle, shuffle, shuffle. This cannot be it. Can it? Tonight, the kookaburra's song is mocking me. I knew I mightn't like the answer. But *no* answer? What kind of an answer is that? For the James boys, for Ron and all the officers who've worked this case, for all the sexual-abuse survivors who've dredged up all their shit, for me and my obsession that's driven my bosses, family, and mates nuts?

Shuffle, shuffle, shuffle, shuffle. Such a mess. At the very start of all this, I wondered what margin I should allow for human error. But when I questioned the detectives' conviction that the male blood on Maria's pillow *had* to be her killer's, I was more thinking, *What if a lover had a blood nose and Maria hadn't got around to washing her pillow-slip?* I certainly wasn't thinking it was because that bloody pillow was from a completely different crime scene. How could the cops have got this so wrong? How could this random pillow have found its way into Maria James's evidence bag?

Shuffle, shuffle, shuffle, shuffle. It's like nearing the end of a difficult puzzle, only to find that the last piece is missing, and that it was never in the box to begin with. 'The answer's always in the file,' says Ron. *Maybe it's not this time.* I think of him tearing up every time he talks about Elvira Buckingham. Promises can be our undoing.

11 July 2017: Episode 4

Everyone is back in the frame.

— *Trace*, Episode 4

No episode drop can be punctuated with a night off for beers, because we're always quickly moving on to the next one. We have to keep investigating, verifying leads and rolling them into the next episode. And each time, the stakes get higher. For the whole month, I've woken feeling nauseous. Week 1: introduce listeners to the case, and hope they'll be invested enough to offer leads. Week 2: link a priest to the crime scene. Week 3: hit listeners with satanic cult rituals. This week, Week 4: reveal the DNA bungle that's hamstrung this case for decades. I can probably kiss goodbye any future support from Victoria Police, if any was ever going to come. I'd emailed the Homicide Squad another list of questions, asking for a confirmation or denial by Tuesday night, that there'd been a bungle with the evidence. But two days pass without a peep.

Just after 6.00pm Tuesday, when I'm bundling take-away dinner into my apartment, Mark James's name lights up on my phone. It turns out that, just as the deadline I'd given Victoria Police ticked over, two officers landed on Mark's doorstep. I quickly put him on speaker phone and tape the conversation, as, chances are, I'm going to have to re-script the entire back end of Episode 4, which Marty Peralta is currently putting finishing touches on, ready to upload to iTunes. Mark James says the officers came bearing an admission.

'What they told me was there had been bungle in the DNA testing, and as a result Father Bongiorno and a few of the other suspects are no longer eliminated.'

Everyone is back in the frame.

'They said to me that a pillow from another crime scene—and this pillow had blood on it—was accidentally put into a bag, a sealed bag, and labelled as part of my mother's exhibits. And this pillow was where they got the blood from, that they were using for various tests to eliminate suspects.'

'Did you ask how this happened?' I try, but I can't keep the incredulity out of my voice. 'How can something from a completely separate case be put into her evidence bag?'

This is DNA 101. Yes, I know, I stuffed up on the whole bagging-samples front—Ron's instruction, 'paper, *not* plastic', will forever ring in my ears. But these are police officers. They've had special training in forensics. How did they get it so wrong?

Mark's similarly baffled. 'I've always had the utmost confidence in Vic Pol, and I recognise the human-error element, but it's shaken me up. They also told me that when they moved all the evidence from many cases across from Russell Street to their new offices, there were OH&S risks with blood being in these evidence bags, and some of this evidence was destroyed. But, fortunately, that did not occur in my mother's case. They have said all the other exhibits that were seized from the crime scene are still intact.'

'So are they going to test those to get a new sample?'

'Yes, they've assured me they're going to be bringing each item into the lab for DNA testing. They mentioned, I think, nine suspects need to be re-tested, based on this error, and Father Bongiorno is amongst them. I'm just hoping, despite this bungle, the DNA of the killer is still amongst those exhibits. There were bags of evidence, blood and everything—there'd have to be the killer's DNA somewhere in there. But I tell you one thing, if it turns out that the killer's DNA is not on any of the other exhibits, I'm going to be asking some questions. There'll be probity issues.'

'Have you told Adam? How's he taking all this?'

'I've just got off the phone with him. He was glad to hear that all the previous suspects including Bongiorno are back on the list. But when I told him about the bungle with the evidence, he was a bit disheartened.'

'When did police become aware of this DNA mix-up?'

'Three to four months ago, and it was a result of the police taking an objective new look into Mum's murder, which I think they mentioned started late last year. Maybe September? I would've rather been told a bit earlier, but I'm relieved. I recognise they have a difficult job. I just hope they expedite this matter and give us justice for our mum.'

All of Mark's thoughts have a bitter-sweet tinge. On the one hand, it's back to square one; on the other, now he knows what the stumbling block's been for so long.

'I'm upset, but I also have a renewed sense of hope. I'm hoping the coroner will set aside the finding [of the initial

1982 inquest], and police will move forward with their investigation. If it wasn't for the ABC running this podcast, none of this would've occurred—it was in the too-hard basket. Police are working with limited resources—what's occurred is predicated on the podcast and the good community support it's received.'

There is one important question, though, the answer to which he's none the wiser about.

'The question I put to police, was, "Did this bungle with this DNA exhibit occur before or after Bongiorno became a suspect in this case?" They answered that Bongiorno became a suspect in 2013, when Adam made his sexual-assault allegation, but I have information to the contrary that police felt Bongiorno was a suspect many years before that. They've just said to me the DNA error occurred somewhere in the [Victoria Police] move [around 1994] from Russell Street to the new St Kilda Road premises.'

'But how can they know when it happened?'

'That's what I was trying to pin down, when, and I couldn't get a definitive response.'

This may well turn out to be the million-dollar question.

An hour later, an email from Victoria Police lands in my inbox. After all the emailed questions I've sent the organisation in the past year, this is the only time it's ever replied in writing:

Homicide detectives have today met with the family of Maria James to provide them with an update on the investigation.

The meeting followed the discovery of an error in the handling of an exhibit.

The exhibit in question had been forensically tested and used to eliminate suspects. A recent review by the Homicide

Squad however has shown that the exhibit was in fact unrelated to the Maria James case.

A small number of persons of interest who had previously been eliminated will now be re-assessed in accordance with normal investigation procedures.

Victoria Police would like to stress that this was an isolated human error, and not the result of any flaws in the forensics testing process.

Homicide Squad detectives remain absolutely committed to this case and achieving justice for the family of Maria James.

As the case remains unsolved and is subject to an active investigation it would be inappropriate to comment further.

I call Marty Peralta and ask him to start unpicking his handiwork. We have a long night ahead.

July 2017

Of course it's an embarrassment to us. It's really difficult, particularly for investigators.

Victoria Police press conference, 13 July 2017

Assistant Commissioner Stephen Fontana's press conference is patched live to ABC News Breakfast. Episode 4 dropped yesterday evening—after the *Trace* team's midnight-oil burn to re-script, voice, and edit a new ending—and Victoria Police is in damage control.

'Our investigators have worked really hard, on this

particular case and other cases, so it's disheartening when something like this happens.'

I wonder whether the assistant commissioner is silently cursing me. He's the one who had the grace, and guts, to offer Victoria Police's blessing for this podcast. But now, possibly because of it, he's having to answer for an error of his predecessors.

'We're extremely disappointed for the family; it must be very difficult for them. They've had their hopes up that we've had a DNA profile of a suspect, and unfortunately that's not the case. Yeah, it's pretty hard to take.'

Mark James sits across from me in the ABC's green room. He's hard to read today. I can't tell if he's crushed or quietly determined. We were set to be interviewed on the ABC News Breakfast couch, but we've been trumped by this red-eye Victoria Police press conference. The alert hit chief of staffs' desks around 6.30am. I can almost hear the collective groan of Melbourne's media having to rush to the 7.30am conference.

'It [Maria's exhibits bag] was stored adjacent to another exhibit, and they were similar types of exhibits in both cases, and one ended up in the other. They were appropriately sealed, there's no cross-contamination, it was just pure human error.'

Because Mark and I were due on air, Kerri Ritchie raced off to the press conference to ask the question …

'As you know, there is a Catholic priest on the suspect list. Can you assure the family, who might be fearful—you know, the Catholic Church, very powerful—that there could've been some sort of influence, that this might've been a deliberate act by someone?'

'Oh no, this is not—this is a human error, it's got nothing

to do with the Catholic Church or any other.'

I watch Mark James. He's not convinced. I bustle him from one interview to the next. First, live on the ABC News Breakfast couch, with presenter Michael Rowland. Mark once told me he always gets stressed during interviews about his mum, because he's desperate to get it right, to be eloquent, to hit a nerve within whoever knows something but isn't coming forward. In the past, we've always had a debrief in which I've reassured him that he did great. This time, as he walks out of the TV studio, that worried look is gone. He knows he nailed it. Perfect priming, really, for his hallway encounter.

He bumps into the deputy commissioner, Shane Patton, who's filling in for his boss for the chief commissioner's monthly radio slot with Jon Faine. Mark tells the deputy commissioner that he wants his mum's exhibits re-tested. That he wants an assurance they'll be kept safe. And that if police don't find any male blood, serious probity questions will be asked. The deputy commissioner's minder shuffles beside him a little uncomfortably. I usually try to intervene in such encounters. They're awkward, and the ambushed party is often caught too off-guard to offer any solace anyway. But this time, I let Mark go. This is his moment. He's calm, determined, and unfazed by the power imbalance. Maria, you would've been so proud.

Thirteen hours of media interviews and news reports later, I'm home, surveying neglect. Three days' worth of dirty dishes are piled in the kitchen, and there's a sandwich crust in a takeaway box in my bathroom sink. Outside are the withered brown ghosts of geraniums, basil, and lavender. The yucca is the only thing that's fought on through, but even it's yellowing. It all reminds me of the final scene in the TV series *The Fall*. The protagonist, Gillian Armstrong, wins—well, kind of. She nabs the serial killer, but he's shot dead in the series' crescendo. So, as she cradles a chilled white wine back in her empty apartment, with unopened mail piled at her door, the viewer, through her empty stare, is left wondering whether it was all worth it. I know it's just a TV show, but I wonder if that's how detectives feel in the wake of big cases, when they return to their lives.

Then the tears come. A lot have been shed this past year, but these are the first proud ones. We did it. The idea that some people initially said 'wouldn't work' has helped unearth a DNA blunder and maybe, just maybe, will inspire the coroner to have another look at all this. Yes, I've devoted more time to the life of a woman I never met than I have to my own, but we did it. *Trace* is out there in the world, with a power that none of us fully realise.

Part IV
The Wait

July 2017

— Text from Kerri Ritchie to Rachael Brown and Jeremy Story Carter, 13 July 2017

Kerri Ritchie is not usually one to cry wolf, so her text message suggests this is big. When Mark James and I walked out of Jon Faine's studio, and bumped into Shane Patton, that goldmine of a talkback line was flashing red again, waiting for us, so Kerri took the call.

'Just when we thought things couldn't get any weirder,' she says, as Jeremy Story Carter and I plonk ourselves down in an alcove at the top of the stairs.

'This book dealer, "Chris", says he had this sweet deal with removalist companies back in the day—and that he might still have books from Maria's shop with blood on them.'

What the hell? I have so many questions. How on earth was Chris allowed into the crime scene? And why would he take books with blood on them? And keep them? Something

235

feels off. When I tell Ron Iddles, he sounds sceptical, and his tone suggests we should be careful. This is from the guy who had no problems with me rocking up on the doorstep of a former gangster who'd done jail time for being an accessory to murder. Maybe we do need to be more cautious about the leads that are coming in. Because, with *Trace*'s momentum, I guess now is the risky time when people might start trying to insert themselves into the investigation, trying to be part of something—or, worse, trying to shut us up. But when I do a Google search of this guy's name, the articles I find suggest his story might be legit. Odd, but legit. So I call him. And that's when things get even stranger.

'When I heard your program, it jogged my memory,' he says.

I ask Chris how he managed to sneak into the crime scene. 'No, I went in in 1997,' he tells me. So this was 17 years *after* Maria James's murder. Had the bookshop been empty all that time? He describes a particular wardrobe.

'I just remember seeing flecks of things across the edging of the front of the wardrobe.' He says it looked like dried blood. 'There definitely were books which I think had blood on them, too.'

The loot he took home included weird sci-fi horror comics with pop-pulp covers for his son, and fashion magazines for his wife.

'There was one particular book that she didn't want in the house anymore because it did seem to have a splotch across it. It was one of the fashiony books. She said, "Let's get rid of that." And I just wonder about the other comics we may still have in a box somewhere; if there's a splotch or a splatter, could that be any help?'

It might be, given that the DNA bungle has left cops

without a sample from the killer. The chances are, if these were Maria's books, and if the blood was from the attack, it's most likely her blood. But there's also a very slim chance that the pages could hold blood specks from her killer. And a slim chance is better than nothing at the moment. I'm still confused, though, why bloodied books would be inside 736 High Street, 17 years on.

'It's common in deceased estates where somebody will be a bit of a hoarder, or maybe they have no close relationships with family. Or maybe they don't even die—maybe they go into a nursing home, and the books have been there for 10, 15 years. It's not uncommon.'

In the days following this chat with Chris, I dig into the land title records of 736 High Street. From what I can gather, when Chris rummaged through it in 1997 it was owned by a Ms Pond, who Chris thinks was moving into a nursing home. Maybe when she first bought the place she'd never bothered to clear away all the books? And when Ms Pond moved on, it appears the next owner was a Melbourne restaurateur. At least he was easy to track down. He tells me he remembers seeing dull smudges that looked like blood on a wardrobe and a wall when he lived there. So maybe the existence of remnants of Maria's murder, 17 years on, isn't as strange as it sounds. I call Dadna Hartman from VIFM, who I now have on speed dial, to check if blood found on paper would be testable for DNA after 37 years. Would it be as useful as fabric?

'It's certainly a possibility. Biological material can survive on things like paper—once a bloodstain has dried on a piece of paper, it can be stored at room temperature for many years. I mean, we store a lot of our samples on what we call FTA paper, because it's a good substrate to keep biological material such as blood on, and store it indefinitely.

I guess the biggest issue, or concern, would be the issue of contamination. Because I guess, ultimately, you've got to be able to reassure yourself that someone hasn't tampered with those books and deposited other material on them. The chain of custody is quite crucial. So, depending on the age of the blood, how long it's been there, and the amount, all those things start to go against being able to get good-quality DNA. But if there's enough material there, there's no reason why you wouldn't be hopeful of getting a nuclear DNA profile, even if it's a partial profile.'

If police fail to find a male DNA sample in the re-testing of Maria's exhibits, maybe evidence like this, and the O'Keeffe sample I'm keeping safe, could be valuable.

July 2017

I can't exclude the possibility that in the past a conspiracy has occurred.

— Mark James's phone call to Rachael Brown, 16 July 2017

If you had asked me a month ago, 'Cock-up or conspiracy?' my money would have been on the former. Yes, it's incredibly convenient that Homicide detectives who should have been looking at a priest, among others, were led down the garden path by a rogue pillow. But think about this. If someone from the Catholic Church, or an officer acting on its behalf, wanted to plant this decoy, they would need access to the forensics storage room, opportunity, and specific exhibit reference numbers. They'd also need foresight into just how powerful DNA technology would become. And they'd need insurance; it wouldn't be enough to plant the pillow, surely, because what about Maria James's stained exhibits? They could hold traces of the killer's DNA. So these bloodied clues would have to be taken out of the equation. Last month, I would have said that it's far more likely this was a cock-up. Moronic, yes, but an innocent mistake all the same. Now, I'm not so sure.

Not only was something added to Maria James's exhibits, but something potentially invaluable was removed—her bloodstained quilt. A detective has just called Mark James to kindly keep him in the loop, but now Mark is even more confused. He tells me that the rogue pillow was found in an evidence bag labelled 'quilt'.

And now, that quilt is missing.

'The bag was part of Mum's exhibits. It was labelled as 'Maria James bloodstained quilt', or something of that nature, and somehow the quilt has been taken out of that bag, and this pillow from another case altogether has been substituted in that bag.'

Mark is finding it harder to accept that this was all 'just an accident'.

'This DNA bungle-up, well, what if it was deliberate? And what if all the killer's blood, that was all over the place, apparently, what if all those exhibits have gone missing? I might never have an answer.'

I'm presuming this is the same quilt I saw that day while I was flicking through the crime-scene photos with Ron Iddles. Maria's floral bedspread had new dark blooms on the bottom left-hand side, which looked to be bloodstains. Now that photograph might be the only evidence it ever existed.

'Victoria Police at this stage appear to have lost it—they don't know where the quilt is. They've told me one theory, that because of OH&S concerns, the quilt may have been destroyed because of something to do with mouldy blood on exhibits.'

Mark is referring to the property-office relocation in 1994, when evidence in up to 40 cold cases was destroyed. But if cops can be so sure about where the rogue pillow is from—a 1975 murder case, apparently—why aren't their records as meticulous for Maria James?

'I would've thought,' Mark says, 'that if exhibits were destroyed, there'd be some records. As part of OH&S procedures, one would think there'd be traceability, even if it was just a simple note on the file, or something like that.'

'Have you been given any reassurance that the two pillowcases belonging to your mum are still in the exhibits bag?'

'Ah, no. No, I haven't been given any reassurance of that at all.'

I submit another list of questions to Victoria Police. Again, I get no satisfying answer. This time, it says that, while it is re-examining Maria James's exhibits, it would be inappropriate to comment. While I respect this, as open cases have to be handled with sensitivity, I can also understand how this strange series of events, and the accompanying deafening silence, is only fuelling Mark James's suspicions about a past conspiracy.

'If someone had asked me if that could happen today, my answer would be definitely no. But in the past the Catholic Church has been accused of covering things up, so I can't exclude the possibility that there was some type of a cover-up.'

1998

A TV show re-enacting Maria James's murder calls for new information from the public, and clues flow in that could hopefully revive the 18-year-old cold case:

> Several people rang Crime Stoppers and suggested Father Bongiorno knew something about the murder. The then Premier, Jeff Kennett, received written information in 1998 that nominated Father Bongiorno as a child molester. Mr Kennett passed the letter, which contained a photograph of Father Bongiorno, to police. That helped prompt police to speak to Father Bongiorno again about the Maria James murder. He came into the Homicide offices and appeared more helpful this time. (*Herald Sun*)

While the priest is less hostile than he was in 1980, his line hasn't changed. He doesn't know the identity of the killer, and he won't be drawn on whether he's heard whispers about it in the confessional. He does, however, lob in a bizarre accusation. Father Bongiorno suggests a possible murder motive might have had something to do with Maria working as a prostitute from the back of her bookshop. While some detectives think this might explain the lock on the back of her bedroom door, the barb contradicts everything they've learned about Maria's character and her morals. They check it out anyway, just to be sure, but don't find anything to support Father Bongiorno's claim.

For some reason, Ron Iddles isn't told that his squad has called in the priest. When he finds out about it later, he thinks the 'prostitute' angle is odd. In his whole time working this case, he's never heard anything of the sort. Then again, it's not the first time the priest has spoken ill of Maria James. In hindsight, this will make sense, cementing Ron's belief that attack is the best form of defence.

July 2017

> I am seeking information about the record of interview/meeting (typed transcript and/or audio and/or video) of the August 1998 interview/meeting conducted by Homicide Detective Sergeant ___, with Father Anthony Bongiorno, regarding the 1980 murder of Maria James

— Request lodged with Victoria Police's Freedom of Information Office, 12 February 2017

Let's consider the theory that the rogue pillow was planted to eliminate any trace of Father Bongiorno's involvement in Maria James's murder. One mental block for me is this: the priest didn't become a key suspect until Adam James's bombshell in 2013. So, *before* 2001—when Ron Iddles referred all the exhibits to Victoria Police's forensics lab for DNA testing—there would be no impetus for anyone to tamper with evidence possibly incriminating him. Right?

But just after Mark James stuns me with the news that the bloodied quilt—surely one of the most crucial exhibits—is missing, he tells me that the priest was in detectives' sights much earlier than I thought.

'I recall being called into the Homicide Squad. It was

August '98. I learned, apparently just before *I'd* been in there, Father Bongiorno was called into the Homicide Squad and also interviewed by Detective ___.'

Remember, by that stage, Father Bongiorno had been committed to stand trial for the abuse of three boys; acquitted; and then named and shamed by a Victorian crimes compensation tribunal.

'They wanted to know, now that Bongiorno had been exposed as a paedophile, would he be prepared to divulge any information that might've come out in the confessional. And Father Bongiorno didn't co-operate with that.'

I ask about the valuable opportunity that was seemingly squandered.

'The next obvious question is why, back then, did detectives not ask you and Adam, given Bongiorno's history, whether you'd ever been assaulted by Bongiorno?'

'I can't understand why Adam or myself weren't asked if we were his victims, because that would provide a potential motive.'

This all gives me pause for thought. Until recent times, priests have been considered demi-gods, capable of no wrong—not paedophilia, and certainly not murder. But I don't know. Would or even *could* the Catholic Church have interfered in this investigation?

Swoosh, swoosh. Cock-up? Swoosh, swoosh. Conspiracy? Swoosh, swoosh. A cock-up is more likely; a conspiracy *is* possible. Pffftttt. I don't think any amount of running is going to help me muddle my way through this one. I have even more questions than I started with when this project was solely about a murder, before things got really dark. Did cops call in Father Bongiorno in 1998 just for an update, or was he a suspect back then? And if he was a suspect, why the hell didn't the interviewing detective raise the very question that was screaming to be asked. I phoned this detective, but he can't even remember the interview, let alone the things that *weren't* said. Problem #756, when it comes to investigating decades-old cases, is that you're never going to know if vagueness is just a sign of a fading memory, or obfuscation.

Swoosh, swoosh, swoosh, swoosh. At no point has this investigation just coasted. Every single facet has been a slog, although potentially navigable with enough time and patience. But for the answers I *now* need, I think I'd need to own a badge or a Roman collar to draw them out. Like, when *exactly* was the foreign pillow bagged with Maria James's exhibits? Because the longer it was after 1994, the higher the odds it was a deliberate cover-up. Then again, I've heard that the rogue pillow and Maria's exhibits bag had similar reference numbers, so it is feasible an officer thought they belonged together. Yet, if bloodied exhibits were destroyed after 1994 because of biohazard risks, why would Maria's quilt be thrown out, but not this other pillow, from a 1975 homicide? And what about that case — has the missing pillow affected its closure?

Swoosh, swoosh, swoosh, swoosh. Could someone from the Church, or someone acting on its behalf, have snuck into the exhibits room? Some listeners have emailed saying that Father Bongiorno had powerful connections. Is this true? And in my research on Church sexual abuses, I've come across stories about victims' medical records being mysteriously deleted. How far do the Church's tentacles stretch? Many listeners have suggested I speak to one man who had his career destroyed by the Church's reach. Maybe it's time.

August 2017

> I can't help but think about the Casefile podcast, #34: The
> Catholic Mafia. You might like to listen to that.

Listener email to the Trace account, 16 July 2017

I read a quote recently, that asked, 'What if the word "victim" could be redefined into something closer to "hero", recognising that the path some have tread will spare others from the same?' This quote made me think of former detective Denis Ryan. Sex-abuse survivors aren't the only people the Church has reduced to broken shells. Whistleblowers, too, have had their lives irrevocably changed. Sitting at the top of the list of shattered careers is Denis Ryan's. I know a little about him. He'll go down in Victorian folk law as being the cop who forced the state to face up to the existence of a group within its police force colloquially known as the Catholic Mafia. But I've never met him. And I'd like his take on the DNA bungle. Was it a concerted conspiracy or innocent mistake?

There's ample reading time on the eight-hour train/ bus combo up to Mildura, 550 kilometres north-west of Melbourne, up on the Murray River border that divides Victoria from New South Wales. Swathes of iridescent yellow canola flash by, and in the seats in front, two girls in their early twenties debate whether Craig wants to be *more* than just friends.

'Nah, he was only interested in my tattoo,' says girl #1.

'Which one?' inquires #2.

'This one.' #1 points near her groin.

'Pfffft. Yeah, right,' is #2's expert opinion.

#1 shakes her head, 'Anyway, he has a girlfriend—it's serious, it's been *two* months now.'

Denis Ryan's decision to try to out a paedophile priest in the close-knit town of Mildura has cost him 45 years of ostracism by two communities he adored: the Victorian police force and the Mildura township. All because he thought he was doing the right thing. A profile piece in *The Age* penned by crime journalist John Silvester nails what it really means to be brave:

> In policing there are two types of courage. There is the instinctive act of physical bravery and the moral type that requires the strength of character to uphold the law when pressured to compromise ... He refused to buckle when his bosses wanted him to ignore a paedophile priest and then was hounded from the job in a conspiracy that many believe went all the way to the Chief Commissioner's office. (12 August 2016)

I meet my *Trace* colleague Jeremy Story Carter in the Mildura township, and we make our way to Denis's house armed with an orange rough cake, my late nan's favourite. 'Cake calls for tea,' says Denis, and he pads into his kitchen, past a picture of the Virgin Mary with baby Jesus. It's one of those with gold-leaf paint. Like so many people interviewed for this investigation, it seems that the Church and a person's faith are two separate things, and a burn by the former doesn't necessarily mean a dent in the latter. When I point out the painting later, Denis will tell me he's still a Catholic; he just doesn't go to mass anymore.

Denis Ryan is 85 years old, and has a fragile frame and

a warm chuckle. As he lifts three mugs from a shelf, I realise the cake is more trouble than it's worth. Denis doesn't own a kettle, so he slowly fills the mugs with water and shuffles them one by one across the kitchen lino over to the microwave. Forty seconds later, *Ding*. Next. There's something about the way he carefully heats each mug that hurts to watch. This is the man who had the gumption to take on two of the state's most powerful institutions, and they crushed him. Now, simply making tea in his rented flat is an effort. I ask where the plates are for cake. 'I won't have a slice,' Denis says. 'I don't eat sugar anymore.'

After the failed icebreaker, we move into the comfy chairs. 'The Catholic Mafia was a group of die-hard Catholics that unfortunately gave their allegiance to the Catholic cathedral, not to what they were sworn in to do—their loyalty was meant to be to the people of Victoria.' It was back in 1956, on patrol in Melbourne's red-light district of St Kilda, when Denis Ryan met the man who'd haunt his entire career: Father John Day.

'I was on the divisional van, night duty, and we stopped a car entering the old St Kilda Junction. There was a prostitute driving, and another on the other side, and lying across them was a man with his pants pulled down around his ankles, and there was an empty sherry bottle on the floor. The person lying prostrate across the two prostitutes was wearing a Roman collar. One of the prostitutes said, "Oh, he's a regular customer of ours. He allows us to drive his car."'

At the time, such consorting was a criminal offence. Denis was a staunch Catholic. But, for him, like Ron Iddles, black and white have never bled into other shades, so he took Father Day to the police station. Senior officers promptly let the priest go.

'My sergeant, Tom Jenkins, rang the cathedral, and two priests came down and took him away. I asked Tom Jenkins why wasn't he charged, and he said, "You don't charge a priest short of murder. If you do, you'd be ostracised in the police force."'

'Did you challenge that at the time?'

'Oh yes, that rather startled me, really, because irrespective of what denomination they were, if they committed an offence, then they were entitled to be charged.'

'How was this philosophy rationalised? That anything short of murder, priests should walk?'

'Well, I didn't have much more to do with priests, other than at Mordialloc. The priest there was an Irishman by the name of Jim English, and we talked, and he told me of a priest or a brother who'd exposed himself down on the Chelsea beach, and he told me, "Denis, don't ever let a priest go if he's caught like that." So that was the last time, until I was with a group of senior police at O'Connors Hotel in Melbourne, and that's when I was asked by Fred Russell would I like to join this certain group of theirs, and I said I'd give it time [to think] first. And I thought about it, and I later met him and told him no, I wasn't interested.'

'What kind of group was it?'

'Only to look after priests if they got into some form of trouble, and I well believed that trouble would've been DUI or offensive behaviour, or other types of street offences. I had no idea that it would reach the stage which eventually occurred in my time in the police force.'

Welcome to the Catholic Mafia: a secretive cartel with very long and poisonous tentacles.

'How did it exert its influence? Through threats and violence, or was it far more subtle?'

'No, it was extremely subtle. It was there to assist priests who had misbehaved themselves.'

Six years later, in 1962, Denis's path would again cross with John Day's, who was now a monsignor. Denis accepted a detective position in Mildura. His son, Michael, had asthma, and doctors thought his lungs would appreciate the drier climate. On Denis's first day, meeting the locals, guess who the Mildura parish priest turned out to be?

In 1971, Denis learned that the priest had switched his appetite from hookers to children. The vice-principal at St Joseph's College told Denis that Monsignor Day had molested a female student, adding that Denis shouldn't tell his boss, detective sergeant Jim Barritt, who was apparently part of the Catholic Mafia. Denis started investigating, and found that there were a dozen boys and girls who'd been molested.

'The offences were not just groping and indecent assault, which was bad enough, but buggery and gross indecency on young children. I took 12 statements, and I could have taken 100.'

Yet it was all swept under the carpet. Denis presented his findings to the district's most senior officer, Swan Hill-based superintendent, Jack McPartland, and requested help with the complex inquiry, explaining why Detective Sergeant Barritt should not be involved. Denis was told he'd breached the chain of command and that he should drop the case.

'They failed to investigate; they failed to do their duty, which they're sworn to do; they conspired. What they did was criminal. First I was shocked, then I became extremely disgusted that this could occur, and I was so disappointed in my fellow policemen to think they were part of this vast conspiracy. And it went further than that. It went to the commissioner of police, who was not a Catholic, but at that time an election was occurring, and the Liberal coalition were in some sort of trouble, and if this came out it wouldn't have helped them very much at all. It was a major conspiracy, and it engulfed the police force from the highest-ranking officer down. From the chief commissioner, Reg Jackson, to former assistant commissioner Jack O'Connor, to former superintendent and CIB head Fred Russell, to former commander Frank Holland, and I can't go on with all the names.'

Denis refused to budge, and senior police grudgingly compiled a report that found 'insufficient evidence' with which to charge Monsignor Day, who would elude justice until his death in 1978. The matter was chalked up to a 'personality clash between two headstrong detectives'. Detective sergeant Barritt was transferred to Echuca, and Denis was ordered back to Melbourne—a move that senior police knew he couldn't make because of his son's health, forcing Denis's resignation.

John Silvester wrote, 'They'd rid themselves of the honest cop and protected the cover-up artist.' And as is all too common, as the professional life crumbles, so does the personal.

'I committed the unforgivable sin of taking my work during this crisis home to my wife, who had been a victim of a guardian, and I think that started her off and she became an alcoholic. It got to the stage where she left me and we were divorced, and she died a short time later of cirrhosis of the liver.'

Denis has more recently lost his second wife to brain cancer.

'And what about your boys? Did they respect what you were trying to do?'

'Yes, they did, but without a doubt it damaged them to some degree.'

Denis takes a hanky from the pocket of his trousers and dabs under his glasses at the inner corners of his eyes. On top of losing his colleagues, half of the Mildura community turned its back on him, too.

'I've had a local chemist rush out of his shop and challenge me to a fight because of what I'd done. Well, I stood back and laughed, because I don't think he could've beaten a paper bag.' Denis laughs, still clutching the hanky. 'He turned out to be a good fella—he finally saw that I was right.'

'It'll be stone cold,' I point at the tea that Denis has not once reached for as he's steered himself through all the questions, all the memories. But he has no regrets. He'd suffer it all again, in a heartbeat.

'Of course I would. You can't have children buggered and offences committed on them, most disgusting. It was something that any person, in my opinion, should have done. To allow a depraved paedophile like Day to do what he did is unforgivable. Nah, I'd do it again without a doubt. I wouldn't even think about it.'

'A lot didn't. You put yourself on the line; you put yourself out there.'

'Well, that's on their conscience, not mine.'

Denis finally found an ally in former chief commissioner Mick Miller, who read *Unholy Trinity* by Denis Ryan and Peter Hoysted in 2013, and married the book's events with conversations he remembered from the 1970s and his knowledge of the structure of the police force. In 2015, Miller told the Royal Commission into Institutional Responses to Child Sexual Abuse that Victoria's 15th police chief commissioner, Reg Jackson, had become corrupted by undue influence:

It is my opinion that the Chief Commissioner Reg Jackson was the architect of Victoria Police's response to Denis Ryan's investigations into Monsignor Day. It couldn't have operated in the manner it did without his knowledge and consent. The book documents ... misconduct by senior Victoria Police officers, including dereliction of duty, conspiracy to pervert the course of justice and inciting other members of the police force to join the conspiracy against Denis Ryan in order to conceal the crimes committed by Day.

He recommended to the commission that Mr Ryan be compensated for this 'shameful event in the history of Victoria Police'.

An apology finally came in 2016, with just a few words and a handshake behind closed doors. Only one journalist was allowed in.

'Look, what [chief commissioner Graham] Ashton did I appreciate, but the apology was more or less in-camera—a dozen people there, that's it. The apology ought to have been one that was public, on the air, for any reporter who wanted to be there to ask questions—that's what I call an apology—so the people of Mildura could see it on TV. So John Silvester was there, and he put a nice piece in the paper. I had my speech, and I read that out, and that didn't say I was pleased with them. And then as to my compensation, the Police Association had hired an actuary to work out how much money I'd lost by being forced out of the police force, which they all accepted, and it came to $3.1m. Now they said, "you wouldn't get that, you'll get half of it," and so it went on, and they gave me $90,000.'

Denis Ryan's is one of the best case studies of the toxic fallout that can follow wilful blindness. *They failed to investigate; they failed to do their duty.* So he knows what officers protective of their secular interests are capable of. But that doesn't mean it always happened. Denis's career was cut short—he left the force eight years before Maria James was murdered—so he doesn't know the case well. But I'm keen to get his take on whether the Catholic Mafia's CV *could* have extended to protecting a murderer.

'Do you think the group protecting priests at the time would've been prepared to protect a priest who might've been responsible for more than paedophilia?'

'I don't believe they would try to collaborate to such an extent as to cause a conspiracy in the case of murder. But I am a victim of what they can do, and they certainly can do it in the most heinous of all crimes.'

I run Denis through what I've discovered: Adam's abuse by Fathers Bongiorno and O'Keeffe, and Maria's plan to confront the parish the day she was murdered. But, to Denis's credit, he's not a man to speculate.

'I can't comment on something when the only thing I know about it is what I read or saw on the TV, and what you've told me. It would be wrong of me to make a comment.'

'I respect that, but given the evil you've seen within the Catholic Church, for a very long time it was thought priests couldn't be capable of paedophilia, and sadly now we know differently. Do you think a priest could be capable of murder?'

'Yes, anyone can be capable of murder, irrespective.'

I have absolutely no proof that the Church has in any way influenced this murder investigation. Even throwing the missing quilt into the mix, if you ask Ron Iddles what he thinks, 'Conspiracy or cock-up?' his answer is the latter. But I tell Denis I've been wondering if it's a theory that's at least worth *consideration.*

'The quilt that's missing had blood on it, possibly the killer's blood. Would that strike you as suspicious?'

'Rachael, as I said earlier, it would be wrong of me to make a statement in relation to this offence. I wasn't there. I know nothing about it other than what I read.'

'It strikes me as strange that something from one case could end up in a bag of another case … or do I take the police's word that it was an innocent mistake, and stop asking questions?'

'As you well know, anything is possible. Whether it happens or not, I don't know. I think you're entitled to go ahead with your investigation, and I congratulate you on it.'

As we leave for the long trip home, he wishes us luck, with a slight twinkle in his eye that suggests the fight will never really leave Denis Ryan.

August 2017

> I'm looking at this podcast really as a final chance to get an answer. In fact, I think that if this podcast doesn't succeed, it's never going to be solved.

— Mark James's thanks to Rachael Brown and the *Trace* team, interview on 26 May 2017

Tunnel vision can cripple a police investigation, and journalists can't afford to have it either. I've concentrated on Fathers Bongiorno and O'Keeffe because they have the strongest motives we've managed to find so far. The *Trace* team's central question became, 'Was Maria James murdered to cover up the sexual abuse of her son?' But, remember, I haven't been allowed anywhere near those ten cold-case boxes. There could be evidence in them that points to other suspects, with equally compelling motives. As I stress in the podcast, should criminal charges be laid against someone, I'd hate for any prior sustained focus on other suspects to be seized upon by a defence lawyer as an exculpatory reason why their client should walk. So let's look at everyone who's back in the frame.

Mark James tells me police are now focussing their efforts on a small group.

'They've told me, in addition to Bongiorno, they've termed what they call the top five.'

I'm guessing that this top five includes the local loner, Mario, who had twine in his backyard and possibly bloodied trousers. He'd given a DNA sample, which is now redundant, and I've had word that he's since died. So if police need a new DNA sample, it'll have to come from a relative.

I'm unsure if Peter, the real-estate-agent lover is back in the frame, given he had an alibi. Muddying the waters are the security guard, Frank Todd, and the 5.00am man—but I doubt they were ever considered solid suspects.

As for the Telecom worker, police told Mark he'd been involved in other crimes.

'They said he had been found in Queensland to have sexually assaulted two females, and he had, I understand, some twine and a knife in his car.'

A *Herald Sun* article by Keith Moor reports that this man picked up two female hitchhikers in Queensland, a month and a half after Maria's murder, and tried to rape them at gunpoint. The women wrestled the gun from him and managed to escape. Police searched his car and reportedly found rifles, handcuffs, nylon cord, tape, and a knife similar to the one missing from Maria James's kitchen.

Apparently, Jeanette Hodson, the driver who nearly crashed into the white-shirted sprinter, was flown up to Queensland for a police line-up. The story goes that she picked out the Telecom worker, who does look a little like the 9:10am face-fit issued by police. However, there are two problems with this. One, Ron Iddles is adamant that this is a different Telecom worker from the one who committed suicide a few months after Homicide detectives interviewed him. Two, Jeanette Hodson apparently also picked Peter, the real estate agent, out of a line-up, throwing her reliability as a witness into question.

And then there's the late Peter Keogh, a convicted killer. Mark James thinks he's also back on the list of suspects, so I'm keen to meet with Phil Cleary, who inspired Ron Iddles to get a sample of Keogh's DNA before his cremation. When I pay Phil a visit, it's nearly 30 years to the day since Keogh killed his sister, Vicki, outside a Coburg kindergarten. While I haven't been allowed anywhere near Maria James's file, Phil Cleary says that years ago he spent days poring over it, to check for signs of Keogh's possible involvement.

'High Street was his [Keogh's] patch. He knew it like the back of his hand; he drank at the Junction Hotel. I was told by an old crim who did time in Pentridge that he [Keogh] worked as a butcher, not far up from the bookshop, and he was identified as the boyfriend, or, in the vernacular, "She was his missus."'

Butcher. Why does this stir something in a back drawer of my memory? Michelle O__, that's right. She was charged with falsifying a story about Maria having a relationship with a Mordialloc butcher who was into kinky sex. Maybe she *was* telling the truth? Then again, Mordialloc is a very long way from Thornbury. While I'm musing about this, Phil Clearly ploughs on, telling me that Keogh's psychotherapist suspected him of Maria's murder, and in order not to breach patient/client confidentiality, she asked a colleague to tell the police that they should question him. Phil says the police failed to properly follow up on this, as well as on a 1982 Crime Stoppers call about Keogh.

'The police did not do their job properly. We should reflect on how it is that women get murdered in such a way, and we don't find the killers. The Easey Street murders, only a handful of years earlier—astounding. I think it raises bigger questions about violence against women and the inadequacy of our society's response historically.'

Phil thinks his sister would still be alive had police fixed their sights on Keogh.

'It would've made it onto the grapevine, no doubt. In the northern suburbs, word travels, you know, and in those days it did travel. So when my sister said, "Oh, I've met a bloke, Peter Keogh", the word would've been out.'

The most intriguing thing that Phil tells me is this, a story he's heard second-hand from a source he, annoyingly, won't name.

'Keogh said to someone, "I killed Maria James." I think it was said in a skiting moment, and was said to frighten someone, which doesn't mean he was telling the truth—he may've just been using it because he knew the person knew of the bookshop. But I am told reliably that Keogh said, "I will do to you what I did to the woman in the bookshop."'

I press Phil for his source, but he asks if I'd ever reveal *my* sources. Touché. So I can't corroborate this.

'Can police relook at him … do they still have the DNA they took?'

'I don't know. I had to pressure the police to take his DNA—they took it off the corpse.'

'Does Keogh have any relatives—living siblings, or nieces or nephews? That could be another way to get DNA.'

'Yes, he does. He has sisters, so we would hope they'd be happy to pass on their DNA, wouldn't we?'

An obvious problem, though, is that no clear connection was ever proven between Keogh and Maria. There's an absence of a little thing called motive.

We're back to exactly where we started. With *everyone* in the frame. With more questions about the Church's reach and how it wields power. With suspicion hanging over how a rogue pillow danced its way across a shelf, sending officers on a 16-year wild-goose chase.

I meet Ron Iddles and his wife, Colleen, for dinner at the Termo pub in Richmond, near the biscuit factory where he used to live as a young cop, in the streets that feature in his recurring nightmare. They're a good match. She's warm, funny, and feisty, and the way he speaks of her is how we all wish to be spoken of: adored, respected, and appreciated for carrying what she did, which allowed him to keep doing what he did best. I get the sense the long coach trips still sting, those times when Ron finally got a break from the murders and chose to hit the highway to nurse his mind instead of spending more time with his family. But we pick our poison, don't we? And Colleen used to be a psychiatric nurse, so she's seen it all, too. And heard it all.

Ron called her once, to apologise for having to miss dinner. His crew had found a decapitated body in a bath, but they couldn't find the head. 'A head's heavy,' replied Colleen very matter-of-factly. 'It won't be far. Have you checked the toilet?' Ron flipped up the toilet lid he'd been standing near. Sure enough, it was there. 'I'll be home after all,' said Ron. The things they must've weathered, thanks to each other and their dark humour. She was the constant for their three children all those times he got dragged away and he had the self-described honour of investigating the death of Victorians. Now they're enjoying a quieter life up north, with more sunshine and more sleep.

Ron's reply when I tell him over a chicken parma about the missing bloodied quilt isn't what I'm expecting. Through a resigned sigh, I hear, 'Maybe time to let it go?'

'What, you?' I ask, shocked, given that Ron matches me in the stubbornness stakes.

'And you,' he replies softly.

7 September 2017: Episode 5

At the end of Episode 5, just as in Episode 4, I explain there are things that need to happen now, which I simply cannot do, nor can I rush the only people who *can* do them:

> This investigation has taken on a life of its own, and we have to wait and see if the coroner decides to reopen Maria's case, or if Victoria Police finds a trace of the killer's DNA. When they do, we'll bring you an update. So to everyone who's called or emailed, thank you, the *Trace* team is grateful for your leads, and Mark and Adam James are blown away by your support.

Listener leads keep flowing in. And more people reach out to me, saying that they too have been the victim of church abuses. But for the institutional responses I'm after it's a matter of hurry up and wait. Wait, especially, for the coroner to decide whether to hold a new inquest. Mark James wants one for transparency, if nothing else.

'There are just too many suss things going on here, you know—DNA bungle-ups, evidence going missing, "Not sure if it's been destroyed", being told different stories about what happened with those exhibits. These are the types of things that I want the coroner to get to the bottom of.'

But his gut feeling, like Ron Iddles', is a stubborn one.

'You have witnesses that put Bongiorno at the scene of the crime before the murder, and after the murder covered in blood. I mean, what more do you want? Do you want a film of him doing it, or something?'

Victoria Police is re-testing Maria James's exhibits, hoping to find a new DNA profile of her killer. If it does, it could then test that against the curious collection of DNA I'm accruing—a bloodied book and Father O'Keeffe's twin brother's ___.

Adam James has given his police statement about Father O'Keeffe, and hopes his story helps bring some clarity.

'We've been hanging on, waiting for a long time for this, and I think coming here talking with you, I think it's going to bring a lot of perspective.'

One beautiful thing to come out of this mess is that the James brothers don't feel as alone anymore. Mark tells me he's been moved by the number of strangers, including police officers, who've approached him, when he's out shopping.

'Comments like "We're all behind you", "Good luck", "Keep at it", "Don't give up" have been personally touching, and emotional for me.'

Mark's old school mates have reached out, wanting to reconnect. And a former teacher of Adam's emails me, asking to be put in touch with him:

> I always had the utmost respect for his desire to 'be liked and wanted' but of course I never had any idea of what he had gone through.

Some podcast listeners, however, are a different story. The iTunes reviews that used to buoy me are now peppered with some that taunt:

> Where's the story gone … ? Waiting!

> Don't hold your breath for upcoming episodes, sheesh

Maybe I should have stressed more often that the research for the first four episodes took me 16 months?

> Great podcast. Only downside is the delay between casts. There's been no further episodes for months. It just stopped. No explanation. Considering the media coverage when this first came out. I really thought we would hear more about finally solving this case, As a podcast it's one that's been left half finished.

Nazza82, I'd *love* to be able to bring you that update. But this is not a show, folks. This is someone's death. And I can't invent an ending—it's real-life nonfiction. I want to scream, 'Imagine how the James boys feel?'

After the brothers, there is no one more desperate than me to see this case finally solved. Well, maybe there's one person more desperate. Ron Iddles cannot wait for that moment when he can call Mark, one last time. 'I'd go and visit him, and we'd probably have a big hug and sit down and have a drink. Yeah, it would be a magic moment.'

As for the *Trace* team, my producer, Tim Roxburgh, now has a baby girl. The podcast wins a Walkley Award. And we enjoy a little bit of light for a few weeks. Until we hear the devastating news that our series producer, Jesse Cox, has been fighting his own demons, but has kept mum about it. I learn he has a form of rare soft-tissue cancer, alveolar soft part sarcoma, in an email from Sophie Townsend—who placed me and my investigation in his trusty hands in the first place. Her email says that Jesse has suffered a seizure, caused by a brain-tumour bleed, and he's intubated.

I have to read it twice. This can't be my Jesse? Then the guilt sets in. For not knowing. For not asking why his beard looked white at the Walkleys. For bugging the shit out of him this year, calling at all hours, and on weekends, stealing him away from his wife, Que, and their two-year-old son, Alfie. For all the creative tussles. But then, there were way more laughs, through every edit waltz. And he looked so bloody proud on stage accepting the Walkley Award—proud that we'd managed to knock this podcast, which had early wobbles, out of the park. There's a photograph I love, of us in our finery before we climb the stage stairs: I've just whispered, 'We did it!'

The next email from Sophie ends the breath we've all been holding. She has said goodbye to Jesse. From all of us. Because he's not going to make it through. And I lose it. I sit outside during a Melbourne thunderstorm, farewelling another generous genius. He wanted to change the world, and he did. With his tireless enthusiasm, he brought people's creative dreams to life. So much so that, from now on, when producers get stuck, they'll ask 'What would Jesse do?' I can't manage to leave the house for three days. He was 31, for Christ's sake. None of us know the hand that life is going to deal us. And few of us know of the battles that others are fighting.

January 2018

The court may not have jurisdiction to hear your application.

— Letter from the Victorian Coroners Court to Mark James, 16 January 2018

It's been six months since Mark James lodged a Form 43: his request for the coroner to set aside the 1982 finding—that Maria James was murdered by 'a person unknown'—and hold a fresh inquest. He thought it would be a no-brainer, given the new facts and circumstances revealed by *Trace*, but he's heard nothing from the Coroners Court. I learn there's a 'sticking point', but just what that is … is a mystery. Seriously? These brothers have spent enough time in the dark.

Exasperated, I reach out to both the Victorian attorney-general and his shadow counterpart, then ask in an email if they'll help the Jameses achieve some clarity:

As I understand it, such applications (Form 43) are usually determined within three months. The James brothers are calling for a fresh inquest, in the interests of transparency,

to clear up whether the Catholic Church was involved in the
DNA bungle, given two of the murder suspects are priests who
sexually abused Adam James.

A week later, Mark gets his answer, from the State Coroner
of Victoria. And her answer is … 'I don't know.'

[T]he Court may not have jurisdiction to hear your application.
That is because the finding into Maria's death was made under
the Coroners Act 1985 [this should have read 1958], which
was repealed when the 2008 Act came into operation on 1
November 2009.

'If it's not the coroner's job, whose is it?' Mark asks me.'
'No idea,' I sigh. I feel like every time these brothers
get close to answers, the goalposts shift. The coroner's
letter invites Mark to make a submission on this matter at
a directions hearing at the end of the month. This informal
hearing will help chart the case's course. 'At least that's a
lifeline,' I say, trying to keep his hopes up. 'It's better than
your application being quashed entirely.'

But when the directions hearing hits the Coroners Court
list, seven other names are on it as well as Maria James's:
JAMES, M (1980); ABBEY, D (1987); ABBEY, R (1987);
DIAZ, O (1996); JENSEN, G (1988); PRENDERGAST, L
(1989); DAWSON, B (1980); and MCCRYSTAL, M (1997).

Six families in the same boat as Mark, living in the same
holding pattern. How long have they been waiting? Who's
been speaking up for them?

Dorothy and Ramon Abbey were shot at their West
Heidelberg home, while their children were just metres away
in their bedrooms.

Oswaldo Diaz-Lopez was crushed under a car when a hydraulic trolley jack slipped.

Bank robber Graeme Jensen was shot by the armed-robbery squad.

Underworld figure Laurence Joseph Prendergast disappeared and is presumed murdered.

Barbara Dawson's throat was slashed, and her naked body was found wrapped in garbage bags on rocks in shallow water in Altona North.

Mary McCrystal from Maffra suffocated with a toxic volume of drugs and alcohol in her system.

These crude lines tell us nothing about the pain left in their wake. Mary McCrystal, for example: her daughter, Cheriekah Ramirez, has dedicated almost two decades to trying to prove that her mother's death was not suicide, but murder. Cheriekah has studied science, forensic biology, forensic psychology and toxicology, and has undertaken a Bachelor of Criminology so she can find the answers that the authorities have denied her. 'I've run out of doors to knock on,' she tells me, adding she's been so consumed by this she's forgotten to live her own life. And she's become estranged from her siblings because of it. Cheriekah says she's given birth to six children, three since 2014, to make up for lost time, to remind herself of what really matters in life—family.

Then there's Fay Spear. She's the sister of Graeme Jensen, shot dead in his car by the armed-robbery squad in 1988. The fatal bullet was fired by the now-asssistant commissioner of Victoria Police, Robert Hill. Police say they shot him in self-defence, because Jensen was wielding a gun. But no civilian witness saw him with a gun. And Fay Spear now has an affidavit from a former surveillance officer who claims he saw a detective plant a sawn-off rifle in Jensen's car.

Fay Spear says of the affidavit, 'It's a huge deal, it's the first bit of truth that's come out. I lost faith in the system, I guess, and didn't know if anything would happen or not.'

When I visit her one sunny afternoon, she offers me tea and biscuits. Her kitchen table is covered with folders overflowing with newspaper clippings, court documents, and hand-written notes—the trail of a crusade. I thought Mark James had waited a long time, but Fay lodged her application for a new inquest in 2015, asking the coroner to probe the 'planted gun' claim.

'It's just horrible hanging there, year after year after year,' Fay whispers.

She's softly spoken, with blue eyes, fine grey hair pulled into a bun, and tasteful, chunky jewellery. If a memory's painful she'll reach for her cigarettes to still her trembling fingers. While Fay has a delicate frame, there's a heaviness about her that reminds me of Mark—exhausted but determined.

'It's taken a big toll. I'm certainly not the person I used to be. And my children, they're sick of seeing me going through it.'

The other traumatising thing about her brother's death is its legacy. Graeme Jensen's shooting was the catalyst for the revenge execution 11 hours later of Constables Steven Tynan and Damian Eyre, better known as the Walsh Street shootings. The ambush of the two young constables responding to a report of an abandoned car in South Yarra was random and barbaric. Fay Spear says her family is forever tarnished by the association.

'So bad I can't find words for it, really. One day, we were an ordinary family getting up and going to work and saving for holidays and so forth, and the next we were police-killing criminals.'

Fay's not naive; she's the first to admit her brother was no angel. He was a bank robber. But she says he wasn't the ruthless criminal that the police and media made him out to be.

'All of his convictions are from that 10-year-old to a 22-year-old. In his last bank-robbery case, when he saw the witnesses getting so upset, he said, "I didn't even think about them, I didn't realise", so that's how young he was.'

And 'that 10-year-old' she mentions didn't really stand a chance. Graeme Jensen's trajectory was also largely plotted by sexual abuse.

Fay says, 'To me, it was like he was a boy who wasn't meant to be. A day after he was born, he almost died, and just so much has happened to him. He was sexually assaulted, and my mother took him to the police and said you must tell the truth about everything, which he did, and then they charged him with 11 counts of gross indecency. He was 10 years old when he was put into a boys' home, when he hadn't really done anything wrong.'

In the boys' home he fell in with the wrong crowd, and we all know the rest. Fay says her younger brother deserves the final chapter of his life to be written truthfully, as everyone does.

This makes two Pandora's boxes the coroner will be prising open if she grants new inquests to the James and Jensen families. Is that what the sticking point is? In the James case, the bungle with the DNA sample raises serious questions about potential interference by the Catholic Church. In the Jensen matter, was his shooting—which led to the revenge killing of two of the force's own—lawful?

The Victorian Coroners Court maintains that the current holding pattern is solely due to a gap in its legislation. Maria

James's inquest was determined under the 1958 Coroners Act, when it was up to the Supreme Court to decide whether to set aside findings and hold new inquests, and it's ambiguous as to whether that power was repealed by the current 2008 Act. This confuses me because I know of a handful of cases in recent years where coroners *have* made rulings on historical cases. So were those rulings made in error?

February 2018

10am Coroners Court – jurisdictional argument

— Diary note, 27 February 2018

Two families are noticeably absent as the State Coroner, Sara Hinchey, hears submissions on the powers afforded by Section 77 of the current Coroners Act, in relation to new inquests. It seems an amendment in 1999 affords her the power to grant new inquests for cases *after* that year; but for inquests determined earlier, it's anyone's guess.

The James and Jensen families have decided to short-circuit the process, applying instead to the Supreme Court for some clarity. Which means more time, more money, and more waiting. There is another way. The attorney-general could draw up an amendment to bridge the legislative gap. But that again would take time, and couldn't happen before next month's Supreme Court hearing, and possibly not even this year, given that Parliament will be preoccupied with the state election coming up in November.

As the complicated legal argument plays out in the Coroners Court, a journalist, looking a little lost, asks me, 'Have you been following this case?'

'A little bit,' I answer him. *I'm the reason you're here.*

I cradle the package—carefully wrapped in brown paper by an eccentric book dealer—as one would a newborn. I sit with it in the back of a cab, a little freaked out to think that this bundle could hold both the blood of the woman I've devoted my last two years to, and possibly also her killer's. This is the fashion magazine that 'Chris' has kept for me, the one he grabbed for his wife that day in 1997 when he was racing the rubbish-removals guy who was gutting number 736 High Street. 'Top right-hand corner,' he'd said, handing me his find. 'There's quite a big splotch, and then you'll see splattering as well.'

I deliver it into the trusty hands of Dadna Hartman at the Victorian Institute of Forensic Medicine, and she guides me into her office to explain what she'll be looking for. 'But first, PPE,' she says. Personal protective equipment. A lab coat, mask, and hair net. Lab chic. Next, I'm asked to do a buccal swab, and handed what's essentially a long cotton bud so I can collect some skin cells on the inside of my cheek. This is a sample so I can be eliminated as a potential donor of any DNA that might be recovered from the magazine. Finally, I'm led into an air-controlled laboratory for the unwrapping.

With my heart in my mouth, I watch one of the scientists, Michelle Spiden, carefully peel back the brown paper. Her shoulder is partially blocking my view of the 1947 *Ambassador Magazine* with its special on 'Versatile Velvets', and I can't see any staining. *Oh God, this will be embarrassing if Chris has just talked this up.* On tiptoe, I strain to get a closer look, and there they are. The largest stains are on the top-right hand corner of the cover: two brown mottled circles, the larger one having seeped through, leaving lighter-brown shadows on subsequent pages. There's also splattering underneath, as if someone has flicked a paintbrush. And on the magazine model's nose is a small, thicker dollop in a darker reddish-brown.

'Does that look enough of a stain to give a viable sample?' I ask Michelle.

'If that's blood, there's definitely enough there. We should be able to get a profile from that.' And then I ask her what I really want to know: 'Will you be able to tell if there's both male and female blood?'

'I guess we could see a mixture if it's a victim and a perp, or somebody else who's actually handled the magazine. But if there is male DNA there, we should be able to pick it up.'

Michelle says she'll either swab the samples or cut them from the cover. Then she'll lyse the cells and perform PCR, [polymerase chain reaction], which makes multiple copies of the areas of DNA needing targeting. Finally, the samples will be run through another machine, for capillary electrophoresis, which separates the DNA fragments by size, to generate a DNA profile. She'll be doing both nuclear and mitochondrial testing, so she gives me a quick refresher.

'So, you have your nuclear DNA, which is like what you see on TV, the whole double-helix, and half of that comes from Mum and half from Dad. Whereas mitochondrial DNA is only passed along the maternal line.'

Michelle delicately lifts the *Ambassador Magazine* into a Tamper Evident Bag, and tells me the testing should take a few weeks, depending on the number of urgent requests that come into the lab.

It will be morbidly poetic if the mystery of Maria James is solved by a bloodied magazine.

March 2018

I have an update. Do you want to call me to discuss?

— Email from VIFM's Dadna Hartman to Rachael Brown, 7 March 2018

'I've been very nervous about this. What's the upshot?' I ask, sitting down in Dadna Hartman's office.

She rips the bandaid off fast. 'Unfortunately it's not great news.' *Dammnn.*

'It's not too surprising, given the condition of the book,' Dadna adds. 'Its age, how it's potentially been stored in the past. DNA is biological, so it can degrade. It's affected by a number of factors: heat, humidity, all these sorts of things.'

She opens a folder containing pages of graphs, and points at one of the peaks on a electropherogram (EPG). 'Although we're seeing some DNA information there, it's not reportable, in that the peak heights are quite low.'

She tells me that she repeated the test four times to check if those same peaks appeared in multiple analysis. But no luck.

'We would say there might be some really low-level DNA present, but unfortunately our current methodology is not at the sensitivity that we can detect it. In the future, perhaps, it might be an option to retest the exhibit, when things improve or our methodology becomes more sensitive.'

I was hoping for something. *Anything.* 'Can you tell from these results whether there are two separate DNA profiles?'

'No, we can't. For example, here you can see it's XX [chromosome], so that would indicate a female. In another one, we did see an XY, which would be indicative of male DNA present — but it wasn't reproducible, so it's not something I could say is definitely a male sample.'

'Sample? So it's not necessarily XY blood? It could've been, say, a skin cell, of the man who handled the magazine?'

'Correct. So at this point we really can't discern anything from the data.'

I let go of a breath I haven't realised I've been holding for six weeks. 'Thanks for trying. I appreciate all the work you've put into it. I'm just so disappointed.'

'So are we.' And they are — it's written all over her face. Her team has gone above and beyond. It's humbling that some of the best brains in the business are now just as invested in getting answers for the James brothers. Especially Dadna, who really wanted her science to solve it, whose folder bears a sticker that's somewhat of a talisman: *A match between the suspect and the evidence is 9.46 trillion times more probable than coincidence (Dr Mark Perlin, Cybergenetics).*

Then Dadna throws me a lifeline. 'There's a lab in the UK, Cellmark, that does extra testing to see if it can target low-level DNA. So there could be an opportunity to send the sample there, but obviously that would come at a cost.'

You little ripper. And that gives me an idea. 'This DNA wasn't strong enough to test against the Australian population, but could it be tested against what police have on file for Maria James's profile?'

'No, with what we have, we couldn't. And Victoria Police

doesn't use low-level or low-copy DNA techniques. But if you were to send the exhibit overseas, and they were able to get even a partial profile—let's say maybe five or six regions of DNA—the police could certainly compare that to a DNA profile they might hold for the victim, or a DNA sample from the crime scene.'

In short, it'll take more sophisticated technology, or more time, to have any hope of cracking the DNA secret that this magazine is harbouring.

The hopes of Mark James and Fay Spear currently hinge on the 1958 and 1985 Coroners Acts. They ask the Victorian Supreme Court to determine their applications for new inquests by exercising the same powers it held back then.

'The answers to this case are out there,' Mark says. 'We know they're out there. We just need a new inquest to get to the bottom of it.'

Fay is similarly dogged. 'We need a door that can be open for the families—not just mine—for the truth to come out and to get justice. If we don't have that door opened, we've got nowhere to go.'

Once the legal proceedings are over, I introduce Fay to Mark and Adam James. In normal circumstances, the sons of a second-hand bookseller and the sister of a bank robber might never have met. But here, under the dome of the Victorian Supreme Court, they're united in a common purpose.

Fay doesn't tell the brothers this, but she's worn her crucifix necklace under her shirt, for Maria. 'Oh you poor boys,' she says, her voice wavering, reaching up to hug Mark. 'Your mum would be so proud of you.' And this fragile woman breaks into sobs, burrowed into the neck of a burly stranger. Fay's arm reaches out and brings Adam into the hug. The brothers seem so touched by the empathy that they're lost for words. It hurts so much to watch that I have to look away. The peak-hour flurry in the corridor stops. Everyone—including lawyers with their wheeled briefcases, and court journalists trailing the families for an interview—gives the unlikely new allies their space.

I wish the judiciary could see this part, away from the creaky pews and tedious argument about the nuances of Section 10 of the 1958 Coroners Act, which became Section 59 of the 1985 Act, and then Section 77 of the 2008 Act. This is the toll of a cold case; the weight of the wait.

April 2018

Counsel for James family applying for suppression order on some police files.

— Text message from Lauren Caulfield to Rachael Brown, 13 April 2018

The Supreme Court decision is handed down faster than I expected, catching me while I'm on a media exchange trip in China's southern province of Guangzhou. In the thick of peak-hour traffic, piggybacking off a colleague's internet, I depend on text-message updates from Lauren Caulfield, who's part of Fay Spear's legal team.

Finding of no jurisdiction.

The Supreme Court has ruled that it doesn't have the

power to reopen the inquest of Maria James nor of Graeme
Jensen.

So now it's up to parliament to amend legislation.

I text back, *Oh no, how long will parly* [parliament] *take?
This is ridiculous.*

*No it's not great. So many years and such a huge toll on
families. Fay is too frail and unwell to be in court. I'm outside
court with laptop liaising with Fay now.*

The s77 coroners court question remains open.

This is the other prong of the argument: whether the
Supreme Court can declare that the power to order new
inquests for historical cases does indeed lie with the coroner.
More waiting. Just before Lauren has to rush off, she kindly
keeps me in the loop.

*Counsel for James family applying for suppression order
on some police files.*

News to me. A lot of the material being relied on by Mark
James's legal counsel is research I've provided, so whatever
it is they want suppressed, I probably already know about
it. Justice Niall denies the suppression-order application,
so when I'm back on home soil I ask Mark's lawyer, Naty
Guerrero-Diaz, what part of her affidavit she wanted kept
quiet. And it's a pearler. Paragraph 10:

> Victoria Police has told Mark James that the remainder of
> the exhibits which have been verified as being from Maria
> James' murder scene have been tested to see if they contain
> DNA of the murderer. There is some male DNA that has been
> identified, however the current tests have not yielded sufficient
> DNA to allow them to be tested against suspects' DNA with
> current technology.

It's news to me that they've found male DNA. Since Victoria Police's promise in July to retest Maria's exhibits, I've been denied an update, with the force replying each time that it's 'not in a position to release details as the investigation is ongoing'.

Naty tells me she called Victoria Police to double-check Mark's notes.

'They've said my wording is not quite correct, and that they've found some *substance* in some of Maria's exhibits, but it's not sufficient to test, so they can't say whether it's DNA. So there is something there, but current technology doesn't allow them to test it against other exhibits.'

Again. *Yes, we've found something. No, we can't test it.*

Naty also asked about the missing quilt. 'There's been an extensive search done, and the quilt is not in Victoria Police's possession. But it can't confirm that this means the quilt was destroyed—they don't have records of its destruction.'

I'm baffled. 'But you'd assume they'd keep destruction records, right, for chain-of-custody management?'

'Look, I would expect that if the quilt was destroyed today that we'd see records of it, but I don't know what Victoria Police's practices were at the time.'

Something else is missing. I've been eagerly awaiting responses to two Freedom of Information requests I lodged in February. And I strike out on both. I'd asked for Max Schiavon's information report:

The Information Report filed by Geelong CIB Detective Max Schiavon to Victoria Police in late 1998 or 1999 regarding his inquiries into the claims of James Shanahan. In late 1998, James

Shanahan rang Max Schiavon at Geelong CIB and told the
detective that between 1961–1963 he was forced to participate
in cult rituals in the Sandringham and/or Dandenong regions,
in which three or four people were murdered. Mr Shanahan
says present at the rituals was Father Thomas O'Keeffe, who
was a Curate at Sacred Heart Parish in Sandringham, and
then later a Chaplain at CBC College in East St Kilda. I seek
the Information Report Detective Schiavon filed regarding his
inquires into and/or assessment of Mr Shanahan's claims.

And this was the verdict from the force's Freedom of
Information officer:

I have made enquires with the Homicide Squad and as a result
I have been advised that following an extensive search the
information report you have requested cannot be located ...
no other documents could be located that match the scope
of your request.

As I understand it, information reports are supposed to
be kept until a case is solved, and in many homicides they're
kept forever.

I'd also requested the transcript of an interview that the
Homicide Squad conducted with Father Bongiorno, which
Mark James says police told him occurred in August 1998.
I'd asked for:

The record of interview/meeting (typed transcript and/or audio
and/or video) of the August 1998 interview/meeting conducted
by Homicide Detective [name redacted], with Father Anthony
Bongiorno, regarding the 1980 murder of Maria James and/or
Father Bongiorno's recent acquittal on paedophilia charges.

This was the one I really wanted, proof that the Homicide detective had called in the priest. Proof he was on their radar in the late 1990s. The reply:

[O]ne document comprising 2 pages could be located. The document comprises:
    Crime Stoppers Information Report from August 1997
    I have been advised that Superintendent [name redacted] has no diary entries in relation to this matter.

The letter goes on to deny me access to this report because the case remains open, and because giving access might discourage people from calling Crime Stoppers in future if callers know tip-offs can be accessed under FOI. This I understand, and completely respect. However, the absence of a diary note from Superintendent ___ is baffling.

'Oh come on,' Mark James laughs angrily, rocking back in his chair, when I visit him to deliver this news. Mark is adamant that it was this detective who called him into Homicide's St Kilda Road office in 1998 to buoy his hopes about the progress of his mum's cold case.

I move on to the Supreme Court affidavit, and ask Mark about what's been found in the re-testing of his mum's exhibits. He elaborates on what he told his lawyer: a detective visited him, with what looked like a traceability matrix.

'He had a whole bunch of sheets of paper, and on them was the police's investigation into these exhibits. I wasn't allowed to look at the findings, but the detective was referring to them. There was somewhere like eight pages of A3, and we're talking about font size number seven, so there's an enormous amount of information on those pages.'

'So what have they found?'

'They found a sample of what I understood to be male DNA on a pillowcase. But the bio lab technician said the sample wasn't good enough for actual testing. And the police's position is that they can't take it any further unless there are advances in DNA testing technology.'

Mark continues, 'I was also told that on the twine—twine was used to tie up my mother's hands—there was another sample found. But the opinion of the lab technicians and police was that this twine would have had DNA samples from so many different sources—including the manufacturer, sales people, anyone else that handled it—so it wouldn't be worth trying to test it.'

'But if that's all they've got, wouldn't it be worth it?'

'I know. There have been advances in DNA technology overseas. There've been cases where police and even the FBI haven't been able to get definitive DNA samples, and it's been referred to European specialists, and they've been able to get DNA from those samples, which has then been used in court to prosecute people.'

'Dadna Hartman from VIFM was telling me there's a company in the UK that does low-level testing,' I tell him. 'Did you put that to the detective? Would Victoria Police consider sending the exhibits overseas?'

'I did put that to them, and they declined. That was disappointing. I would've thought, you know, coming so close, they'd be pushing it to the very edge, to the very limit of what science could do.'

Looking at all this through Mark's eyes, it's incredibly hard not to be sceptical about the handling of his mother's case. This is how it looks, laid bare:

- The Homicide Squad spoke to Father Bongiorno in 1998, after his paedophilia had been revealed. Yet the detective never asked the priest if he'd abused the James brothers, nor did he ask the brothers.
- There's no diary note of this meeting, and the only associated record that does exist can't be released.
- Sometime before 2001, a red herring in the form of a bloodied pillow is put into Maria James's evidence bag.
- A bloodied quilt is taken *out* of that bag. It's missing, yet no record of its destruction exists.
- An information report of satanic-cult allegations levelled at Father O'Keeffe is also missing.

'Things do not add up,' Mark says. 'Something is going on, back in 1997, 1998, that implicates Father Bongiorno in the murder of my mother. Since that time, there's been interference with evidence. Now, I'm not attacking the police—I have a great deal of respect for the police of today—but that doesn't preclude the possibility that something untoward occurred many years ago. And that's why it is critical in my mum's case and for the sake of justice, accountability, transparency—all of the words we *say* we live by—that the cards are put on the table. And the best way to do that is through a coronial inquest.'

The next phase of legal proceedings was due to play out in mid-June, after this book went to press, with the Supreme Court being asked to rule that the coroner *does* have the power to reopen a historical inquest that was decided under a previous Act. And Mark James tells me his team have one more move up their sleeve: they've reported Maria James as a new death, because it's never been reported under the 2008 Act, because back in 1980 that Act didn't exist. Ingenious.

It reminds me of Ron Iddles' novel idea to skirt exhumation prerequisites by applying for a search warrant for Father Bongiorno's cemetery plot. I feel he'd appreciate this creative thinking.

May 2018

Call when you can. It's about Bongiorno.

— Voice message from Ron Iddles for Rachael Brown, 28 April 2018

'A guy came up to me after a talk I did last night,' Ron Iddles tells me when I return his call. 'Reckons Bongiorno told his dad the killer was in his confessional box'. For a priest who swore he couldn't divulge anything about the confessional, he sure seems to have spent a fair bit of time talking about it. So I get the man's details, and a week later I'm at his kitchen table eating quiche.

'You really shouldn't have,' I say of the impressive lunch spread. 'Please, come again,' says Tony Gale. 'It's the only time I get fed.' His wife, Lyndie, smiles and shakes her head. After the tea cake, Tony tells me about an odd lunch at his parents' home in the early 1980s that has always stuck with him.

'Now, before going there,' Tony says, backtracking a bit, 'I used to talk a lot with my father over the phone. One time, we started talking about this case. Before she [Maria James] was murdered, I think Trisha [Tony's late wife] and I went into that bookstore. Dad said that Bongiorno knew who the killer was, because the killer confessed to him. "And he can't divulge anything," Dad said. "He can't tell the police anything about it. He can't reveal the name of the killer because it was under the confessional. That's the trouble with our doctrine."'

This revelation was apparently dropped during one of the priest's regular lunches with Tony's parents. At the time, Tony was working as a private investigator, and had a lot of questions about this case.

'I thought, hang on, Dad, why would a killer confess to a priest that he'd killed someone within his own parish? Firstly, the priest can't give him absolution, because it's a murder case. Also, it would've been his [Bongiorno's] duty to tell the murderer to give himself up. So I said to Dad, "I doubt very much anybody would've confessed to him. Secondly, you don't shit in your own backyard." If you're going to confess, you'd go to, say, St Francis in the city—they don't know you, see. I found it very strange that he said that to my dad.'

'Was your dad supportive of Father Bongiorno?' I ask him.

'Well, he used to be', says Tony. 'I said to my dad, "What did you do about it?", and he said, "What do you want me to do about it?" And, of course, it turned into an argument, because my dad was such a staunch Catholic. He'd say to me, "Oh Tony, where's your faith? The priest, you know, he can't [divulge confessional secrets]" … we had that disagreement. My dad, I loved him and all that, but sometimes he used to frustrate me.'

Tony says that some time later he dropped in unannounced to his parents' place in Northcote.

'Mum's meals, she used to feed an army. And Father Bongiorno was there, and he was eating away, happy as Larry—he was talking about the Virgin Mary. And I walked in and said, "Hi Dad, Mum," and they introduced me to Father Bongiorno. I think I had seen him celebrating mass.'

Tony says that when the priest asked what he did for a living, everything changed.

'My father popped up straight away, "Oh, he's a detective", and—Tony thumps his fist on the table, nearly sending a china teacup dancing—that was it. He nearly choked on what he was eating. His whole persona changed. It was as though I'd walked in, and I was the Devil ready to take him to hell. The vibes I got from him, I thought this bastard's up to something—he's trying to hide something.'

Tony says the priest jumped up, flustered, said he had to go, and left behind an unfinished lunch and bewildered hosts.

'My father said, "What's the bloody matter with him? He comes here all the time." He said to Laura, my mother, "Did you say something to offend him?" "No," she said. "What's the matter with him?"'

The priest never returned for another of Laura's home-cooked meals. And Tony remembers his mum being upset after a later church service, because Father Bongiorno had refused to give her Communion.

Tony Gale says he never said anything at the time, because he thought police knew this story about the apparent confession.

'That's what really pisses me off. When Lyndie was reading the stories and all that, I said, "Bullshit. I heard, through Dad, that he [Father Bongiorno] knew who the killer was, and the police were trying to find out from him."'

Tony Gale's feeling is that there was no confession. Or, at least, not one from a penitent stranger. He thinks Father Bongiorno made the claim to deflect attention from himself.

'My belief is that the confession that he heard was his own soul. He was confessing to himself and asking God for absolution, which he wouldn't get—you can't give yourself absolution. But I think he made that up, thinking the word would get around.'

All this makes me think of Rita Constantini, and the "Do I know? Don't I know?" jokes that Father Bongiorno used to make about the killer being in his confessional. I call her to touch base, to check whether the podcast's revelations over the past year have changed her mind about 'Bonj' being a murderer.

'Definitely not, not the man I knew,' Rita says. 'Maybe he dropped in to say hello [to Maria James], found her, picked her up, then ran for his life out of fear.' But she's now less certain about everything else.

'I believe Adam [James] more than anyone else,' Rita whispers before dissolving into sobs. 'I only knew him [Father Bongiorno] as *I* knew him. I couldn't see it, but it brings me to tears if he's hurt someone. I'm quite distraught for Adam—I'm so sorry for him.'

Also, recently, the Victorian government revised Denis Ryan's compensation payment. While it's a lot less than the $3.1m initially calculated, Denis says he's satisfied with the offer. *Go Denis*, I think when I read the news. I wonder if he'll move out of his rented flat and buy himself a kettle. Slowly but surely, society is starting to face up to some hard truths.

The confession that he heard was his own soul.

Was it? Was Father Bongiorno a master in the art of deflection? Was he crying out for help? Or did he really hear the killer—or *know* him—and have to shoulder that alone? Or was this just another joke? Was the killer someone else in the police files? Or someone *never* looked at?

I've landed precisely back where I started, but with many more questions. Murakami would find a delicious 360-degree irony in all this. But I don't. Nor, as they keep reminding me, do *Trace*'s listeners.

I appreciate their passion, and their yearning for an ending. Most people need closure. But this is messy. Like life. The final chapter about the woman who ran a bookshop in Thornbury remains, for now, unwritten. And each day, her sons have to lug around that incredible weight.

But as Jesse Cox's mum said to me, when loss is unfathomable, stories become treasures. And for the James brothers, stories also bear witness.

So now, just as *they've* done for 38 years, we wait.

Acknowledgements

To Mark and Adam James, thank you for entrusting me with your mum's story. I dearly hope it helps you find answers, and peace.

To Ron Iddles: Victorian families have been so lucky to have you, as they've faced the monster that is grief. For your generosity, integrity, and care, I am forever indebted. And thanks to Colleen Iddles, too, for your endless warm support.

To all the brave abuse survivors who let me into your hearts and nightmares: your compassion floored me. I hope I've also given you a voice. And to Denis Ryan, and Chrissie, and the late Anthony Foster: you've shown that quiet grace can be an unstoppable force.

Thanks to the dedicated staff at VIFM, the Victorian Coroners Court, and to those past and present members of Victoria Police who could help. The work you all do is incredible.

Thanks to the Thornbury locals, victims' advocates, and everyone who helped me understand all the layers of this investigation.

To the Scribe team, thank you for seeing the importance, and heart, of this case, which paints the worst but also the very best of humanity. You've helped tell Maria's story with great respect. To Wendy Hanna (who suggested I should write this book), Barrie Cassidy, Kate Wild, and Margaret Wieringer — you cleverly shooed away first-time-author doubts. To my writing havens, Elba Island and Frankie Says.

To Mum, Dad, Sam, Nick, and Mel, and the extended Brown, Caldwell and Jaques families: thanks for raising me to believe I could achieve anything, and for having my back, despite the investigation's confronting content.

Very special thanks goes to Kerri Ritchie, for always knowing what to say, and for your unshakable faith in me, and this project.

To some incredible women who held me together: Sarah Notaro (Detective Puttick), Mazoe Ford, Amanda and Dani Isdale, Anna Allbury, Jennifer Robinson, Jemima Fox, Johanna Johnson, Emily Smith, Brooke Bowman, Emma Doyle, Tiki Menegola, and Antonella di Bello.

For the welfare checks and dinners, thanks to Nerida Cain and Vinay Gehi, Pete Brown, Chess Cradduck and the Crosbie Crew (I never trained, but you cheered me anyway), Bethan Davies, Ryan Sheales, Annalise De Mel, Alan Duffy, Ami and Jamie Smith, Pat and Mon Carrarini, Kate Ablett, Pete Wells, Grant Sammut, Peter and Pam Woods, Anna Priestland, Peter Cave, and Justine Ford. For your sage advice, thanks Hamish Macdonald, Charlie Pickering, Jill Gordon, Sandro Demaio, Nial Fulton, Ivan O'Mahoney, and Jacinta Waters.

And thanks to my ABC podcast posse: Jeremy Story Carter, Rach Carbonell, and Andy Burns — trusty allies through what was the darkest of projects. To David Burgess and Sophie Townsend for championing my idea, and to

Craig McMurtrie, Gaven Morris, Tanya Nolan, and Radio National for their trust. To Jesse Cox, Tim Roxburgh, and Marty Peralta for the waltzes and making the work sing. I've never enjoyed fighting with anyone more. To Emma Lancaster and Grant McAvaney for ensuring the work pushed the envelope safely. To the ABC News Breakfast team, Jon Faine, Fran Kelly, Samantha Donovan, Paul Kennedy, the newsroom, and my wider ABC family: thanks for urging me on and helping this important story resonate with Australian audiences. Special thanks to all the external outlets (kicked off by Channel 10 and KIIS FM) that helped *Trace* tap into the community. And to Jesse's family, I hope you take heart that his legacy lives on through everyone he has helped to fly.

For my late Nanny Anne and Pa Sid, from whom I've got their beautiful curiosity. They taught me that questions are a precious way to show care.